OPEN AND EQUITABLE SCHOLARLY COMMUNICATIONS

CREATING A MORE INCLUSIVE FUTURE

Prepared by Nancy Maron and Rebecca Kennison
with Paul Bracke, Nathan Hall, Isaac Gilman, Kara Malenfant, Charlotte Roh, and Yasmeen Shorish

Association of College and Research Libraries
A division of the American Library Association
Chicago, Illinois 2019

Advancing learning
Transforming scholarship
Association of College & Research Libraries
A division of the American Library Association

Open and Equitable Scholarly Communications: Creating a More Inclusive Future.

Citation: Association of College and Research Libraries. *Open and Equitable Scholarly Communications: Creating a More Inclusive Future.* Prepared by Nancy Maron and Rebecca Kennison with Paul Bracke, Nathan Hall, Isaac Gilman, Kara Malenfant, Charlotte Roh, and Yasmeen Shorish. Chicago: Association of College and Research Libraries, 2019. doi: 10.5860/acrl.1

Association of College & Research Libraries
A division of the American Library Association
Chicago, Illinois 2019

Contents

Foreword

ACRL has a longstanding commitment to accelerating the transition to a more open system of scholarship through education, political advocacy, coalition building, and research. In January 2000, an ACRL task force on scholarly communications began discussing how ACRL might contribute to shaping and envisioning the future of scholarly communications. In the task force's January 2002 report, they recommended that ACRL, as one of its highest strategic priorities, be actively engaged in working to reshape the current system of scholarly communications.

Based on the recommendations in the report, ACRL launched its scholarly communication initiative in spring 2002, establishing a new standing committee of the ACRL Board of Directors. Now, nearly two decades since that task force was formed, ACRL's commitment to reshaping the system of scholarly communications remains strong. With leadership from ACRL's Research and Scholarly Environment Committee (ReSEC), the association has developed numerous programs and services to address what has remained one of ACRL's primary strategic goals, including issuing scholarly communications research agendas in 2004 and 2007. In spring 2017, ReSEC recommended not only updating the 2007 research agenda but also broadening the scope to specifically include voices from historically underrepresented communities and those with different ways of knowing and making meaning.

Designing an Inclusive Process

In exploring approaches that would ensure a diversity of voices and use an inclusive process, member leaders of ReSEC interviewed a dozen individuals from organizations representing African American, American Indian, Asian American, and Hispanic library groups, as well as representatives from historically black colleges and universities, community colleges, technical schools, women's colleges, and various diversity initiatives and units. It was decided that a call for proposals for the design, development, and delivery of the new research agenda would be issued, and ReSEC members thought it important to share an excerpt of the draft call itself for public feedback prior to issuing it to show the depth of our commitment to being inclusive and community-driven at even the earliest stages. In December 2017, ACRL issued the call for an agenda that would engage the community in thinking about the full span of the research environment and scholarly communications system, to make it more open, more inclusive, and more equitable. We specified in the call that the process of creating the agenda should itself be inclusive and open, with the priorities of the research agenda being defined by members of the community.

We are pleased to release *Open and Equitable Scholarly Communications: Creating a More Inclusive Future* and are confident it does reflect a much broader understanding. The researchers ACRL selected to undertake this work engaged in a robust community-based process, interacting with more than 1,000 ACRL members and other stakeholders in scholarly communications systems. They sought input from experts as well as people who are not always consulted in the development of a research agenda: those working in academic libraries at the front line of scholarly communications work; those at smaller institutions, not just major research universities; people of color; and people with disabilities. From April through September 2018, they undertook a thorough review of the scholarly and practice literature and conducted interviews with experts, seven focus groups, workshops at three major meetings, and an online survey. Once prepared, a draft of the research agenda was shared publicly and received robust input from both individuals and representatives of groups such as ALA ethnic caucuses and other historically underrepresented groups. We thank and recognize the valuable input of all these people, listed in Appendix 4, and are proud to issue a report that was co-created with the people it affects the most, our community of academic and research librarians.

Recognizing All Contributors

As this report notes in the section on people, it is important to acknowledge all contributors to a work being published, beyond those listed as authors. To raise the visibility of the labor involved in an undertaking such as this, the citation for this report names Nancy Maron and Rebecca Kennison, the consultants ACRL hired to lead the research and writing, and also includes members of the ReSEC subcommittee and staff who contributed their intellectual work through many rounds of detailed and careful comments and revision (Paul Bracke, Nathan Hall, Isaac Gilman, Kara Malenfant, Charlotte Roh, and Yasmeen Shorish). Former ReSEC Chairs Amy Buckland and Patricia Hswe deserve credit for spurring the committee to take on this project, developing the inclusive approach, and drafting the RFP (members of the previous subcommittee were Paul Bracke, Mary Galvin, Nathan Hall, Lori Critz, and Amy Nurnberger).

Beyond dedicated ACRL volunteer leaders, ACRL staff members played important roles over the life of this project. Kara Malenfant, as liaison to ReSEC, and Mary Ellen Davis, ACRL's Executive Director, were closely involved at all stages, from evaluating possible approaches, drafting the RFP, reading proposals, and contracting the finalists, to reading and commenting on drafts in progress. Staff support from Erin Nevius and Kara Malenfant ensured that the community was engaged with drafting the RFP, participating in the survey and focus groups, making comments on the public draft, and in organizing conference presentations. Additionally, as with all ACRL reports of this nature, we benefitted enormously from the talents of Erin Nevius in her publishing role; Dawn Mueller for design, layout, and production; and freelance copyeditor Judith Lauber. David Free contributed greatly by promoting the work in progress and the final release of the publication through ACRL communications channels. ACRL initiatives benefit greatly from a team approach and we are grateful to and proud of this team of devoted ReSEC members who volunteered countless hours, consultants, and staff, who, working together, were able to bring this project to fruition.

Collective Responsibility for Change

Open and Equitable Scholarly Communications, like other ACRL publications and programs, suggests to academic librarians that they can and should focus on the power of taking a scholarly approach to their own professional work. ACRL is committed to seeing this research agenda challenge the profession and encourages readers to take action—whether by implementing the practical actions in this report or investigating a recommended research question. In tandem with the release of this report, ACRL is issuing a call for proposals for research grants intended to spur inquiry in these areas. More information on these grants can be found on the ACRL website. Additionally, a group of ALA Emerging Leaders is currently developing materials to help extend this reach of this report and encourage the community to take it up through use cases.

We invite you to peruse, review, and engage with these important questions to further the advancement of the transformation of the scholarly communications system.

Mary Ellen K. Davis
ACRL Executive Director
mdavis@ala.org

Lauren Pressley
ACRL President 2018-2019
Director of the University of Washington Tacoma Library and Associate Dean of University Libraries at the University of Washington in Tacoma
pressley@uw.edu

Executive Summary

For many years, the academic and research library workforce has worked to accelerate the transition to more open and equitable systems of scholarship. While significant progress has been made, barriers remain. The Association of College and Research Libraries (ACRL) seeks to stimulate further advances through this action-oriented research agenda, which is designed to provide practical, actionable information for academic librarians; include the perspectives of historically underrepresented communities in order to expand the profession's understanding of research environments and scholarly communication systems; and point librarians and other scholars toward important research questions to investigate.

This report represents a yearlong process of reviewing the scholarly and practice-based literature to take into account established investigation coupled with extensive public consultation to identify the major problems facing the academic library community. Through interviews, focus groups, workshops, and an online survey, over 1,000 members of the ACRL community offered their thoughts and expertise to shape this research agenda. Incorporating guidance and input from ACRL's Research and Scholarly Environment Committee and an advisory panel, this document recommends ways to make the scholarly communications and research environment more open, inclusive, and equitable.

Reading This Report

The research agenda is organized into three major concepts—People, Content, and Systems—and each of these priority areas opens up into several specific research areas to address.

The section on **People** approaches diversity and inclusion from several directions.

- *Embracing Diversity and Inclusion* addresses ways to better understand and improve upon the success of those who are hired and work in academic libraries and scholarly communications functions. It also calls for greater clarity and acknowledgment of the range of roles and skills of those who engage in scholarly communications work.
- *Improving the Working Lives of People Engaged in Scholarly Communications* explores incentives necessary for people to change behavior and participate in new, open models of scholarly communications. This section also highlights the challenges presented when the labor required to produce new works is donated or informally compensated.
- *Increasing Awareness Concerning Creators' Rights* brings to the fore the need to understand creators' rights and responsibilities, whether that means educating authors on managing their intellectual property or developing a more nuanced approach to "open" content that respects the privacy of those whose ideas, images, or culture are being discussed.

The section on **Content** acknowledges the opportunity for greater inclusion and openness, given the many ways in which materials are created, collected, and evaluated.

- *Rethinking What "Counts"* asks researchers to consider the ways in which value is assigned to scholarly materials, particularly as they relate to promotion, retention, and tenure decisions, and to consider the role librarians might play in influencing ongoing efforts to refine them. This section also suggests avenues of inquiry to better understand the implicit and explicit bias that can operate in evaluating scholars and their work, particularly when the scholars are from underrepresented communities or geographies.

- *Creating More Representative and Open Collections* outlines the need for further examination of collection building to ensure diversity in the materials created and acquired and to revisit overly restrictive copyright provisions that limit access.

The section on **Systems** identifies several avenues to explore, each representing a different type of system that undergirds scholarly communications work.

- *Supporting Technological Infrastructure That Is Sustainable* explores the support needed to sustain core infrastructure and the increasing importance of data and data management in the scholarly communications workflow.
- *Creating Systems That Permit More Access to More People* discusses the systems that encourage and facilitate greater access by users, whether through addressing specific disabilities or through a renewed and proactive focus on building a deep understanding of user and stakeholder needs into any new product creation.
- *Building Mission-Aligned Organizational and Financial Systems* offers suggestions for new research on the financial models that support scholarly communications, specifically highlighting the current interest in community- and academy-owned infrastructure.
- *Advancing Innovation in Academic Libraries* acknowledges that in order for new ideas to take hold, organizations themselves will need to take active steps to understand the environments they create that can foster (or impede) innovation and change.

For each of these research areas, this report presents an overview of the topic, highlighting areas of progress and practical actions that libraries can take, as well as specific lines of inquiry, each including research questions that would help advance understanding and problem solving around that topic. Finally, each area offers an illustrative suggestion for an actual research project, suggesting a framing and methodology that might be used.

Readers will notice that the topics covered, by their nature, often seem to be relevant to more than one of the thematic sections. Indeed, while the agenda's authors offer the categories of People, Content, and Systems as a way to start thinking about all the ways in which the scholarly communications system could be improved, they readily acknowledge that the topics within them are deeply interconnected. A full discussion of what makes scholarly communications technical infrastructure sustainable, for example, requires addressing its technical requirements, the organizational systems in place to support it, the financial models that fund its ongoing operations, the responsibilities and labor practices concerning the people who create and manage it, and the range of materials and content types the infrastructure could support. Elements of these issues appear in more than one section of the agenda; we hope that this categorization, rather than causing frustration, serves to spur creative thinking about different approaches to address the most pressing questions of our day.

Accompanying the report are extensive appendices, including an essay on issues of social justice in scholarly communications that have informed this agenda, findings from the online survey, and an annotated list of recommended readings.

When considering what needs ought to drive the selection of topics for inquiry, we have not assumed that academic libraries' scholarly communications staff will be the only ones who undertake the research paths suggested. Instead, we assumed that the questions might inspire academic and research library workers to dive in as well. The topics outlined here are of great interest to the broader academic library community, and ACRL urges members, whatever their role, to participate in undertaking the research needed to develop a system that is more open, inclusive, and equitable.

Introduction

A research agenda captures a moment in time, identifying current problems to solve and potential paths to solving them through sustained inquiry. The Association of College and Research Libraries (ACRL) issued a call for proposals in spring 2017 seeking proposals for the design, development, and delivery of a research agenda in the scholarly communications and research environment.[1] This effort was to build upon an earlier ACRL research agenda, developed and published in 2007, entitled *Establishing a Research Agenda for Scholarly Communications: A Call for Community Engagement*, which pinpointed several emerging topics at the time, all vital to the scholarly communications space in higher education.[2]

The agenda produced in 2007 was developed at an invitational meeting involving leaders of academic libraries and of library-focused organizations, including the Association of Research Libraries, the Council on Library and Information Resources, the Scholarly Publishing and Academic Resources Coalition, the Coalition for Networked Information, the Andrew W. Mellon Foundation, and ITHAKA. The agenda outlined several broad areas of inquiry, from evaluation and metrics to preservation and infrastructure. Even if not all the specific research topics suggested in the report have been undertaken since its publication, the broad strokes of that agenda are no less relevant today.

The research agenda outlined in this report differs from earlier approaches in a few ways.

First, **the scope is broader**. Earlier definitions of "scholarly communications" focused on research outputs, such as understanding questions concerning digitization or fee models for supporting the distribution of digital content. Today we recognize scholarly communications begins with the process of creating the work itself (research, writing, collaboration); continues through production, distribution, and evaluation of that work; and includes its sustainability. The importance of considering this entire workflow has been thrown into stark relief by recent acquisitions by commercial publishers that have shown strategic business interest in offering products and services to support all stages of research and scholarly work.[3] Academic librarians need to understand in detail this entire workflow in order to determine what academy-based alternatives might be viable and how best to achieve them.

Second, **ACRL has a commitment to issues related to openness, inclusion, and equity.** The *ACRL Plan for Excellence* includes a strategic goal for the area of Research and Scholarly Environment to "accelerate …the transition to more open and equitable systems of scholarship."[4] The research agenda presented here takes up this challenge, helping to identify actionable steps that academic librarians can take to accomplish this. Moreover, ACRL's core commitment to equity, diversity, and inclusion underscores the critical value and importance of meeting this challenge, for the larger mission of the Association.

Finally, in developing the vision for the call for proposals, **ACRL made clear that this agenda should reflect the priorities of the community** in a range of ways: it should be informed by the scholarly literature and take into account the views of "established …experts" but should also reflect both advances in practice and the voices of historically underrepresented communities.[*] To that end, in addition to conducting a review of the literature and speaking with experts in the field, the report authors engaged in a community-based process—interacting with more than 1,000 ACRL members and others in the scholarly communications space—to gain a deeper understanding of the major questions facing academic publishing, as well as the questions of special interest to those working in academic libraries. (For a full discussion of the methodology, see appendix 3; for a listing of those interviewed, see appendix 4.)

* The full RFP is in appendix 2. The researchers have followed ACRL's charge to "take into account established investigation from recognized experts in the priority areas, once identified, but not to the exclusion of other perspectives" (p. 3).

Other research agendas are also addressing key issues in the realm of the scholarly communications and research environment. In recent years, several related efforts have emerged, from Clifford Lynch's provocative editorial in *College and Research Libraries* to the recent Digital Library Federation work on valuing labor and the MIT Libraries white paper proposing a "grand challenges" approach to a research agenda in scholarly communications and information science.[5] The theme of 2018's International Open Access Week was "Designing Equitable Foundations for Open Knowledge."[6] Ongoing research agenda–setting work is underway among members of the Library Publishing Coalition and CNI as well. Other research agendas will undoubtedly be launched by other groups in the near future.

This agenda quite specifically aims to alert, engage, and encourage members of the ACRL community to take on the elements of the questions they care most about by conducting research that is meaningful to them, whether for the community at large or at their own institutions.

Defining Open, Inclusive, and Equitable

Open. Inclusive. Equitable. These terms, at the heart of the charge given by ACRL for its newest research agenda, are extremely broad, leaving open a range of interpretations to what they might mean if they are not carefully defined. As more than one focus group participant noted, it is hard to start talking about what might make scholarly communications more "open" until there is agreement about what "open" means—or, for that matter, what the scholarly communications and research environment encompasses.

The working concept of the scholarly communications and research environment used in this report includes all the steps researchers take, from beginning a new research project and getting it funded; to gathering and analyzing the data; to writing, editing, and publishing the work in some form; to having the work shared and distributed throughout the world, including its being collected and preserved for others to use.

But when thinking about what "open," "inclusive," and "equitable" might mean, rather than impose definitions and ask participants to abide by them, we chose to listen to the community through interviews with a handful of experts in scholarly communications, through discussions in the focus groups, and through the survey process. Using a two-stage approach, first "good-enough" definitions were developed, based on work already done in the field.[7] Then these definitions were tested with the hundreds of participants in the study to see to what extent they agreed with the definitions and how they might interpret the terms otherwise. Participants in the seven focus groups were encouraged to discuss what the terms meant to them. This served as a starting point to encourage discussion of ways to make scholarly communications more open, equitable, and inclusive. The online survey asked respondents to evaluate each definition in turn and to register their level of agreement (strongly agree, agree, not sure, disagree, strongly disagree):

> **Open…** refers to removing barriers to access, especially to the tools of production of scholarly content and to the outputs of that work.
>
> **Inclusive…** refers to (1) creating opportunities for greater participation in systems, institutions, and processes involved in creating, sharing, and consuming research, and (2) removing barriers that can hinder such participation.
>
> **Equitable…** refers to ensuring that systems, institutions, and processes function in a way that demonstrates fairness, impartiality, and objectivity in all their practices.

Eight hundred thirty-two respondents answered these survey questions, and the overwhelming majority were satisfied with the definitions provided. (For the full set of survey results, see appendix 7.) That said, notably there were strong alternative definitions or (more often) tweaks to the language that were worth incorporating. Below is a brief discussion of how people responded to each of the three terms.

Open... refers to removing barriers to access, especially to the tools of production of scholarly content and to the outputs of that work.

While some voiced a preference for definitions of "open" that hewed closely to a specific idea of free-versus-pay models (e.g., "I've always understood 'open' to mean that published materials are available outside of a paywall"), many more supported the broader notion of "open" to mean "removal of barriers to access," though they offered suggestions on further barriers they had in mind:

- *"...removing barriers to access and reuse..."*
- *"Unfettered public access to information."*
- *"It should be expanded to include the removal of barriers to sharing."*
- *"I would also include access to the means to produce scholarly content (e.g., access to the publication system, not just the tools), which is similar to the definition for Inclusive, but with less agency. I read the current definition as covering open source software and open access to use."*
- *"Why only scholarly?"*

Some urged not simply removal of barriers, but also an active process that encourages participation in the systems in question:

- *"It's more than removing barriers—it's about setting up systems and tools to actively INVITE access."*

And some reminded us that, in fact, there are good reasons why "open" can require some qualification:

- *"There are 'tools' and 'scholarly content' which should retain barriers to access on the basis of cultural/spiritual sensitivity, privacy, etc."*
- *"Open (as in access) can be problematic as it can be used to remove or minimize the rights and access of Indigenous people to their own content...."*

Inclusive... refers to (1) creating opportunities for greater participation in systems, institutions, and processes involved in creating, sharing, and consuming research, and (2) removing barriers that can hinder such participation.

In considering definitions of "inclusive," many respondents made the point that for a system to be considered "inclusive," simply removing barriers to access did not feel muscular enough. They wanted to see a more outcome-oriented definition. As one noted, "This is not about making exceptions, it is about re-thinking participation in research generally, from citizen science to the most costly forms of basic science." In particular, they found the idea of "creating opportunities" to be passive rather than proactive:

- *"Again, 'removing barriers' seems like a negative construction. 'Creating opportunities' seems passive—something done by the includers rather than the included. Something more like 'increasing and encouraging full participation in all phases of scholarly research by individuals of diverse nationality, socioeconomic status, gender, race, and other demographic categories or identities.'"*
- *"Inclusion must involve active calls for greater participation ...and removing barriers ...('creating opportunities' is too passive)."*
- *"Inclusive isn't just creating opportunities. It's reaching out and encouraging those who are 'on the outside' to participate."*
- *"I do not equate being 'inclusive' [with] 'opportunities for greater participation.' Being inclusive is more proactive than just providing opportunities, it is reaching out so that all can be enabled to participate."*

And some respondents went further, describing the desired outcomes they would like to see and providing more specificity concerning who exactly needs to be included:

- *"...refers to designing an environment in which people from a wide range of backgrounds feel welcome; includes physical as well as psychological/mental/intellectual aspects of the environment."*
- *"...removing barriers that can hinder such participation, so that everyone no matter background or status can benefit."*
- *"...removing barriers that can hinder such participation, especially among socially disadvantaged people."*
- *"...especially for those whose voices have often been marginalized."*
- *"I'd like some phrasing about 'under-heard voices,' or 'diversity of voices.'"*
- *"Those who are underrepresented due to race, nationality, economic class ...or not currently represented...."*

Still others pointed out the need to not only include people, but also recognize "alternative systems, institutions, and processes involved in creating, sharing, and consuming research as legitimate ...which have not yet been identified as such because they are outside of mainstream academia."

Equitable... refers to ensuring that systems, institutions, and processes function in a way that demonstrates fairness, impartiality, and objectivity in all their practices.

Many more respondents offered improvements to the definition for this term than to either of the others, urging us to be more precise about the use of the term and reminding us that a focus on "impartiality" and "objectivity" does not do enough to address the historical and social conditions that drive unequal usage or access in the first place. This is neatly summarized by the following comment:

- *"This seems like the right definition of Equitable; but I'd like to see institutions of higher education (and all institutions) working towards equality, which cannot function solely on 'impartiality' but must take into account the inequities our social-political world has created and work to undo those."*

Many noted the distinction between "equitable"—as in "fair"—and "equal," underlining places to explicitly make things "less equal, in order to make them more fair," particularly for "scholars and readers who have traditionally been marginalized in the production and use of scholarly content," and doing so "in a way that demonstrates fairness by working against current and historical inequities":

- *"[To create equity, systems, institutions, and processes must function] in a way that demonstrates fairness, impartiality, and objectivity in all their practices and strive to make their practices and services equally known to all potential user groups."*
- *"[Digital humanities] won't always be totally equal—for example the Mukurtu project manages access unequally, making access to community-sensitive content available only to that community, and not site visitors from around the world. Is that fair and impartial? Not strictly speaking. Going back to the root equity, it seems like there is a justice component missing."*
- *"Ensuring that systems, institutions, and processes function in a way that gives everyone what they need in order to successfully participate."*
- *"Equitable means taking into account historical and current structural barriers to certain populations."*

As a result of this feedback, a revisiting of the original definitions suggests the following revisions to each:

> **Open...** refers to removing barriers to access **and encouraging use and reuse**, especially of the tools of production of scholarly content and of the outputs of that work.

Inclusive… refers to (1) creating opportunities for greater participation in systems, institutions, and processes involved in creating, sharing, and consuming research; (2) removing barriers that can hinder such participation; and (3) **actively encouraging and welcoming people to participate, particularly those whose voices have often been marginalized.**

Equitable… refers to ensuring that systems, institutions, and processes function in a way that **gives everyone what they need in order to successfully participate.**

Aiming for Change

Following the discussion of the terms "open," "inclusive," and "equitable," research participants identified where the scholarly communications and research environment was not sufficiently open, inclusive, or equitable. They were encouraged to identify the barriers keeping it that way. Finally participants answered these questions: What might make it better? What needs to change? (For more information about the methodology used, see appendix 3. For the focus group guide that was used, see appendix 5.)

We prompted participants in these face-to-face discussions to think about stages of the scholarly and publishing workflow: creation, production, credentialing, sharing, and preservation. Through an iterative process of synthesizing and summarizing the excellent conversations from this approach and incorporating feedback from both the face-to-face engagements and the online survey, we refined our understanding of the community's priorities. Conversations at the Third National Joint Conference of Librarians of Color* helped clarify that the commonly expressed themes were part of these three larger concepts:

- **People.** To encourage a more open, inclusive, and equitable system of scholarly communications, a first step is to focus on the people who are involved in that system, with the premise that greater involvement by more people in more roles at more levels throughout the system will eventually result in a fairer and more equitable system. Research to bring about such changes should emphasize an even greater focus on hiring and even more so on retention and promotion, including a better understanding of type of environment and level of support needed to do this work. Additionally, the community must empower creators of scholarly content, better understand labor practices, and honor the multiplicity of roles people have today that contribute to the scholarly communications environment.
- **Content.** Creating a more open, inclusive, and equitable scholarly communications landscape requires broader thinking about what constitutes scholarly content, how works are evaluated and valued, what content is deemed important enough to be collected and preserved by libraries and archives, and how to address the limitations imposed by intellectual property laws on accessing, using, and sharing content. Research in this area could look at reevaluating PRT criteria† and all the issues that such a reevaluation might raise, especially when it comes to rewarding openness and public scholarship and the creation of works in a greater diversity of formats by a wide array of participants in the scholarly process (not merely "authors"), as well as suggesting changes in the way these materials are collected, preserved, and shared.

* The five ALA associations of librarians of color, who collectively comprise the Joint Council of Librarians of Color, are the American Indian Library Association (AILA), the Asian Pacific American Library Association (APALA), the Black Caucus of the American Library Association (BCALA), the Chinese American Library Association (CALA), and the National Association to Promote Library Services to Latinos and the Spanish-Speaking (REFORMA). They hold a joint conference every four years, the most recent in September 2018 in Albuquerque.

† While the *P* and the *T* are uniformly recognized as *promotion* and *tenure*, what the *R* stands for varies from institution to institution, where it can be either "retention" (as we've chosen to use here), "reappointment," or "review."

- **Systems.** Some researchers feel that the quickest way to make scholarly communications more open, equitable, and inclusive is to improve the systems that undergird it. If cheaper, more efficient, transparent **technological systems** (e.g., those that allow for capacity, innovation, infrastructure, accessibility) existed, this could lead to lower costs and greater access. This argument suggests research into methods of supporting innovation and shared infrastructure, such as "academy-owned" infrastructure built for use by the greatest number of users. Other researchers feel that the key to greater openness lies in developing **business models** that offer greater access to the tools of creating and sharing intellectual work; this approach suggests the need for research into methods for lowering costs in the system or parts of the workflow, for measuring costs of certain activities within a system, or for looking beyond the academy to identify other models of financial support. Other systems that play a critical role and require further investigation include **organizational and legal models.** An academic library and the institution it is part of represent organizational structures that deeply inform the possibility and pace of change that is possible.

The categories of change listed above cover a lot of ground and address what we heard were the most pressing problems to solve. That said, despite all the efforts to explore these themes, a key determinant in whether or not things will actually change as a result may well lie in people's ability and willingness to effect and accept change. Understanding what motivates or hinders change is an important issue that has been tackled from a variety of angles.[8] But all librarians, activists, and library workers who engage with this agenda should be aware that identifying the problem and conducting the research are but first steps; reaching consensus and gaining support for implementation provide a set of challenges that must be addressed strategically if change is to be made.

Situating Research in Practice

While this research agenda seeks to pinpoint major challenges facing scholarly communications in and beyond academic libraries, it also embodies a second aim: to encourage practitioners—that is, in-service librarians—to actively identify key issues that need further study and to begin themselves to design and undertake research projects.

The academic community has not always recognized connections between scholarship and practice, though scholars have long made the case that some of the most important insights come directly from reflection on professional practice itself. The Institute for Research Design in Librarianship was funded in 2016 by IMLS to promote exactly this aim.[9]

Indeed, the notion of action research—"a participatory, democratic process concerned with developing practical knowing in the pursuit of worthwhile human purposes …[that] bring[s] together action and reflection, theory and practice, in participation with others, in the pursuit of practical solutions to issues of pressing concern"[10]—could be a powerful framework, particularly for academic librarians seeking to accelerate change in the system of scholarly communications through their research. The method design for this research agenda explicitly involved the community, broadly defined—from directors to domain experts to participants in a range of library roles—engaging actively in the work of priority-setting so that the resulting agenda is truly a community-based process and one that the community will continue to develop.[11]

Similarly, the concept of social justice is woven throughout this research agenda, and its tenets are reflected throughout the topics highlighted.* Therefore, it is important that just as its aim is to propel movement toward more open, inclusive, equitable systems and practices, the research processes that develop those systems and practices should themselves exhibit those qualities. The *Core Values of Librarianship*, outlined by the American

* For a review of the literature concerning social justice in scholarly communications, see appendix 1.

Library Association, enumerate access, confidentiality/privacy, democracy, diversity, education and lifelong learning, intellectual freedom, preservation, professionalism, the public good, service, and social responsibility as "values ...[that] have been embraced by the majority of librarians as the foundations of their practice."[12] Many elements of social justice—especially its emphasis on fairness, justness, and equity in behavior and treatment, specifically in terms of the distribution of wealth, opportunities, and privileges—are reflected in these values. This research agenda, focused as it is on people, content, and systems, requires that librarians not only take on research but also take up action embedded in these values.

Many of the "big picture" research areas outlined in this report are intended to address the major issues facing the scholarly communications and research environment ecosystem writ large. Changing not only practices but also systems requires wholesale cultural shifts at every level of the academic enterprise. It therefore often makes sense to undertake large-scale studies; when looking for examples of innovation, for example, one needs to seek out places where innovation is taking place. Major system-wide studies or even studies of exemplary cases might tend to favor researchers at well-funded institutions or might seem disproportionately to result in recommendations for practices and actions that can be undertaken only by those with considerable resources. Nevertheless, there are valid and valuable objects of study at institutions of all sizes and types—which can be undertaken by those at community and technical colleges, those at liberal arts colleges and at teaching-intensive universities, as well as those at research-intensive universities. The work of research can be done at a range of scales, from individual research projects that may take a few weeks to large consortial grant–funded projects that may take years. In the sections that follow, the research questions offered as well as the sample projects suggested are written with all these possible librarian-researchers in mind. Some questions and projects are local, some are regional, some are national, some are global. ACRL expects that this research agenda will resonate broadly across the community and that interested librarians will feel empowered to advance the topics and aspects put forth through this work.

Research Agenda

At the heart of this research agenda are three main organizing notions of People, Content, and Systems, each offering a different direction for interested researchers to engage with the issues they care most about.

*Topics concerning **People** include embracing diversity and inclusion, improving the working lives of people engaged in scholarly communications, and increasing awareness concerning creators' rights. For those who wish to tackle issues concerning **Content**, we suggest approaches to rethinking what "counts" for recognition and reward within the academy (and how best to measure that) and to creating more representative and open collections. Potential researchers whose interests, talents, and/or expertise lie in the area of creating better **Systems** will find research questions addressing how to support technological infrastructure that is scalable and sustainable, to create systems that permit more access to more people, to build mission-aligned organizational and financial systems, and to advance innovation in academic libraries.*

PEOPLE

No content would be created, no systems would run, and no culture could be changed without the people who are engaged with each of these areas, and any set of solutions will necessarily revolve around people. This section identifies several topics that explicitly take on the roles people play—as employees from a variety of backgrounds and cultures, as participants in the creation of knowledge, and as those whose work is undervalued in the scholarly communications and research environment—to better understand how addressing people's concerns, inequities, and challenges can help support a more open, inclusive, and equitable system of scholarly communications.

Areas of Progress

Commitments by ALA, ACRL, ARL, and other library organizations to diversity and inclusion. Numerous statements, standards, guidelines, and reports over the last decade (e.g., ACRL's *Diversity Standards: Cultural Competency for Academic Libraries*) have affirmed the commitment by library professional organizations to encourage diversity and to develop cultural competencies in the profession at all levels.[13] Efforts include implementation of diversity and inclusion plans, active recruitment from the five ALA ethnic caucuses, residency programs (such as those hosted by the ACRL Diversity Alliance*), opportunities for networking, professional development and staff training, and mentoring and leadership programs. These efforts are areas for continual improvement, thanks to input and challenges from the community and the genuine and often unseen work of association champions.

Empowering creators through copyright tools and education. In the last decade or so, SPARC and the Big Ten Academic Alliance, among others, have urged the use of addenda by academics to retain their rights when they submit their work to a publisher.[14] This work, as well as other efforts, including fair use best practices and increased licensing options, has also resulted in more opportunities for education and outreach on copyright and creator rights.

Discussions about intentional limitations to openness and sharing. Alongside progress in opening up content, awareness has increased about the need to respect limitations. The creation and adoption of Traditional Knowledge Labels,[15] for example, helps noncommunity users of Indigenous cultural heritage better understand its signifi-

* The ACRL Diversity Alliance program, founded in 2017, unites academic libraries committed to increasing the hiring pipeline of qualified and talented individuals from underrepresented racial and ethnic groups. Learn more at the ACRL Diversity Alliance webpage, accessed March 6, 2019, http://www.ala.org/acrl/issues/diversityalliance.

cance to the communities from which it derives and where it continues to have meaning.[16] Similarly, an appeal for "open ethics"[†] has begun to be discussed alongside the calls for "open access" and "open data," particularly when research is based on publicly available data that may not ever have been intended for research purposes.[17]

Increase in academic librarian activism to address social justice issues. Through community advocacy and organizing, public engagement via social media, task forces and committees, and other everyday activities, academic librarians are increasingly engaged in working to address and correct the sociocultural, political, and economic factors that influence academic libraries, particularly those that contribute to systems of oppression. The extensive work done in the area of social justice and academic librarian activism is outlined in appendix 1, "Social Justice and This Research Agenda."

Practical Actions

All libraries can make diversity, inclusion, and equity core to their strategic plans, can put into place practical steps to address concerns, and can set actionable targets to measure their success in the area of people.

1. Librarians can develop multicultural programming on scholarly communications issues that engage the local community in planning and presentation.
2. All librarians can be trained on creator rights and responsibilities, and those who engage with faculty and students can become more active as part of a "copyright first-responders" team.[‡]
3. Librarians can educate themselves about Traditional Knowledge Labels through existing training modules and begin to use them.
4. Librarians can develop or point to existing guides for avoiding biased language in writing.
5. Editors of library journals can request that all contributors to the work being published be acknowledged in some way, not merely those who had a hand in writing the article and are listed as authors.

Next Directions for Research

Embracing Diversity and Inclusion

Both diversity and inclusion encompass not only race and ethnicity, but also gender and gender identity, sexual orientation, ability, language, religious or ethical values systems, national origin, age, social and economic class, and ideas. Diversity recognizes the range of human differences; inclusion acknowledges the inherent worth and dignity of all people and promotes a sense of belonging that recognizes the talents, beliefs, backgrounds, and ways of living of all as valued and valuable.[§] Research might look in particular at the intersection of these social categories and their effects in the academy.

† The concept of "open ethics," which originated decades ago in media and journalism studies with the emergence of online communities, has increasing relevance today when almost everyone has a smartphone and can easily both upload and access material that may never have originally been intended to be seen publicly. For background on the concept from several different perspectives, see, for example: Janneke Adema, "Practise What You Preach: Engaging in Humanities Research through Critical Praxis," *International Journal of Cultural Studies* 16, no. 5 (2013): 491–505; Jennifer Jacobs Henderson, "Toward an Ethical Framework for Online Participatory Cultures," in *The Participatory Cultures Handbook*, ed. Aaron Delwiche and Jennifer Jacobs Henderson (London: Routledge, 2012), 272–80; Stephen J. A. Ward and Herman Wasserman, "Open Ethics: Towards a Global Media Ethics of Listening," *Journalism Studies* 16, no. 6 (2015): 834–49.

‡ The first to launch this program was Harvard (see "Copyright First Responders," Harvard Library Office for Scholarly Communication, accessed March 6, 2019, https://osc.hul.harvard.edu/programs/copyright/first-responders/), but it has now been adopted by colleges and universities of all sizes.

§ These definitions for "diversity" and "inclusion" are the standard ones offered by offices of diversity and inclusion at many academic institutions in the United States. The emphasis presented within these definitions on celebrating difference and on embracing the dignity, worth, and value of all human beings is in keeping with the feedback we heard on the need to expand the original definition of being "inclusive" beyond (1) creating opportunities for greater participation in systems, institutions, and processes involved in creating, sharing, and consuming research and (2) removing barriers that can hinder such participation—in other words, on the importance of placing the emphasis on the people, rather than on processes and practices.

Diversity and inclusion for scholarly communications staff in the library include two aspects: the diversity of the staff itself, and the inclusion of scholarly communications staff (however they may identify) within the broader library workplace. While a great deal of work is already well underway at both the institution and library levels,[18] when thinking specifically about how the scholarly communications ecosystem would benefit from greater diversity, two main areas came to the fore: striving to ensure (1) that those making decisions concerning the creation and sharing of intellectual content are themselves representative of the broader social context within which they work; and (2) that the notion of "scholarly communications" as a professional role is understood to have implications for many library-based roles, whether or not workers are explicitly in a "scholarly communications" unit.

Enhancing representation within academic libraries

A step toward improving representation in the materials libraries create, collect, distribute, and share is to continue to improving inclusion in the workplace. This effort applies to all library staff engaged in the scholarly communications system, no matter what their position or title or in which unit they work. While much research has already been done in this area, much more work remains to understand how best to move from policy to practice.

Some specific research questions to address on the topic of **diversity and inclusion** include

1. How successful are diversity fellowships and residency programs longitudinally in terms of retention? Do fellows or graduates from residency programs do better (e.g., job satisfaction, tenure, or financially) over time than librarians who do not participate in such programs? What other metrics for success are there?
2. What management practices and beliefs influence recruitment and retention of librarians of diverse backgrounds?
3. How can "diversity" be measured in an academic library? What are the most diverse roles specifically tied to scholarly communications in college and research libraries? How is such diversity determined? What practices are undertaken to achieve this diversity? Is this diversity reflected at all levels of the organization?
4. Given what we know about librarians of color leaving academic libraries,[19] are some jobs more prone than others to attrition? Where do academic librarians go when they leave the academy?
5. What are the hallmarks of successful retention practices and programs for underrepresented minority librarians?
6. Does opening up the required qualifications for academic library positions (e.g., degree requirements) improve recruitment and retention of underrepresented populations?
7. How have other professions improved the recruitment and retention of people of color, and how well do those practices transfer to academic and research libraries?

Sample Research Project: Case Studies of Publications and the Career Paths of Librarians of Color. This project would compile the number of library publications written by librarians of color and how their careers have been impacted. It would include follow-up in-depth interviews with librarians of color who have achieved tenure at institutions where librarians have faculty status or who have worked in an academic library for more than twenty years. The profiles would seek to understand common challenges librarians of color have faced in the scholarly communications system and in their careers in order to make recommendations for best-practice strategies specifically aimed at participation in scholarly communication systems and in the retention and promotion of librarians of color.

Creating a broader scholarly communications workforce

Several community respondents, particularly in workshop settings, made it clear that those with "scholarly communications" as part of their professional description often feel marginalized within larger library organizations. However, publishing-related work frequently takes place in different library units, such as scholarly communications, digital initiatives, digital publishing, digital scholarship, publishing and data services, or library technology, which "indicates the experimental and highly context-dependent nature" of much scholarly communications work.[20] While even large organizations might have only a few people with "scholarly communications" or similar terms in their job titles, the activities encompassed by "the scholarly communications and research environment" suggest the broad sweep of library roles that are integral to this work, including metadata services, collection development, information literacy, data curation, information technology, and more. This current narrowness of the definition—or lack of awareness of its breadth—can make it difficult for scholarly communications librarians to get the support and acknowledgement they feel they need throughout an organization.

Some specific research questions to address on the topic of a **broader workforce** include

1. Is there a shared understanding of how scholarly communications is defined in the profession? Who does this work? Who does not?
2. Whose work and labor are valued most within the library organization and why? Does this answer change depending on who is being asked and what role that person plays organizationally? Who defines "value"?
3. How do those working within the library interact with the scholarly communications system? Are there barriers as to who can do research and publish? What are those, and how might they be addressed?
4. How do the various units within the library coordinate their scholarly communications efforts? Who leads this coordination effort? What is the role of management and library leadership in this effort? Can this coordination be improved?
5. What is—or could be—the role of consortial groups or professional associations in broadening the definition of scholarly communications? How can these networks of professionals be better connected?

Sample Research Project: Mapping the Scholarly Communications Network. It takes a village—or at least a number of people—to create and distribute a scholarly work and to make that work discoverable, and yet many of those roles are not officially "scholarly communications" jobs. A national study could capture the range of publishing and other scholarly communications activities in libraries and the people and roles involved. Such a study would be best done by having several campuses of different types and sizes choose different formats of scholarly outputs or platforms—for example, a book, a journal article, a data set, a digital humanities project, a science gateway—and try to catalog the roles and departments or units of all those who have been involved in any way at different stages. At the campus level, the results of this study would offer a deeper understanding of the resources needed to produce and support these works or platforms, information important for budgeting and staffing decisions; at the broader community-wide level, this work would offer a valuable state-of-the-field look at trends and staffing models at different types of institutions.

Improving the Working Lives of People Engaged in Scholarly Communications

In many of the focus groups and workshops, participants highlighted the need to think about what it means in the library workplace to be involved in "scholarly communications." As mentioned above, given the broad understanding of what scholarly communications encompasses, it would be difficult to point to many—perhaps any—librarians, faculty, or students who are not in some way part of the scholarly communications and research environment. And yet job titles and descriptions, time allocations, salaries, and status can vary greatly among those who do this work, resulting in challenges both for managers who try to lead people who do not report to them and for workers who do not feel acknowledged. These individual challenges can add up to managerial and leadership challenges, as library administrators seek, for example, to direct major grant-funded initiatives across multiple institutions and guide in-kind cross-institutional open-source software projects with staff who are working under a variety of arrangements.

Creating incentives for participation

Considerable research shows that getting people to change is difficult. Scholars may choose not to deposit content in repositories; publishers may choose not to adopt open-access models; faculty may prefer to keep using commercially published textbooks in lieu of less costly alternatives; library administrators may keep budget lines funding established (often commercial) publishers rather than supporting newer, innovative publishing models. None of them act out of malice; they have their reasons for acting the way they do. For change to take place, and to increase the likelihood of success for those in scholarly communications who are working hard to effect change, we must first better understand the needs, motivations, and sources of resistance of those whose behaviors we hope to influence.

Some specific research questions to address on the topic of **incentives** include

1. Building on recent work,[21] what do faculty care most about when deciding what course materials to use? Do preferences and perceptions vary across disciplines?
2. Given any particular innovation—for example, adopting open textbooks for courses, depositing published content into an institutional or subject repository, creating a disciplinary culture of "preprints"—what are the underlying motives or barriers to participation? What incentives to participate would be effective for researchers, for institutions, for university administrators, and so on?
3. What factors are most important for faculty and students making decisions about where to publish? Do preferences and perceptions vary across disciplines? How quickly are attitudes changing, and what might further accelerate this shift? What concerns or disincentives still exist to keep scholars from engaging in open-access or other recommended efforts?

> ***Sample Research Project: Understanding Participation.*** Many great ideas fail when people choose not to participate. A research study would examine a particular initiative—the broad adoption of open educational resources, for example—to explore the outcome of the initiative from the point of view of participation or uptake. How many people participated? In what ways? To what end? Did the amount and type of engagement measure up to what was hoped for or anticipated? These questions can first be answered by a simple online survey. Follow-up interviews could delve into the motivations or concerns that led to people's behavior. Interviews would be conducted with those who participated as well as those who did not. Questions would seek to surface both the motivators for participants and the habits, fears, obstacles, and other reasons underlying nonaction. Better understanding why some people participate in an initiative and others do not would suggest new ways to incentivize participation. It might also reveal fundamental changes that the innovation would require to be successful.

Understanding the costs of un(der)recognized and un(der)compensated labor

Despite a general agreement that producing freely available content is a good thing, the labor required to produce that content is not free. The ideals that underlie much open-access and open-source work—and the often highly collaborative nature of academic partnerships—can leave the impression that even quite complex undertakings can be accomplished without properly compensating (monetarily or reputationally) some of the people involved. Project teams thus operate with constant risk of losing key players with little notice. Librarians in particular realize the risks of this arrangement. Scholarly communications workers, including those who write and maintain the code, who manage digital projects, or who provide the metadata that allows the works to be discoverable, may be underrecognized or not properly rewarded, in no small part because the work they do is "invisible" to the success of the project: the code works seamlessly, the project appears on time and looks great, the site is well ranked by search engines and therefore well visited. Research is needed to understand the "invisible" labor of librarians in making content available, discoverable, and reusable now as well as viable and usable in the long term and the related issue of ways to address the lack both of recognition and of reward mechanisms.[22]

Some specific research questions to address on the topic of **labor** include

1. What are the costs of the labor invested in creating and maintaining open-source infrastructure to support scholarly communications workflow? Who is engaged in these projects? How is unpaid labor taken into account? Who is providing this labor, and how are they rewarded for this work? What are the costs, benefits, and risks of staffing projects with small fractions of many people's time?
2. How much in-kind staff time, at institutions of different types, is being allocated to support community-based open-source initiatives and scholarly communications projects (e.g., digital humanities, OERs)?
3. How do we define the "workforce" that is needed to produce and maintain core infrastructure for scholarly communications? What library and other campus-based staff are involved and in what roles? With whom do they most often collaborate?
4. What labor goes into hiring, training, and mentoring interns and student workers? How and by whom is the work of interns and students assessed and rewarded? What are the short- and long-term implications of these particular practices?
5. What jobs are given primarily to interns? What are the decision-making practices that go into that determination? How are interns primarily compensated, and who makes these determinations?
6. How do student workers and interns experience their work in scholarly communications? To what extent is the training seen as an entry to the profession? How does—or could—the work support students in the rest of their academic and professional formation?

Sample Research Project: Understanding the True Cost of a Digital Humanities Project. This project would undertake an analysis of the labor that went into creating and maintaining a specific digital humanities project that has been in existence for at least five years. In addition to capturing the ongoing storage and hosting costs, researchers would calculate the labor of all who participated in the creation of the project, no matter what their role, as well as those who contribute to its ongoing maintenance and who will ensure its long-term viability.

Increasing Awareness Concerning Creators' Rights

Much of the effort expended by librarians engaged in scholarly communications work focuses on educating faculty and students about both national and international intellectual property law. They urge researchers and scholars to be aware of their rights under the law (often specifically copyrights). They encourage them to retain the rights to reuse their work (in the classroom, in future publications, and in other scholarly and professional activities) or to deposit their work in an institutional repository or some other online sharing site. The goal of this training is often to encourage practices that will permit more open access to the content being created.

A focus on "creators' rights" goes beyond those rights accorded to "authors," a term that privileges writing in a fixed form, and applies to the concept of intellectual property in its broadest sense. (Copyright cannot be applied to ideas, for example, although the concept of plagiarism is.) A creators' rights focus fosters greater awareness of one's own rights of ownership—which allow one to give the work away and to determine how, if at all and under what circumstances, it might be modified, reused, or even leveraged for financial gain. Such a focus also reminds us to be alert to the rights of other creators. We benefit from others' work in a range of ways. We need to be aware and respectful if we use or reuse knowledge produced by others that may not have been intended to be used for research and scholarship.

Retaining and protecting intellectual rights

Although libraries encourage rights retention, authors regularly sign over all rights to written work without much thought to the ramifications. While education about copyright is commonly offered in libraries with a scholarly communications person or office, smaller institutions are less likely to have access to this guidance. Even at the best-resourced institutions, notions of intellectual ownership would still benefit from increased focus where creators may be authors of articles, dissertations, or monographs. More focus would also be valuable in the less-resolved space of digital initiatives, databases, or other innovative digital works, or where ideas may be presented in an "unfixed" form (e.g., a conversation) that is not afforded legal copyright protection. Finally, where certain scholarly content involves nontext formats (audio, video, performance, or multimodal pieces), issues of embedded rights, fair use, and the implications for reuse come to the fore. As forms and formats evolve, so will librarian and faculty needs concerning best practices to protect not just the rights of the author or creators, but also the rights of all those whose work contributed scholarly outputs.

Some specific research questions to address on the topic of **intellectual rights** include

1. What have been effective strategies for rights retention on campuses? What has not worked? What metrics are in place to gauge success? Do all strategies work similarly at all types of colleges and universities, or are some more successful at one type of college (e.g., community colleges) than at another (e.g., liberal arts colleges or research-intensive universities)?
2. What copyright policies and copyright transfer agreements are currently in place for library and information science journals? How well do librarians keep their rights to their own work?
3. How do dissertation repository mandates, and their implications for publication with a university press, impact perceptions and behaviors for early-career scholars?
4. How prevalent is the appropriation of knowledge or practice from the Global South by the Global North* or from other underrepresented practitioners by the majority? What concepts or practices were first introduced by those marginalized in scholarly communication, only to be accepted and recognized when reintroduced or appropriated by those dominant in the system?

Sample Research Project: Rights Retention, Ten Years Later. A decade ago, SPARC and the Big Ten Academic Alliance issued addenda for authors to use when negotiating contracts with publishers. This project would capture data on current faculty and librarian practices concerning rights retention, including what rights they retain, with which publishers or types of publication; whether or not they use publishing addenda, or otherwise modify publisher agreements; and how successful they are in asking for the terms they prefer. This project could be undertaken as a survey instrument, issued to faculty and librarians on just one campus or across many institutions of all sizes.

* Although the terms "Global North" and "Global South" are imprecise, they are terms common in current usage. For more on the "North-South divide" more broadly, see Wikipedia, s.v. "North-South divide," last modified February 18, 2019, 09:21, https://en.wikipedia.org/wiki/North%E2%80%93South_divide.

While it would not be possible to prove directly the value of addenda, this study would capture the range of influences that have helped to change author practices (if they have changed), and it would establish a benchmark for future studies of the question. If followed up by some in-depth interviews, such a study could also surface more detail concerning the obstacles authors experience in seeking to retain rights, as well as the motivations or tactics that have been successful in doing so.

Intentionally limiting openness and knowledge sharing

"Openness" and "sharing" are often put forth as positive values to be actively promoted, but there are circumstances when the creators of an idea, performance, or work neither intend nor desire to share it beyond the audience they define. This is most often the case with forms of knowledge that are created without any explicit expectation of publication or use in research, such as religious rituals or personal histories. While some excellent work has already been done within this area, particularly when it comes to work done with Indigenous and other cultural communities by archivists and museums,[23] what is the role of academic librarians when it comes to these these activities, particularly those librarians engaged in scholarly communications?

Some specific research questions to address on the topic of **limiting openness** include

1. How can the cultural heritage community better enforce and reinforce desired limitations to access? What steps need to be taken to ensure such limitations are respected by researchers and the public, while still providing for long-term access to this knowledge by the intended communities? What is the role of librarians in particular in this work? How does this role differ from that of archivists?
2. How well are best practices being followed when collecting and making public traditional forms of knowledge (e.g., "nothing about us without us")? How many libraries have these policies in place, and how many do not? How is the community engaged in working with libraries (other than archives and museums) to establish respectful research practices based on these materials? Do these practices vary depending on the type of college or university engaging the community or the particular community being engaged? Who typically participates from the library in these discussions, and what decision-making authority do they have? Who typically participates from the community?
3. What works currently in the library collection used research that may not have respected the knowledge-sharing practices and desires of the peoples who were the subjects of this research? What are the criteria for making such a determination? What local, national, and international policies might be established as to what to do with these materials?
4. What does an "open ethics" look like when it comes to publicly shared materials (especially those online) not intended for research purposes? What role can librarians play in developing such ethical guidelines?

Sample Research Project: Developing Common Agreement Practices for Open-Limited Communities. Building on previous work,24 assess practices and agreements between institutions and open-limited communities (e.g., LGBTQA+, Indigenous people, anarchists) and determine if there is a core set of common practices or universal elements that could be shared across the GLAM community (galleries, libraries, archives, and museums), or if each constituency requires tailored approaches, which must be determined on a case-by-case basis.

CONTENT

"Content is king." Bill Gates popularized this phrase, which has become a mantra in online marketing, including for those in the academic publishing industry. The idea that content has primacy of place has also become embedded in neoliberal assessment practices within the academy that center on market indicators of productivity and value. As a result, research output—that is, content—is the central evidence of such productivity and value. But increasingly within the academy itself, questions about content—its creation, distribution, selection, and preservation—have come under scrutiny, especially the role that content (whatever its form) plays in both encouraging and discouraging openness, inclusion, and equity within the scholarly communications system.

The desire for rethinking metrics based on content, especially when it comes to promotion, retention, and tenure (PRT), has been especially strong in our discussions with the academic library community. Change within that system is needed in a number of areas: in openness to innovative and nontraditional modes of communicating knowledge, including publication outside the established system; in greater understanding of "excellence" and "quality" in different contexts (e.g., disciplines, cultures, traditions, non-Western knowledge systems); in an emphasis on public scholarship; and in the need to develop recognition and reward mechanisms for all who participate in the research process and its communication, not just those listed as "authors."

Areas of Progress

Encouragement of open scholarship and an increase in transparency. The Review, Promotion, and Tenure Project[25] and the push by the Indiana University system to reward public engagement[*] are but two examples of a welcome move toward rewarding more openness in the PRT process. Among several projects designed to increase transparency throughout the scholarly communications system that might then lead to better practices within it are the JISC OpenCitations project[†] and the Peer Review Transparency project.[‡]

Reward in the PRT process for creation of different types of output. Some institutions (e.g., University of British Columbia[§]) have begun to allow open educational resources to count for tenure and promotion. Many journals have begun to call for reward to be given for the creation of data sets and software. Publons[26] was created by publishers to provide a mechanism for giving credit to those who engage in peer review. CRediT (the Contributor Roles Taxonomy), created in 2014, has been adopted by many academic publishers as a way to provide visibility to the broad range of contributors to published output.[¶]

* "The emergence of 'public scholarship' expands the range of audiences to whom a scholar/artist may direct their research/creative activity, and sometimes the best of this work does not appear in narrowly-defined professional outlets. Candidates should describe how their research/creative activity targeted for non-academic audiences intersects with work targeted to a scholarly community" (p. 6). Read the full guidelines at Office of the Vice Provost for Faculty and Academic Affairs, Guidelines for Tenure and Promotion Reviews at Indiana University Bloomington, March 19, 2015, https://vpfaa.indiana.edu/doc/pt-revised-review-guidelines.pdf.

† The JISC OpenCitations project is "dedicated to open scholarship and the publication of open bibliographic and citation data by the use of Semantic Web (Linked Data) technologies" and is "engaged in advocacy for semantic publishing and open citations." (OpenCitations homepage, accessed March 6, 2019, http://opencitations.net/.) See the OpenCitations homepage for more about this project.

‡ The Peer Review Transparency project is led by MIT Press director Amy Brand and Amherst College Press director Mark Edington with the goal "to create agreed definitions of how peer review is conducted, and to disclose clearly and efficiently to readers the kind of review a published work has undergone." (Peer Review Transparency homepage, accessed March 6, 2019, https://www.prtstandards.org).

§ Contributions that should be considered for PRT include "publications in peer-reviewed and professional journals, conference publications, book chapters, textbooks and open education repositories / resources" (University of British Columbia, Guide to Reappointment, Promotion and Tenure Procedures at UBC [Vancouver: University of British Columbia, updated July 2018], 16, http://www.hr.ubc.ca/faculty-relations/files/SAC-Guide.pdf). Read the full criteria in the online PDF.

¶ CRediT has developed a high-level taxonomy designed to be used to "describe each contributor's specific contribution to the scholarly output" (CRediT webpage, CASRAI, accessed March 6, 2019, https://casrai.org/credit/). The taxonomy can be found on the CRediT webpage.

Development of strategies that promote not only openness but also inclusion and equity. Such strategies include, for example, leveraging libraries' purchasing power to provide broad access to online materials; advocacy for nonpejorative taxonomies; selection of materials that culturally and linguistically reflect the local user community; and support for research and publishing that includes marginalized perspectives.[27]

Experiments in evaluation. Although not without their issues alternative metrics are emerging as a way to tell a more immediate story about a scholar's work and its impact than does the much-derided journal impact factor. Efforts to define and capture value in research outputs are beginning to dramatically change the evaluation landscape. Experiments in new measures include the pilot project Humane Metrics in Humanities and Social Science,[**] which is looking to create and support a values-based framework for academic evaluation.

Community-based guidance on best practices in library publishing. The Library Publishing Coalition in 2018 issued the first version of *An Ethical Framework for Library Publishing*, intended to be a living, community-based document to offer resources and recommendations to library-based publishers.[28]

Practical Actions

- Library deans, department heads, and faculty (if applicable) can regularly review the criteria they use to reward open scholarship. This could mean revising language for hiring, tenure (if applicable), annual reviews, and promotion to ensure that contributions to open scholarship are rewarded.
- Libraries can regularly review collections to ensure they include the full range of voices and experiences. Collection development plans can explicitly describe strategies for acquiring work created by diverse authors, illustrators, and publishers.
- Libraries (particularly in their library-publishing operations) can prioritize support of the research and publishing by and about members of marginalized groups.
- Library-based publishing operations and university presses that report to libraries can be among the first to utilize and promote a transparent peer-review system, such as those developed by MIT Press (PubPub)[29] and by Simon Fraser University (OJS),[30] among others.

Next Directions for Research

While content discussions among scholarly communications practitioners often are framed around questions of openness, the most frequent barrier to a more open, inclusive, and equitable system reported by study participants was the current PRT system and its focus on productivity and quality, defined almost exclusively as multiple traditional publications (i.e., journal articles and books) in venues perceived as high prestige. No greater frustration was voiced than that with the current PRT system, which focuses on quantitative measures of productivity, rather than on quality or novelty. Hundreds of studies[††] demonstrate

** The HuMetricsHSS initiative "endeavors to create and support a values-based framework for understanding and evaluating all aspects of the scholarly life well-lived and for promoting the nurturing of these values in scholarly practice," focused particularly on the humanities and social sciences ("About HuMetricsHSS," HuMetricsHSS Humane Metrics Initiative, accessed March 6, 2019, http://humetricshss.org/about/). See the HuMetricsHSS Humane Metrics Initiative website, http://humetricshss.org/, for more information.

†† For a list of many studies addressing the challenges within the academy to those who are not straight white males to succeed in a world created by that dominant class for that dominant class, see the extensive bibliographic resource being developed by the Publication Ethics Project: "Publication Ethics Project Bibliography," Google Docs, https://www.zotero.org/groups/2272596/publication_ethics. While focused on philosophy (the straightest, whitest, and most male of the disciplines), this bibliography provides a wealth of studies that have very real impact on hiring and promotion for all disciplines, including library science. Addressed within the bibliography are diversity (or lack thereof) in citation and engagement practices; varieties of plagiarism

that prejudice is encoded in the scholarly communications system that even today globally privileges and rewards those who originally founded the academy: white males who speak European languages. (This bias toward white men in publication practices plays out even in a female-majority profession such as librarianship.[31]) Global issues of openness, inclusion, and equity in terms of content creation, publication, and use are of considerable importance.

Rethinking What "Counts"

Although faculty are told that teaching and service (where time-consuming scholarly communications activities such as editing and peer reviewing normally are included) are important, both tenure and promotion are almost entirely based on productivity metrics that are solely about research output (i.e., publications) and about the "impact" of such output, as difficult as that is to determine.[32] Recent studies about the angst involved in research assessment and faculty productivity, particularly when it comes to PRT,[33] have prepared the groundwork for institutions to revisit current ways of assessing such productivity metrics and to rethink how they should measure value and impact. Librarians (tenured or not) are as concerned about these issues as are their faculty colleagues, and thus can work alongside faculty to create the change they want to see. Our participants emphasized the importance of addressing implicit and explicit biases, especially within publishing practices, and of introducing a values-based approach to metrics and rewards.

Addressing implicit and explicit bias

Research in this area might consider the implicit and explicit biases throughout the scholarly communications process that have limited content discovery and reinforced the inequalities of the gatekeeping in publication practices that tend to privilege white men (e.g., submissions, panel acceptances, peer review, citations, etc.). Investigations into the North-South divide are considered especially pressing by many ACRL members, particularly the need to examine the inherent biases of the Global North countries that marginalize the contributions of the Global South, but such biases exist throughout the system. While much research has been done already, progress toward equity has been slow, and more research is needed to enable systemic change.

Some specific research questions to address on the topic of **implicit and explicit bias** include

1. What are effective strategies for addressing biases against the research being done or the work being produced in the Global South? How are these strategies being implemented, particularly within library and information science publications? Are these strategies proving successful in increasing acceptance of research produced by scholars (particularly librarians) in the Global South? What evidence can be offered of success?
2. Given the limitations on discoverability of content written in languages other than English and other European languages, what solutions could be implemented? Who should be responsible for implementing those?
3. What biases exist with respect to "gendered" language and "nonwhite" production, including (or especially) within publishing practices undertaken by librarians?
4. What are the cataloging and archival description biases that limit discoverability? How might those be best addressed?
5. Are there ways to assess which vendors or search engines are the best at providing the least biased results? What do these vendors or search engine programmers do right? What might still be improved?

(including taking without attribution the ideas of another); implicit or explicit bias in research, peer review, editorial practices, or professional status; and so on.

Sample Research Project: Making Library-Published Publications More Open, Inclusive, and Equitable. This project would survey library-based publications to assess the degree of diversity—demographic, geographic, educational, or other measures chosen—among the authors published. In addition to gathering data on published work, the study would gather data on the yield—for example, the ratio of submissions to accepted papers by category. As a means of controlling for disciplinary variety, the study would compare the "diversity" measure to other assessments that capture the relative diversity of the scholarly discipline itself.

Creating metrics built on value: Expanding which values we measure

The systems to evaluate the quality of scholarly work have remained unchanged for decades. Peer review remains firmly in place as the primary determiner of quality, taste, and research integrity.[34] Citations are counted and reported in a variety of ways as a proxy for the impact or reach of the ideas contained in the work. Recently interest has been increasing in including in evaluations of impact the data that can be gathered from "real-time" mentions of the research (on social media, in mainstream media, and so on). While peer review, bibliometrics, and altmetrics may all play a useful role in the evaluation of scholarly content, they can often reinforce the current power structures of the academy, part of the incentive structure undergirded by the PRT system. Consequently, any proposed change to create a more open, inclusive, and equitable system of scholarly communications needs to start with a change to PRT, in particular what is measured and what is deemed valuable.

A critical aspect of this reevaluation will need to include reconsidering what is evaluated and how, and what is included and why, and then determine the means to incentivize the scholarly outcomes and behaviors we would like to see. Two notable projects underway are examining these questions. ACRL's Impactful Scholarship and Metrics Task Force is evaluating promotion and tenure manuals from a variety of institution types,[35] and the Humane Metrics Initiative is exploring a "values-based framework for understanding and evaluating all aspects of the scholarly life well-lived," including collegiality, quality, equity, openness, and community.[36] These initiatives have yet to answer the crucial questions of how to assess values and what role content continues to play in evaluation. Much research remains to be done, both within these initiatives and outside them.

Some specific research questions to address on the topic of **evaluation** include

1. What would a new evaluation system look like? What forms of evidence might be created or adopted to enable this new system to succeed? What would success look like?
2. What additional types of intellectual products should be considered as part of an evaluation of a scholar's contributions? Are there types of content that might be rewarded that currently are not (e.g., data sets, software, exhibitions, performances, preprints, OERs)? What are the barriers to PRT committees changing any evaluation practice? What are strategies to overcome these resistances?
3. What are the particular values within LIS that could form the basis of a values-based PRT system within the profession? What are the particular challenges within LIS to enacting this change? How can these be addressed and overcome?
4. What are the most effective ways for librarians to influence change in the academy, outside of LIS scholarship?
5. Are there disciplines that might be first movers in recognizing and rewarding openness, inclusion, equity, and other values? What are possible approaches to enact change among these disciplines? What local, regional, national, and international conversations would be required? And with whom?
6. What professional associations and organizations outside of librarianship are having these conversations, and how can librarians advocate for PRT changes in those venues?

Sample Research Project: Librarianship Core Values in Practice. This project would compare stated values with what is rewarded in PRT and seek to develop model PRT guidelines that are consonant. Using an agreed-upon framework (such as that provided by HuMetricsHSS), this project would develop a set of core values for academic librarianship, collect representative PRT guidelines, and then compare these guidelines with the core values, creating a new set of guidelines that best represent core values of librarianship.

Creating More Representative and Open Collections

A library's collections are a reflection of the priorities, strategy, and values of the institution. Many participants in the community consultation emphasized the need for library leaders to prioritize developing collections that better represent a broader range of scholars and scholarship, a range that fully reflects the communities of scholars and learners that these collections serve.

Ensuring diversity of collections

Research in this area would examine collection policies, priorities, and practices for both general and special collections, with a focus on representation and diversity.

Some specific research questions to address on the topic of **diversity of collections** include

1. What is the impact of the Big Deal on representation in serials collections?
2. How do consortia approach collection development decisions to diversify representation? Is this a consideration in collection development? If not, why not?
3. What would a review of collection development policies across institutions reveal about collection priorities? How are openness, inclusion, equity, and social justice considered within those policies?
4. What historical influences have contributed to closed, exclusive, and inequitable systems of scholarship?
5. Are there nonwritten or otherwise nontraditional cultural heritage works being produced locally that should be acquired? In what formats do these exist, and how might they be preserved? What intellectual property concerns should be considered?
6. What role does work being produced in the Global South play in collection policies and practices for libraries in the Global North? How much content from these sources is being used to inform research done locally? How are collection policies impacted by what division initiates their acquisition (e.g., area studies, public services, special collections)?
7. What are the priorities for what gets bought, for what gets cataloged and processed, for what gets digitized, or for what gets cut when budgets are tight? What are the mechanisms for making these decisions, and who gets to be involved?

Sample Research Project: Collection Diversity Assessment Tool. A research project could develop an assessment tool to be used at any institution, in order to assess "diversity"—as defined by the researchers—and alignment with the mission of the institution. A campus might begin to develop this tool by examining trends in the demographics of the student body, recent faculty hires, and enrollment in majors and compare how well both the collection and collection development policies reflect the local environment. An assessment tool would be designed to develop a profile of the current collection, some means of evaluating its alignment with current local trends, and a mechanism to identify gaps to be filled. The tool would be piloted at a cross-section of institution types, based on size, geography, and collection type (e.g., research-focused collections, teaching-focused collections).

Enacting effective strategies for revisiting copyright

Limitations on content collection, use, and preservation are often the result of overly restrictive copyright laws. Although much work has been done on teaching about and encouraging rights retention, not much research has addressed how best to go about challenging the current legal system by encouraging authors to renegotiate their agreements with publishers and by pushing within libraries the boundaries of fair use and institutional property rights. This area of research would focus on content that may or may not be under copyright or that might be renegotiated. It would help clarify some directions for action.

Some specific research questions to address on the topic of **copyright** include

1. What are the best strategies for making older copyrighted materials publicly available? What exemptions to the US Copyright Code have been most successful in resisting challenges? What lessons can be drawn from these exemptions?
2. How are libraries encouraging their communities to fully exercise fair use? Which strategies have been most successful and what are the barriers to engagement?

Sample Research Project: Creators, Copyright, and Fair Use in OERs. The landscape of textbooks has changed dramatically, particularly at the community college level, due to the use of open education resources (OERs). What are the practices and challenges for creators and users (both instructors and students) at community colleges around copyright, fair use, and licensing? How are issues of use and reuse being addressed and by whom? How are libraries partnering with people and programs on community college campuses to provide resources and education on these topics?

SYSTEMS

Participants in our interviews, focus groups, and survey identified many barriers in the scholarly communications and research landscape that might be reduced by addressing some challenges related to the systems we rely on to create, produce, and distribute intellectual work. Some see the key to unlocking today's challenges lying in access to the tools of publication and distribution; others would like to see intellectual outputs made freely available. Solutions might be open-source systems that are free to use (if not to install or maintain) or financial models that fund the creation of works, making them free or low-cost to all readers.

This section addresses two different kinds of systems that undergird the scholarly communications environment: (1) digital infrastructure—the technical systems that form the virtual roads and bridges where content is created, hosted, accessed, and stored; and (2) the financial systems that permit organizations, companies, and individuals who invest their time in creating intellectual works to be fairly paid for their labor.

It has already been noted in the sections on **People** and **Content** that systems built to privilege those in power reinforce the status quo and present persistent obstacles to innovation and change, particularly to creating a more open and equitable environment. We confront this issue again here, with the focus on technical and financial systems.

Areas of Progress

Digital Infrastructure

In 2007, ACRL's *Establishing a Research Agenda for Scholarly Communication* cited the need to examine issues concerning cyberinfrastructure, the "layer of enabling hardware, algorithms, software, communications, institutions, and personnel [that] should provide an effective and efficient platform for the empowerment of specific communities of researchers to innovate and eventually revolutionize what they do, how they do it, and who participates."[37]

These issues are still at the forefront within the academy, and investments by national funders have sparked the creation of many elements of the digital infrastructure described in the 2007 research agenda, from building large-scale support structures for scholars in the sciences, to offering access to high-performance computing capacity to all researchers, to supporting data repositories that host and preserve data sets, to creating middleware intended to support those who wish to create "gateways" to more broadly share their tools and data. Private foundations—including the Alfred P. Sloan Foundation, Andrew W. Mellon Foundation, Ford Foundation, and Laura and John Arnold Foundation—have also played a major role in this space by funding scholars and librarians who are exploring and building elements of this infrastructure.*

Grants from the Andrew W. Mellon Foundation have spurred the creation of publishing platforms by academic libraries, university presses, and scholarly societies, including the Vega Academic Publishing System at West Virginia University (now residing in the Wayne State University Libraries), the University of Minnesota Press's Manifold Scholarship platform, the Fulcrum project from Michigan Publishing, the Editoria project from the University of California Press and California Digital Library, and Humanities Commons and its Commons Open Repository Exchange (CORE), a joint project of the Office of Scholarly Communication at the Modern Language Association and Columbia University Libraries.[38]

Aiming for scale. In recent years, some good examples of infrastructure or platforms have emerged that are approaching critical mass. The notion of a "digital research commons" has begun to take form. Examples like the aforementioned Humanities Commons are gaining momentum, with over 17,000 registered users in spring 2019.[39] While some approaches to scale are relying on cloud-based third-party hosted platforms, others are taking a distributed approach, offering open-source software so that users can install and run their own platforms. The Public Knowledge Project's Open Journal Systems open-source software has for nearly twenty years made it possible for users anywhere to set up their own journal publishing platform; as of 2018, the organization has identified 10,000 journals in over 150 countries using the software.[40]

Investments in repositories. If the preferred metaphor for digital communication is still a superhighway, repositories are often the unsung parking lots where content can be deposited, stored, and cataloged and from which it can be retrieved as needed. The last decade and a half has seen a flourishing of institutional repositories as well as domain-specific repositories, places where scholars are increasingly encouraged (or required) to deposit the work they have done. Preservation solutions, like Portico and LOCKSS/CLOCKSS, have emerged to encourage content holders to invest in preservation. While the enthusiasm for retaining, preserving, and hosting content is to be commended, the relative value of institutional repositories versus domain repositories or even "preprint" servers is still to be determined.[41] Standards for IRs are still emerging and may not be easy to implement for all institutions. Even larger-scale efforts and domain-specific repositories that may appear to be "success stories" struggle mightily to attract users and sustainable funding sources.[42]

---

* In the sciences, see related efforts to address the sustainability of cyberinfrastructure, including the NSF-funded Science Gateways Community Institute (SGCI website, accessed March 6, 2019, https://sciencegateways.org) and work of the UK-based Software Sustainability Institute (Software Sustainability Institute website, accessed March 6, 2019, https://www.software.ac.uk).

Movement toward standards. Standards such as those for open data and facilitation of discovery solutions are premised on the notion that data and content have been stored somewhere and can be easily found and retrieved. For example, the Arnold-funded FAIR initiative, led by the American Geophysical Union, is intended to "connect researchers, publishers, and data repositories in the Earth and space sciences to enable **FAIR** (findable, accessible, interoperable, and reusable) data" on a large scale.† NISO's Open Discovery Initiative, which "simplifies the process of data exchange between participating discovery vendors and content providers," is only one of many NISO efforts in the last decade to increase discoverability and use.‡ Broad coordination across disciplines and across stakeholder groups in developing these standards is encouraging. And not all standards are technical in nature; the Trustworthy Digital Repository (TDR) ISO 16363 outlines a certification process that includes a self-evaluation reporting on organizational and staffing practices.[43]

Accessibility for the people with disabilities. Other standards that have arisen deal with accessibility. The American with Disabilities Act standards, which have been evolving over the last two decades, provide design criteria for both the built environment and information technology. In addition to the work being done globally by the W3C, criteria for web accessibility specifically have been spelled out in Section 508 of the ADA; these were most recently updated in January 2017, and the newly redesigned Section508.gov (launched in July 2018) provides excellent tools.[44] The Association of Specialized Government and Cooperative Library Agencies (ASGCLA) has clear policies in place to develop and implement standards within the library environment in particular and has created robust tool kits and resources to address the entire range of physical and cognitive disabilities, including a fifty-minute webcast tutorial, "AccessAbility Academy."[45] Similarly, ACRL's Universal Accessibility Interest Group, established in 2009, offers networking and information sharing and supports programming to promote accessibility in academic libraries, including web accessibility, assistive technology, reference and instruction for users with disabilities, and captioning processes.[46]

Investment in innovation. For a long time, research agendas have paid lip service to "innovative" publishing formats, while publishers remained caught in a very long print-to-digital transition, remaining committed to a print-mimicking PDF format. In recent years, however, we have seen some traction and interest in the newest crop of innovative platforms to emerge, particularly as partnerships among universities, libraries, and university presses. One example among many is Project Editoria, an open-source, digital-first book production system from the Collaborative Knowledge (CoKo) Foundation, a not-for-profit entity working in close partnership with libraries and university presses.[47] Efforts to support data management, including hosting, curating, storing, and discovering, have been no less active, with a burgeoning of institutional repositories, domain-specific repositories, preservation solutions, and science gateways over the last decade. The emergence of innovative platforms is not without challenges, however, as rapid proliferation can mean a lack of cohesion or standardization.

Development of tools to support strategic decision-making. Actually taking good ideas and putting them into practice can be extremely difficult, but some institutions are developing and sharing the tools they use. University of California Libraries has a Scholarly Transformation Advice and Review Team, who "evaluate and

---

† "Enabling FAIR Project Overview," Coalition for Publishing Data in the Earth and Space Sciences, accessed March 13, 2019, http://www.copdess.org/enabling-fair-data-project/enabling-fair-project-overview/. The Arnold grant supporting FAIR "will allow the coalition to develop standards to connect researchers, publishers, and data repositories across the sciences. These standards are meant to render data findable, accessible, interoperable, and reusable (FAIR), with the aim of enhancing the integrity and reproducibility of data and accelerating scientific discovery" (JoAnna Wendel, "Grant Will Advance Standards Promoting Open, High-Quality Data," Eos: Earth and Space Science News, August 28, 2017, https://eos.org/agu-news/grant-will-advance-standards-promoting-open-high-quality-data). Find out more in Wendel's article.

‡ "ODI: Open Discovery Initiative," NISO, accessed March 13, 2019, https://www.niso.org/standards-committees/odi. For more about NISO's Open Discovery Initiative, see "Open Discovery Initiative: Promoting Transparency in Discovery" workroom, accessed March 6, 2019, https://groups.niso.org/workrooms/odi/. The Open Archives Initiative (OAI) "develops and promotes interoperability standards that aim to facilitate the efficient dissemination of content" (Open Archive Initiative homepage, accessed March 6, 2019, https://www.openarchives.org).

make initial recommendations on UC consortial investment opportunities" using an agreed set of criteria.[48] ITHAKA S+R's *Sustainability Implementation Toolkit* offers a method for campus stakeholders to assess the current campus landscape in order to identify partnerships and investments needed to support the digital scholarship life cycle.[49] SPARC offers a Big Deal Cancellation Tracking Tool, a spreadsheet that tracks current and resolved negotiations.[50] In each of these instances, the aim is to gather, share, and review empirical evidence so that teams can make important decisions concerning investments of time and resources.

Sustainability and Business Models

Recent work explores requirements to facilitate the transition from paywall models to open-access models and, more generally, to support the creation and widespread sharing of scholarly materials. Progress in recent years has involved many tests and experiments with new models:

Models for funding open-access publications. Over the last decade, author-side fees emerged as an alternative means of funding scholarly journal articles, and today most publishers offer some version of that approach. Some emergent models seek to address costs at the journal level; others, at a system-wide scale. Both approaches have helped to support publishers in developing open-access and hybrid models, but they are not without their detractors. While researchers in the sciences may have grant funding to support these costs, some institutions are beginning to provide at least some of these funds, particularly for scholars in fields where grant funding is less prevalent. Monograph publishing, based on a more complex set of more costly activities, has been slower to enter the open-access arena, but research has helped to illuminate the full costs of monograph publishing as well.[51] Today pilots are underway testing the viability of campus-based book subsidies, including University of California Press's Luminos program and the TOME project, along with Lever Press, an academy-owned open-access monograph publisher for the liberal arts.*

Collective funding models. Several efforts in recent years have emphasized the notion of collective action among academic libraries. Of special relevance is the crop of fairly recent publishing-focused initiatives like Knowledge Unlatched[52] and the Open Library of Humanities,[53] which have seen early successes in drawing together cohorts of subscribing libraries to underwrite the costs of "opening" a group of monographs or journals. Other community-wide approaches are currently being discussed; in particular, the recent Mellon-funded exploration into the so-called 2.5% movement, building on ideas that have been discussed widely for several years, suggests that libraries earmark a percentage of annual material budgets explicitly to support community-run open infrastructure.[54]

Practical Actions

- Librarians can provide outreach and support for faculty seeking to understand the range of funding models available for them to publish open access and to make informed choices about the benefits of publishing in different venues.
- Librarians whose institutions benefit from open-source initiatives in the scholarly communications space should evaluate the cost of supporting these efforts, whether through staff time or direct services agreements. Having a better understanding of the costs associated with supporting "free" software will make it possible to make informed decisions about which efforts to support.

---

* Luminos looks to "offers open access publishing for monographs, with the same high standards for selection, peer review, production, and marketing as for our traditional books program" and works "as a partnership where costs and benefits are shared between the author, publisher, institutions, and libraries" ("UC Press and the Liminos Model," Luminos Open Access, University of California Press, accessed March 6, 2019, https://www.ucpress.edu/openaccess). The TOME: Toward an Open Monograph Ecosystem project is being funded by the Andrew W. Mellon Foundation in partnership with the Association of University Presses ("AAU/ARL/AUPresses Open Access Monograph Publishing Initiative," Association of University Presses, accessed March 6, 2019, http://www.aupresses.org/resources/for-authors-a-faculty/oa-monograph-initiative). Lever Press, led by liberal arts colleges, is an open-access publisher for digital scholarship, accessed March 27, 2019 https://www.leverpress.org/.

- Librarians can provide clear guidance to students and faculty regarding the FAIR principles of data curation and sharing.

Next Directions for Research

The recent burgeoning of new scholarly publishing models and infrastructure developments has led to some soul searching, born in some cases of the success of these projects, as initiatives developed and nurtured within the academy have been acquired by commercial publishers. In 2017, the privately owned digital repository and publishing platform bepress announced that it had been acquired by the commercial publisher Elsevier, triggering an intense discussion among scholarly communications librarians, specifically those who work with institutional repositories and were clients of bepress.[†] Some in the library community who had worked with bepress over the years to refine its repository service had come to see the company as a part of the open-access "community" and responded with a sense of betrayal at its decision to sell. Others simply saw this as an important reminder that organizations and companies are permitted to operate by their own logic and are not guaranteed to remain independent, should more attractive options exist.

Despite a great deal of innovation and activity in this space, many challenges remain. Creation of repositories of all types and sizes does not always—or even often—lead to widespread improvement in faculty compliance with open-access deposit policies. And the number and diversity of options in terms of where to deposit can make the landscape more and not less challenging for those seeking information.

While the last decade has been a source of great activity and innovation thanks to public and private funders, many elements of infrastructure have struggled to secure stable support. Workshops held in 2018 addressed challenges faced by data repositories.[‡] In November 2018, the Digital Public Library of America announced a significant downsizing, part of a plan to "reorganize and right-size our staff."[55] In December 2018, it was announced that the Digital Preservation Network would be winding down after six years in operation, due to a drop in membership.[56] Our experience studying and observing digital initiatives suggests that even those in operation for a decade or more and held up as "success stories" often actively struggle to identify reliable, recurring sources of support. And many more simply languish with low usage and offer uncertain value for those who choose to use them.[§]

These challenges and active areas of debate suggest important new avenues of inquiry for those seeking to help strengthen the academic library infrastructure and ensure maximal access and participation in digital research and discovery and communication of scholarly outputs.

Supporting Technological Infrastructure That Is Sustainable

Infrastructure concerning scholarly communications plays an outsized role in the ability of universities and publishers to do what they do: create, share, and preserve intellectual content. While it is premature to declare the shift from print to digital "complete"—and indeed both formats are likely to coexist indefinitely considering special collections and archives, international or specialized publications that exist only in print, and the physical

† These discussions took place in many settings, such as social media, email lists including LIBLICENSE and SCHOLCOMM, and at in-person events, such as the Coalition for Networked Information (CNI) Membership Meeting in December 2017 and the SPARC Member Meeting at CNI.

‡ The Sustaining Data Repositories: PI Workshop on Creating and Implementing Sustainability Plans, hosted by the Ecological Society of America, brought together twenty-two PIs from a range of disciplines. Case studies on Dryad, TAIR, and the Cambridge Crystallographic Database, developed for the meeting, are available here: "Data Repository Sustainability," Sustaining Biological Infrastructure, Ecological Society of America, accessed March 6, 2019, https://esa.org/sbi/dr_sustainability/.

§ The IMLS-funded "It Takes A Village" study conducted in 2017 by LYRASIS focused on issues concerning sustainability of open-source software projects. (Laurie Gemmill Arp and Megan Forbes, *It Takes a Village: Open Source Software Sustainability: A Guidebook for Programs Serving Cultural and Scientific Heritage* [Atlanta, GA: LYRASIS, 2017]).

objects held locally by historical societies, for example—but many aspects of the publication-to-readership pipeline are now handled digitally and are digital-first. As a result, the notion of a "highway" of infrastructure—of the roads and tunnels and pathways that this information takes—is more valid than ever.*

Determining the right scale and scope for infrastructure

Today there are many instances of software projects that are in use in the scholarly communications space. Some are deeply embedded in academic practice, like Open Journal Systems or DSpace; others, like Manifold, are quite new. And yet nearly all struggle with the challenge of attracting a significant enough base of participants and contributors to guarantee long-term support. At the same time, while larger institutions may choose to build their own institutional repositories, smaller institutions are less able—without staffing or needed expertise—to take advantage of open-source solutions.[57]

Some specific research questions to address on the topic of **infrastructure** include

1. How does institutional capacity to participate in new software/platform initiatives affect representation in development? How are equity and inclusion from an institutional, not a personal, standpoint affecting infrastructure development?
2. How are software creators and their funders evaluating the success and/or impact of the platforms they are creating?
3. Where is the labor for open-source initiatives coming from? How do libraries and their parent institutions determine how much time staff can allocate to contributing code to a community resource and when? Do patterns of participation look different at institutions of different types and sizes?
4. What characterizes communities or collaborations that can develop and sustain infrastructures that can attract a wide range of users? How can those characteristics be developed and supported? Potential characteristics to consider include, but are not limited to, community governance models and the use of open code repositories.
5. How are external technical and social contexts taken into account in the design of infrastructure projects to promote interoperability with existing software and workflows?
6. How much are libraries investing in community-owned infrastructure? How do those investments—financial and nonfinancial—compare to other solutions?

Sample Research Project: Case Studies of Open-Source Software in Research and Scholarly Communications. These case studies would focus on sustainability strategies, specifically how these initiatives have been able to attract a robust user base. Through desk research and interviews with founders, developers, and current maintainers, researchers would develop a series of profiles of open-source projects, specifically examining the question of size: How large is the user base? How many contributors? What strategies might have helped a project get to that size? What associated investments were needed? And can anything be determined about what a threshold, optimal, or minimum viable scale of a project might be?

* This metaphor has been aptly used in the 2016 report from the Ford Foundation by Nadia Eghbal, *Roads and Bridges: The Unseen Labor Behind Our Digital Infrastructure (New York: Ford Foundation, 2016)*, https://www.fordfoundation.org/about/library/reports-and-studies/roads-and-bridges-the-unseen-labor-behind-our-digital-infrastructure. The report is the basis for a joint call issued by the Ford and Sloan Foundations in May 2018 for research proposals (Michael Brennan, "A Call for Research on Digital Infrastructure," *Equals Change Blog*, Ford Foundation, May 30, 2018, https://www.fordfoundation.org/ideas/equals-change-blog/posts/a-call-for-research-on-digital-infrastructure/).

Managing research data and enhancing discovery

Libraries are increasingly grappling with issues related to research data, data management, and discovery. These topics will only continue to gain importance in the years ahead as discussions about accessibility, interoperability, and reproducibility continue.[58]

Some libraries are already deeply involved in offering support for those creating and managing data that result from their research, though how best to do this and to what extent are still being determined. A 2014 survey of ACRL library directors showed that three-fourths of "respondents indicated that their library is not involved in RDS [research data services]," with more engagement demonstrated by institutions with more grant-funded research. Even for those who acknowledged the importance of offering these kinds of services, determining how to staff and fund that activity was often a challenge.[59] Today, ACRL has a flourishing section for members committed to exploring and adapting emerging digital scholarship services[60] and offers a Research Data Management Roadshow, a one-day onsite workshop designed to serve as an introduction for liaisons who are engaging with RDM for the first time.[61]

Some specific research questions to address on the topic of **managing research data and enhancing their discovery** include

1. What standards for data management, metadata standards, and data formats are emerging in different disciplines that need to be further socialized, encouraged, or mandated as faculty engage in scholarly work?
2. How do scholars prefer to find and consume data as part of their research workflow? What are the implications of those preferences for the scholarly communications community?
3. How and when are libraries interacting with researchers (in all disciplines) who are setting up research projects that will generate data sets and other types of data in a range of formats?
4. What types of data come from nonphysical and life science disciplines, what challenges do these data pose for data management, and how are researchers in these fields being supported?
5. How do faculty at smaller or teaching-focused institutions who are actively engaged in data-generating research obtain data management support?

> ***Sample Research Project: Digital Scholarship Support in the Library.*** What library and campus staffing and collaboration models are most effective in supporting the digital scholarship and nontraditional data objects needs of researchers? Case studies across a variety of institution types (e.g., community colleges, liberal arts colleges, tribal colleges) could highlight effective practices for those supporting the "long tail" of data research and digital scholarship. These case studies could articulate a standard set of practices shared across institutions as well as the unique attributes associated with the various types of institutions.

Creating Systems That Permit More Access to More People

Open, inclusive, and equitable systems permit greater access to more content for more people. This section addresses areas identified as important for further examination: accessibility for those with physical disabilities and a general shifting of focus from a creator-driven to a user-focused approach.

Facilitating access for those with disabilities

In June 2018, the W3C issued the Web Content Accessibility Guidelines (WCAG) 2.1, a set of recommendations to "make content more accessible to a wider range of people with disabilities, including accommodations for blindness and low vision, deafness and hearing loss, limited movement, speech disabilities, photosensitivity, and combinations of these, and some accommodation for learning disabilities and cognitive limitations."[62] The most recent updates to US Section 508 now rely on WCAG AA 2.0.[63]

Publishers in and beyond libraries often face challenges when seeking to make content accessible, but these challenges are often less about understanding the standards and requirements than about being able to implement them consistently and effectively. An effort by the Big Ten Academic Alliance funds third-party assessment of vendors and digital products that its members select.[64] The Library Publishing Coalition's *Ethical Framework for Library Publishing* offers an excellent list of resources for best practices for a range of format types, including books, PDFs, audiovisual, and web formats.[65]

Some specific research questions to address on the topic of **accessibility** include

1. What are the greatest obstacles to offering library materials to those who have physical challenges? Taking the broadest definition of "access"—including not only visual impairment and blindness but also neurological differences—how well are academic libraries doing in delivering these services?
2. For library resources that are locally or consortially built, are the staffing, time, and technology sufficient to permit the work needed to make these resources accessible?
3. What processes are in place for working with vendors to improve products that are not accessible or that need retrofitting? Under what circumstances is accessibility a dealbreaker in negotiations with vendors? When should it be, but isn't?

Sample Research Project: Accessibility Decision-Making. Libraries and library publishers can take many steps to make their materials available to all. Are current practices and policies adequately serving all people? Are there potential improvements to universal design and W3C Standards for accessibility? This research project would determine gaps in current provisions through interviews and surveys with people who use access-related improvements provided by institutions that are legally compliant.

Designing systems that focus on users and audience

Just putting content online—even if it is freely available—does not necessarily lead to increased usage or impact. The community needs more critical reflection about how potential readers and consumers of the works they help to create prefer to find and consume information. This "user-facing" process includes digital interfaces as well as any scholarly output and supports current efforts to demonstrate "impact" of scholarship through increased use and reuse. How can librarians, whether working with authors or acting themselves as creators of intellectual works, better reach out to others and communicate the value of their work? Research in this area may take the form of user evaluation to improve digital interfaces or of a study of the reading practices of students in the library. Understanding user experience is not a single event, but rather the result of ongoing engagement.

Some specific research questions to address on the topic of **users and audience** include

1. How does putting content online (and providing the associated infrastructure) intersect with efforts to widen the base of participation in scholarship to be more open and accessible?
2. How are project leads in academia developing online works that are aimed at broader public engagement? What are potential trade-offs when an academic project seeks engagement with a broader, less specialized audience?
3. A common user segmentation in higher education is undergrads/grads/faculty. When is that segmentation appropriate and when is it too reductive? What strategies are employed to determine what user needs are and does traditional segmentation obscure shared/divergent needs across user groups?

4. What are some effective practices for getting useful and usable feedback from users for different types of online resources? How often and at what points should feedback be invited? Who is invited to provide feedback and how diverse is the user pool? What biases affect the collection and analysis of feedback and how can they be mitigated?

Sample Research Project: Putting Users First. Many digital project leaders know they ought to devote time and effort to understanding and improving "user experience." But how deeply committed and attuned to their audiences' needs are academic leaders—including those of library-based digital projects? A campus-based project would start by developing an inventory of practitioners and faculty engaged in digital projects (e.g., websites, science gateways, data sets). A survey of project leaders would surface information about the range of efforts the project team invests in to understand its current audience (e.g., demographics, motivations). It would also cover how the public-facing work will be used, the changes or improvements the project team makes as a result, and (if possible) the impact of these improvements on usage. A deeper examination of practices among the target population could be accomplished through a combination of questionnaires and interviewing.

Building Mission-Aligned Organizational and Financial Systems

The cost of access is a major obstacle to open and inclusive scholarly materials and thus the underlying business models are a fundamental problem.[66] Where scholarly monographs regularly cost over $100, where scientific journal subscriptions reach into the thousands of dollars, and where undergraduate students spend a couple of thousand dollars each year on textbooks, price is an obstacle to accessing content. Yet underfunding the creation, production, distribution, and preservation of intellectual work is not the answer. What business models do we need in order to properly fund the creation of high-quality works of scholarship, while still making them easily available to all?

Building business models to support scholarly communications

The last fifteen years have seen much experimentation and some progress in terms of new funding models to increase access to intellectual content. Nevertheless, many open questions remain about the best business models for supporting the work of authors, publishers—including editorial, production, design, and promotion work—and library-based publishing and making the works accessible. While some working in this space tend to focus on ways to eliminate the cost of content to consumers, future research should also examine costs needed to produce works of the highest quality. This topic includes ways to explore the question from a range of angles—from the value and cost of a particular type of scholarly product (article, book, digital humanities project, or textbook), to the possible models that could support that production across many participating institutions.

Some specific research questions to address on the topic of **business models** include

1. What is the most effective way to measure success of an open textbook? While usage and cost savings are often measured,[67] are student outcomes also as good or better than those in courses using other textbooks?
2. How are library budgets adjusting to funding a range of OA-related initiatives, in addition to carrying ongoing subscription costs? What factors foster or impede budget adjustments?
3. Can we forecast a "tipping point" when the OA initiatives will replace other budget lines?
4. Is the trend towards consolidating collections and scholarly communications budgets and units growing across all institution types? What factors are encouraging or discouraging this trend? What do different models of consolidation look like?

5. What practices and models from the commercial world could be modified to the benefit of academic-led initiatives?
6. What are the limitations and challenges in supporting collective action models across different institution types? What are the financial challenges faced by different groups, in particular those often underrepresented in discussions of scholarly communications or at especially budget-constricted institutions?
7. What motivates institutional leaders to participate and contribute funding to community-based projects (or not)?

Sample Research Project: Funding Academic Open-Source Software. This descriptive project would first gain a deeper understanding of the full cost of academic-owned technology infrastructure by undertaking research to identify existing open-source platforms and tools that are part of the scholarly communications landscape. Further investigation would take place through interviews with key stakeholders of those software projects or platforms to identify ownership, funding models, and revenue sources and gather data on the user base.

Investing in community-owned infrastructure

The terms "academy-led" and "community-owned" have been the subject of active discussion in recent months.* The notion of having the academy not just influence, but actually own and invest in, the ongoing support of core infrastructure elements has reached a critical stage. This concept includes a range of stakeholders who support alternatives to for-profit products and services offered today. Who within the "academy" might be in a position to take on the investment and management of such an effort? What funding models might support it? What elements would it need to include?

Some specific research questions to address on **community-owned infrastructure** include

1. What are measures for the robustness of various elements of infrastructure?
2. How is community-owned infrastructure staffed? How do those staffing levels change based on the "stage"—that is, start-up, expanding, maintaining—of the project?
3. What are the costs of developing and maintaining core pieces of infrastructure? What lessons can be learned from looking at examples of systems and countries where this issue has been resolved?
4. What will make it desirable and possible for a wide range of institutions to commit to the creation and support of collectively owned infrastructure? How would issues of equity and voice be handled? How is academy-owned infrastructure created so that the academy is not split (any further) into haves and have-nots, and all who want to participate are able to, without tiered levels of access or functionality, but as full partners?
5. How do library acquisition practices, which often must prioritize fee-based services, complicate participation in collective funding actions? How are funding decisions for community-based initiatives handled? And how is this process different, depending on size and type of institution?

* On February 7, 2019, the first Academic-Led Publishing Day brought together numerous players to discuss the concept of "academy-led" publishing. For more information about the day and its events as well as numerous resources on the topic, see "About Academic-Led Publishing Day," accessed June 3, 2019, https://academicledpublishingday.com/#about.

Sample Research Project: Assessing the Potential for "Academy-Owned" Infrastructure. The first step in this project would be defining the core elements of what would be included in the concept of "academy-owned" infrastructure and determining which elements may exist already and merit community-based support—and which may not quite exist yet.† Once an inventory was complete, the next stage would involve establishing criteria for evaluating the "value" of each element of software as a means of determining which are most critical to the academy. Some measures to evaluate could include size and engagement of user base, engagement of the developer community, interoperability with other adjacent software elements, and health-checks/assessments of existing infrastructure. Another stage of the project would include a financial assessment of the existing costs to support ongoing maintenance of existing software initiatives. Finally, an exploration of attitudes within the library-based scholarly communications community, concerning the importance and role of community-supported resources, would help identify important differences that may exist among those at institutions of different sizes and types.

Advancing Innovation in Academic Libraries

Encouraging technological innovation and ongoing development

While there are community-based and library-based innovative software efforts, their creation is often grant-supported and may be somewhat idiosyncratic, supported by institutions whose leaders invest in this work or by a team of librarians and faculty who advocate for it. While not every institution may have the capacity needed to lead a major project, faculty and scholarly communications librarians want their needs represented in the tools and platforms that emerge. There is room to more closely examine how best to maximize the capacity of the library community to develop the road map for software the community requires.[68]

Some specific research questions to address on the topic of **technological innovation** include

1. What sources fund innovation, and what models have libraries found for reallocating staff and other resources to encourage experimentation at libraries of all sizes and types?
2. How do the roles and services of consortia need to change to support changes in libraries and scholarly communications?
3. How can libraries develop strategies to encourage innovation while encouraging a more demand- and user-driven mind-set? What incentivizes libraries to engage in community-driven initiatives? What can we learn from library engagement in consortia about drivers of collective investment and the factors that provide sufficient incentive for participation?
4. How can libraries define and measure success of innovative initiatives, or at least the success and value of their participation in them?

Sample Research Project: Campus-wide Support for Innovation. Today, innovation, specifically concerning the research environment and scholarly communications, takes place in many venues across the academy, from research labs, to the library, to academic departments. And yet access to the tools of innovation can differ widely, depending on what department or unit one is in, or what role one has. Working from the assumption that there might be some value to coordinating efforts at some level, a campus-based

† In September 2018, the Andrew W. Mellon Foundation awarded a grant to be led by Michael Roy (Middlebury College) and David Lewis (IUPUI) to map this terrain, including developing a census of infrastructure for digital scholarship. ("Mellon Grant Will Support Revamping Infrastructure for Digital Scholarship," Newsroom, Middlebury College, September 28, 2018, http://www.middlebury.edu/newsroom/archive/2018-news/node/594612).

study could capture and catalog capacity that exists across a given campus for designing, producing, and distributing intellectual work. This could take the form of an inventory of research and scholarly communications tools and platforms: identifying who gets access to what types of support, the resourcing of the different units providing it, and the means of measuring success and impact of the works they help to produce.

Driving transformation within libraries

Where do we see libraries taking action, to rethink and reorganize, so that investments are better aligned with stated mission and ethics?

Some specific research questions to address on the topic of **transformation within libraries** include

1. How do libraries demonstrate that their work in scholarly communications and research support serves to advance their institutional missions? Is resource allocation dependent on this demonstration?
2. What are examples or case studies of campuses where this alignment has been well executed? What can be learned from studying successful examples about processes for aligning, defining, and community building to secure support for change?
3. Are there some key areas of policy that will change (or change quickly) only if mandated? What are the success rates of existing open-access policies and mandates? Is there a need for further laws, regulations, or even guidelines on changes that are unlikely to happen otherwise? What are those areas?

Sample Research Project: Strategy in the Stacks. Aligning library direction and broader institutional mission can be vital to the success of scholarly communications initiatives as well as to the possibility of transformative effects on the library, but the tactics for effectively doing this may not always be obvious. A study of successful cases would offer useful guidance and tactics for others. This would involve identifying specific examples of major library campaigns writ large and speaking with their leaders to document the paths taken, specifically in light of framing work to serve institutional ends. An ideal mix of case studies would include projects led by senior library administration as well as those spearheaded by either librarians, library staff, or faculty members, since tactics needed to advocate from those different positions will be quite different. In addition to documenting the steps taken to advance the project and secure support, researchers would gather examples of useful documentation, for example, talking points memos for meetings with provosts or other senior administrators, or library "road maps" or other planning instruments that are built to support larger institutional aims and considering how those tactics can be applied to scholarly communications initiatives.

Conclusion

This research agenda is intended to encourage the scholarly communications community and all librarians and library workers to work to enact change in the scholarly communications system. The agenda suggests a range of types of inquiries, each of which will help the community create a more open, inclusive, and equitable research environment. The concepts put forth in this agenda, at their core, touch on a broad range of issues—including the challenges of the global digital divide and information inequality, decolonization, democratization, empowerment and social responsibility, ethics and moral responsibility, financial opportunity, intellectual freedom, the politics of technology, privilege (or lack thereof) of all kinds, the public or common good, transparency and accountability, and unbiased policymaking—and highlight the complexity of change in the scholarly communications environment. These were the issues that emerged as most important to the ACRL community, and this agenda's practical actions and future research questions are responses to those issues, to help accelerate change to more open, inclusive, and equitable scholarly communications systems.

This report, based on extensive literature review and on input from over 1,000 individuals, offers many points of entry to library practitioners in institutions of all sizes. Those who engaged with us in the community consultation—whether through workshops, focus groups, or the online survey—had many ways of thinking about what would make scholarly communications more open, more inclusive, and more equitable. Some focused on the need to be more alert to the different contexts in which scholarship is created, to be more knowledgeable and open-minded about what constitutes "good" scholarship. Others felt strongly that the lowering of paywalls would go a long way to removing barriers to access. For others still, the real challenge lies in finding ways to gain more control over the systems and tools that fuel all this creativity. It is also clear that the library itself may well be a viable object of study for many. Finding ways to better understand the extent to which the tasks of "scholarly communications" and the "research environment" have fully permeated the library roster would be only a beginning.

Consider this agenda a call to action! For this to be a success, agenda readers will need to embrace the challenges it highlights. By asking what aspects of the scholarly communications environment are most in need of change and thinking about how that change might be enacted, the community will start to identify the most necessary questions and undertake the research to find the answers.

ACRL expects that all academic library practitioners, no matter what their role in whatever size library they work, will find something of interest to pursue within this document, starting with the practical actions and moving on to investigating the research questions. Exploring the issues raised in this agenda will help move the community ever further toward more open, inclusive, and equitable systems of scholarship.

Appendices

APPENDIX 1: Social Justice and This Research Agenda

What is social justice? It is fairness, justness, and equity in behavior and treatment, specifically in terms of the distribution of wealth, opportunities, and privileges. Where diversity and inclusion are about groups, social justice is about systems.[69]

Putting aside for the moment the sometimes contested terminology of "diversity" and "inclusion" (e.g., Who is being diversified? Is "inclusion" code for white-centricity?), the concepts have deep resonance within the library community.[70] As our survey revealed, while other forms of social justice were not considered as crucial, diversity and inclusion received a resounding response: 138 of 365 respondents (37.81%) considered diversity and inclusion an urgent issue, and another 161 (44.11%) considered this issue very important. We saw a similar response on the question of retention and promotion, particularly of underrepresented minorities: 127 out of 365 (34.79%) considered the question urgent, and 138 out of 365 (37.81%) considered it very important. Diversity and inclusion efforts have been organizational priorities for ALA and ARL, among others.[71] Despite such efforts, much more needs to be done.[72]

As Toni Anaya and Charlene Maxey-Harris pointed out in the most recent ARL SPEC Kit on diversity and inclusion, both terms cover not only race and ethnicity, but also include "gender, sexual orientation, ability, language, religious belief, national origin, age, and ideas,"[73] yet two pressing personnel issues concern primarily librarians of color. The first issue relates to hiring, retaining, and promoting of librarians of color. Lack of diversity in this area is a problem found in academic libraries of all kinds, as well as across the broader scholarly communications system, including academic publishing. Its roots can be found in a lack of diversity within LIS schools among both faculty and students.[74] Specific strategies, such as diversity scholarships and resident librarian programs, have been uneven in their success unless coupled with training and opportunities to advance.[75] In particular, most academic libraries have not done well in allowing librarians from underrepresented groups to embrace their social identities within their professional lives.[76] The second concern is the lack of engagement of librarians of color in any kind of research agenda. Research opportunities are often curtailed for scholars of color, and this reality that has not much changed despite decades of diversity efforts.[77] These fundamental systemic inequalities must be successfully addressed before academic libraries can become a model for a more open, inclusive, and equitable research and scholarly communications system.

Issues of social justice are not related only to hiring and personnel practices; they touch on each of the areas of the scholarly communications workflow: creation, production, credentialing, sharing, and preservation. It is a broader area than diversity and inclusion or even equity when it comes to race and ethnicity, gender, sexual identity, language and geography, or disability. The concept of social justice covers a broad range of issues, including, for example, the challenges of the global digital divide and information inequality, decolonization, democratization, empowerment and social responsibility, equality, ethics and moral responsibility, fairness, financial opportunities available only to some, the fundamental human right to communicate, intellectual freedom, openness to contributions from participants at all levels of society, the politics of technology, privilege (or lack thereof) of all kinds, the public or common good, the reliance of the entire system on "invisible" labor, transparency and accountability, unbiased policymaking—and so much more.

Not surprisingly, openness of all kinds plays a crucial (and sometimes complicated) role in discussions of social justice.[78] But, cautions Audrey Watters, "open" can mean almost anything, depending on who is using the word:

> Does "open" mean openly licensed content or code? And, again, which license is really "open"? Does "open" mean "made public"? Does "open" mean shared? Does "open" mean "accessible"? Accessible how? To whom? Does "open" mean editable? Negotiable? Does "open" mean "free"? Does "open" mean "open-ended"? Does "open" mean transparent? Does "open" mean "open-minded"? "Open" to new ideas and to intellectual exchange? Open to interpretation? Does "open" mean open to participation—by everyone equally? Open doors? Open opportunity? Open to suggestion? Or does it mean "open for business"?[79]

As Nora Almeida notes, "Ideologically, openness is intimately tied up with social justice and the assumption that the internet and higher education are in the business of fixing social disparities."[80] In practicality, however, often those who engage in open scholarship, embedded as it is in an unjust system, are ripe for exploitation. Not all who participate in the commons do so on an equal footing, observe George Veletsianos and Royce Kimmons:

> In the case of open scholarship, issues surrounding the provision of MOOCs, use of open access journals, accessibility and use of OER, participation in scholarly networks, and use of social media by diverse audiences will arise and should be a matter of concern for participants when considering who profits from, and can efficiently and practically use, their collaborative or shared work. As a simple example of this issue, while we can advocate that individuals should publish in OA journals or that they should use social media in their professional practice, we must recognize that if we engage professionally with these practices ourselves, our advocacy [as white men] comes from a position of power and we might be better positioned to benefit from these practices than others whose individual circumstances prevent them from fully adopting such practices.[81]

Similarly, Almeida argues that openness (in all its aspects) is not a magic solution—perhaps far from it. What she says about open educational resources can just as easily be said about other "open" efforts as well: "OER do have value ... [but] OER can also lead to the exploitation of knowledge producers, can reinforce a Western-centric perspective that leads to forms of educational colonialism, can confuse autonomy for liberty, and can privilege a neoliberal formulation of education that precludes real social change."[82] Or, to return to Watters, "What are we going to do when we recognize that 'open' is not enough. I hope that we recognize that what we need is social justice. We need politics, not simply a license. We need politics, not simply technology solutions. We need an ethics of care, of justice, not simply assume that 'open' does the work of those for us."[83]

While "openness" plays a large role in all discussions of social justice, concerns about social justice within the research environment and scholarly communications cover all aspects of the scholarly communications workflow and (crucially!) all the people involved in the process, no matter what role they play. Some of the issues raised in the literature, as well as (in various ways) in our focus groups and survey, are these, listed here in alphabetical order:

- breadth (and limitations) of collections and their impact on knowledge creation and production;[84]
- commitment to high ethical standards, understanding that all aspects of scholarly communications affect real people and real lives;[85]
- complications around intellectual property;[86]
- digital literacy and information literacy as crucial decision-making tools for administrators, faculty, and students to enhance scholarly communications social justice efforts;[87]

- discrimination and harassment (online and offline) faced by scholars of color and gender minorities that can adversely affect their publishing practices and subsequent credentialing and curtail their public scholarship;[88]
- exploitation of knowledge producers and the modes and mechanisms of knowledge production;[89]
- the global digital divide (and other forms of information inequality) placing limitations on the human right to communicate;[90]
- lack of recognition of and reward mechanisms for what is often "invisible" labor, especially by scholars of color and contingent faculty;[91]
- legacy platforms and tools that reinscribe and reinforce bias;[92]
- limitations on equity throughout the entire scholarly communications process that go well beyond access to full participation in the research and publishing process;[93]
- the need for ample funding for numerous projects, not just those that (for whatever reason) garner attention;[94]
- the need to abandon the fiction of neutrality while still maintaining objectivity;[95]
- the neoliberalism at the heart of the current scholarly communications system, including open access;[96]
- the opacity of the role of machines within the system;[97]
- the primacy of English (especially "proper" academic English) for determinations of quality, discoverability, citationality, and so on;[98]
- problematic word choices and terminology;[*]
- technical systems and platforms that privilege some users over others;[99]
- tensions between academic freedom and protection of vulnerable populations;[100] and
- the whiteness of the academy and (even more so) of scholarly communications and limitations of the white-centric "monocultural" experience, especially in decision-making as to resource allocation, priorities, and selection processes (e.g., people, content, materials, collections, services).[101]

Many of these issues are raised in more depth in the three areas we highlight in the new ACRL research agenda: people, content, and systems. Social justice, while offering a smorgasbord of areas of inquiry, is certainly fertile ground for future research. In this research agenda, our focus has been on the spaces where scholarly communications and the research environment cross paths with, or are otherwise affected by, issues of social justice.

* On "ecosystem" as a word with ethical problems when it is applied to humans, see, e.g., Timothy Norris, "Morality in Information Ecosystems," *CLIR Connect (blog), Council on Library and Information Resources, September 18, 2014,* https://connect.clir.org/blogs/tim-norris/2014/09/18/morality-in-information-ecosystems.

APPENDIX 2: Original RFP

Request for Proposals
Research Agenda on the Research Environment and Scholarly Communication System

1. Overview

1.1 Purpose of the RFP

The Association of College and Research Libraries (ACRL) seeks proposals for the design, development, and delivery of a new ACRL research agenda on the research environment and scholarly communication system. With oversight from the ACRL Research and Scholarly Environment Committee (ReSEC) and input from appropriate ACRL staff, the selected researcher(s) will investigate and write an action-oriented research agenda on the research environment and scholarly communication system.

The final research agenda will provide an overview of trends, identify effective and promising practices, and delineate important questions where deeper inquiry is needed to accelerate the transition to more open, inclusive, and equitable systems of scholarship. This research agenda will be informed by scholarly literature, as well as by advances in practice and the voices of historically underrepresented communities. The research agenda should clearly identify priority areas (6-10) where more research is required to effect change and accelerate the transition to a more open system, with background, rationale, and outstanding questions for each.

Applicants must submit an electronic copy of their proposals (PDF preferred) by **January 29, 2018, at 4:00 p.m. (CST).** Applicants will be notified of their status by March 12, 2018. Work will begin in spring 2018 with a final document of publishable quality, 23-40 pages in length, due by December 4, 2018. It is anticipated that the total amount of time devoted to this project will be no more than the equivalent of a ¼ time release position for the 9-month period.

1.2 About ACRL

ACRL is the higher education association for librarians. Representing more than 10,500 academic and research librarians and interested individuals, ACRL (a division of the American Library Association) develops programs, products, and services to help academic and research librarians learn, innovate and lead within the academic community. Founded in 1940, ACRL is committed to advancing learning and transforming scholarship.

1.3 History of the ACRL Scholarly Communication Initiative

ACRL has long endeavored to help academic librarians accelerate the transition to more open and equitable systems of scholarship. In January 2002, ACRL launched its Scholarly Communication Initiative, with goals of creating increased access to scholarly information; fostering cost-effective alternative means of publishing, especially those that take advantage of electronic information technologies; and encouraging scholars to assert greater control over scholarly communications.

ACRL's most recent strategic plan, the *Plan for Excellence*, was adopted in April 2011[†], and one of four goal areas focuses on the research and scholarly environment. A standing committee, ReSEC, is charged with overseeing and coordinating ACRL's Research and Scholarly Environment Initiative as described in the strategic plan; working with the ACRL Board and other ACRL units in creating a comprehensive effort including coalition building, professional

† Find the ACRL Plan for Excellence, updated in October 2017, online at http://www.ala.org/acrl/aboutacrl/strategicplan/stratplan.

development, publications, research, and advocacy; developing the ACRL research and scholarly communications website; and monitoring and assessing the effectiveness of the ACRL Research and Scholarly Environment Initiative.

Among its many activities, ReSEC maintains a scholarly communication toolkit,* edits a regular column in *C&RL News*, plans the SPARC-ACRL forum at ALA Midwinter Meetings and Annual Conferences, and provides oversight for two of ACRL's traveling workshops (on scholarly communication and research data management) and input on a third (on the intersections of scholarly communication and information literacy).

The member group which preceded ReSEC, the ACRL Scholarly Communication Committee, led the development of two research agendas in the past:

- *Establishing a Research Agenda for Scholarly Communication: A Call for Community Engagement*, a white paper issued in November 2007 by ACRL's Scholarly Communication Committee. The report results from a one-day invitational meeting to collectively brainstorm the evidence needed to manage and influence the changing system of scholarly communication.
- *Scholarly Communications Research Agenda*, prepared by ACRL's Scholarly Communication Committee. This research agenda was approved by the ACRL Board of Directors in June 2004.

2. The Project

2.1 Objectives and Scope

With oversight from the ACRL ReSEC committee and input from appropriate ACRL staff, the selected researcher(s) will investigate and write an action-oriented research agenda that will provide an overview of trends, identify effective and promising practices, and delineate important questions where deeper inquiry is needed to accelerate the transition to more open, inclusive, and equitable systems of scholarship. This research agenda will be informed by scholarly literature, as well as by advances in practice and the voices of historically underrepresented communities.

The goals of the research agenda are to: a) provide practical, actionable information for academic librarians; b) include the perspectives of historically underrepresented communities in order to expand the profession's understanding of research environments and scholarly communication systems; and c) point librarians and other scholars towards the most important research questions to investigate.

The research agenda should clearly identify 6-10 priority areas where more research is required to effect change and accelerate the transition to a more open system, with background, rationale, and outstanding questions for each. Some potential priority areas could include topics such as:

- Economics and private values in publishing, such as:
    - research impact,
    - funder policies,
    - reward systems, and
    - commodification of knowledge and knowledge workflows.
- Diversity, equity, inclusion, and intersectionality in research environments, such as:
    - library-led contributions to more equitable research environments,
    - social movements as agents of intellectual priorities and innovation,
    - the social value of scholarship as liberating and emancipatory, and
    - tension between cultural representation/respect and research discoverability/access.
- Data privacy, security, transparency, and ethics.

* http://acrl.libguides.com/scholcomm/toolkit/.

The successful researcher must take into account established investigation from recognized experts in the priority areas, once identified, but not to the exclusion of other perspectives. Of paramount importance, proposals must address how a process for developing this research agenda would be designed in an open manner and steps that would be taken to include meaningful consultation with representatives from historically underrepresented groups, in order to identify systems of scholarship in areas which may have been previously overlooked. Proposals should explain how the goals of diversity and inclusion would be approached.

For example, an invitational gathering could bring diverse voices together as part of developing the research agenda. In such cases, applicants should include a detailed plan for the meeting with proposed dates, agenda, intended outcomes, preliminary invitation list (with rationale), and costs reflected in a budget (note that the facilitator for such a gathering may be different than the researcher/author). Proposals may describe other approaches, such as interviews, focus groups, or other methods that would enhance openness and inclusion. While the person(s) selected to research and write the research agenda will be responsible for planning and carrying out the inclusive approach, the ACRL ReSEC working group will provide guidance while the design is being finalized.

The ACRL ReSEC working group has conducted exploratory interviews with individuals from organizations representing African American, American Indian, Asian American, and Hispanic library groups, as well as representatives from historically black colleges and universities, community colleges, technical schools, women's colleges, and various diversity initiatives/units. Those conversations yielded important insights about engagement within these communities in both traditional and nontraditional forms of scholarly communication and research. These insights include definitions and approaches that may be unique to their communities or organizations and informed by local expertise.† The successful researcher should incorporate these insights and also include the perspectives of other historically disadvantaged communities as appropriate (e.g., disability rights communities, accessibility advocates, and others) and identify ways of operationalizing social justice and values.

See an outline of the research agenda below in **3.1 Specific Deliverables**.

The researcher(s) will hold at least two live online open forums to solicit input while the draft is in progress (spring and fall 2018) and a formal online presentation once the research agenda is final and published by ACRL in early 2019. These events will be recorded and made available on the ACRL web site. Additionally, an in-person update session may be scheduled as part of the 2018 ALA Annual Conference. (See **3.2 Timeline** for more details on these events.)

2.2 The Audience

The primary audience for this report will be ACRL's membership, which includes librarians and other professionals in all types of academic libraries and those interested in libraries. The ancillary talking points should be directed at other audiences, for use by academic librarians. (See **3.1 Specific Deliverables 6** for more details on ancillary talking points.) Findings of this report should be applicable to all kinds of academic libraries, draw upon scholarly and practice-based literature—both formal and informal—and incorporate perspectives from historically underrepresented groups.

2.3 Background Resources

In addition to scholarly and practice-based literature sources, we expect the report will be informed by these ACRL resources:

† For more, see ACRL's Diversity Standards: Cultural Competency for Academic Libraries Standard 11: Research http://www.ala.org/acrl/standards/diversity.

- ACRL's *Environmental Scan 2017* and *2016 Top Trends in Academic Libraries* by the ACRL Research Planning and Review Committee, available at http://www.ala.org/acrl/issues/whitepapers.
- *NMC Horizon Report > 2017 Library Edition*, available at http://cdn.nmc.org/media/2017-nmc-horizon-report-library-EN.pdf.
- ACRL's Diversity Standards: Cultural Competency for Academic Libraries (in particular, see Standard 11: Research) http://www.ala.org/acrl/standards/diversity.
- The ACRL Scholarly Communication Toolkit http://acrl.libguides.com/scholcomm/toolkit.
- The scholarly communication column from *College & Research Libraries News* http://crln.acrl.org/.
- Past SPARC-ACRL forums held in conjunction with ALA Annual Conference and ALA Midwinter Meeting.
- An internal report by a working group of ReSEC which summarizes conversations with representatives of historically underrepresented communities, to be provided to the selected researcher(s).

3. Project Deliverables

A final document of publishable quality, 23-40 pages in length (not including references, annotated bibliography, and talking points), will be submitted by December 4, 2018. It will be published by ACRL (CC-BY-NC) as a free PDF download on the ACRL website and for sale in print in the ALA Store in early 2019.

3.1 Specific Deliverables

The following section describes the anticipated research agenda. For details about the project proposal specifications see **4. Proposal Specifications.** The researcher(s) awarded this work will be responsible for adhering to the timeline and outline described below and following the instructions in **2.1 Objectives and Scope.**

The final research agenda will contain these broad sections:

1. **Executive Summary.** A brief overview of trends, effective and promising practices, and major questions to investigate. 2-3 pages.
2. **Introduction**: A high-level look at the trends in the research and scholarly environment that concern academic libraries and librarians in the broader context of academia, and identification of current academic library responses to the trends. 5-10 pages.
3. **Effective and promising practices.** This section provides recommendations on actionable steps that academic librarians can take to accelerate the transition to and build capacity for more open, inclusive, and equitable systems of scholarship. 5-10 pages.
4. **Priority areas**: The bulk of the report will highlight future-focused outstanding research questions. For each priority area, provide specific research questions, including sample options for investigation, and, at a high level, possible research designs. The discussion of each priority should be a few paragraphs in length. Key research questions should address challenges that the higher education sector is facing, including but not limited to those suggested in **2.1 Objectives and Scope**. We anticipate that this section may include 6-10 priority areas where more research is required, with background, rationale, and outstanding questions for each.* However, the selected researcher could make the case that there are fewer or more based on the literature. 10-15 pages.
5. **Conclusion.** A brief summary of major findings and recommendations. 1-2 pages.
6. **Ancillary and supporting materials**: In addition to the main body of the report, the successful appli-

* As an example of the type of discussion we imagined for each priority area, (in terms of format, length, and tenor), see the 2017-2021 National Research Agenda by the Young Adult Services Library Association, available at http://www.ala.org/yalsa/guidelines/research/researchagenda.

cant will develop materials that will aid and encourage discussion and use of the research agenda, including:

- An annotated bibliography of sources used to inform the research agenda.
- A set of talking points, one page each, for academic librarians to use in conversations with three distinct audiences: higher education administrators; researchers as authors; and scholarly publishers of books and journals, research analytics companies, digital curation service providers, and other vendors disseminating scholarly work outside of the traditional scholarly publishing bounds.

In addition to these components of the report itself, when submitting the revised draft of the report (due October 1, 2018), the researcher(s) should submit a brief memo to ReSEC and the ACRL Board of Directors with recommendations on how ACRL can encourage the community to implement the effective and promising practices, influence other stakeholders via the talking points, and investigate the outstanding research questions.

The researcher(s) will communicate regularly with ACRL ReSEC, which will be sharing updates with the ACRL Board. The researcher(s) will work with ReSEC and ACRL staff to seek feedback on drafts through venues such as online open forums and a possible in person update session at the ALA Annual Conference in June 2018. For more on conference locations and specific points of communication, see **3.2 Timeline**.

3.2 Timeline

ACTION	RESPONSIBLE PARTY	DEADLINE
Proposals due	Prospective researchers	January 29, 2018
Researcher(s) selected and applicants notified	Working group	March 12, 2018
Project begins	Researcher(s)	March 13, 2018
ACRL Online Open Forum (to share progress update with broader community, solicit feedback)	Researcher(s) & ReSEC Chair Patricia Hswe	Late April 2018
FYI update submitted to ACRL office (for review during ACRL Board Meeting at ALA Annual Conference)	Researcher(s)	May 24, 2018
Possible presentation and discussion at ALA Annual Conference (New Orleans, LA)	Researcher(s) & ReSEC Chair Patricia Hswe	June 24, 2018
First draft due to working group	Researcher(s)	August 1, 2018
Feedback to researcher(s)	Working group	September 1, 2018
Revised draft and advice memo due to working group/ACRL Board	Researcher(s)	October 1, 2018
ACRL Online Open Forum (to share draft and progress with broader community, solicit feedback)	Researcher(s) & ReSEC Chair Yasmeen Shorish	Mid October 2018
Feedback on revised draft to researcher(s)	Working group and community at large	November 1, 2018
Final report due	Researcher(s)	December 4, 2018
Public release of final report	Working group	January 15, 2019
ACRL Presents Webcast	Researcher(s) & ReSEC Chair Yasmeen Shorish	February 2019

4. Proposal Specifications

4.1 General Instructions

The successful applicant or team of applicants will demonstrate strong research and writing skills. Preference will be given to applicant(s) with demonstrated experience communicating about the scholarly communication and research environment.

The proposal must comply with the content requirements detailed in this section. The applicant(s) must submit a complete response that provides proof of experience and qualifications to complete the required activities and the project's estimated costs. Applicants should include a letter of support from the applicant's employer indicating support for the time release from other duties to complete this project. If the applicant is a doctoral student, he/she should send a letter of recommendation from a faculty member who agrees to supervise work on this project.

4.2 Proposal

4.2.1 LETTER OF APPLICATION

a. Describe the particular qualifications, knowledge, and experience you bring to this project.
b. Indicate ability and willingness to adhere to the timeline described in **Section 3.2** above.
c. Indicate availability to present at possible forums/conferences. See **Timeline** in **Section 3.2**.
d. Provide a brief description of your (and, if applicable, your company's) experience doing research in the field of academic libraries and higher education and your familiarity with research done in the field of scholarly communication.
e. The letter of application must be signed by one or more individuals qualified to perform the work described. Individuals signing the letter must indicate position title. A contact person for further information must be identified.

4.2.2 PROPOSAL NARRATIVE

The proposal should include a 1,000- to 1,500-word narrative describing your plan to analyze the background material provided above and other significant literature. Address how you would synthesize major ideas and themes to identify trends, effective and promising practices, and priority areas where outstanding research questions remain.

Explain your approach to designing and implementing a diverse and inclusive process. If this would be via an invitational meeting, include a detailed plan with date, agenda, intended outcomes, and preliminary invitation list (with rationale). If via another mechanism, please explain.

4.2.3 PERSONNEL

Identify all personnel to be included in the project by name, title, and the estimated amount of time devoted to each project task. It is anticipated that the total amount of time devoted to this project will be no more than the equivalent of a ¼ time release position for the 9-month period. The response must include curricula vitae or résumés of all project staff.

4.2.4 PROJECT PLAN AND SCHEDULE

Submit a coherent and detailed work plan that adheres to the timeline as described in **Section 3.2**.

4.2.5 BUDGET

The budget for the proposal must contain itemized detail—including the estimated amount of time devoted to each project task—to show how cost is determined. If an invitational meeting is proposed, costs for participant travel and lodging, meeting room, AV, supplies, and meals should be included.

4.2.6 LETTER OF SUPPORT

Unless self-employed, a signed letter from the applicant's employer or faculty advisor granting support for time release from other duties, or project supervision as appropriate.

4.2.7 REFERENCES

Provide complete contact information (name, address, email contact, and telephone number) for three references familiar with your qualifications and experience relevant to the purpose of this work. References must be provided for each individual if submitting as a team.

5. Submission Deadline

An electronic copy of the proposal (PDF preferred) is due by **January 29, 2018, at 4:00 p.m. (CST).** All costs for the applicant's response preparation are the responsibility of the applicant and may not be charged to the budget for the project.

6. Selection Process and Criteria

The contractor will be selected from the proposals submitted to this RFP. A team of appropriate ACRL staff, member leaders, and the ACRL Executive Director will review the responses. The ACRL Executive Director will make the selection based on the following criteria.

6.1 Completeness of Proposal

Proposals must address all elements requested in this RFP. See **Appendix A: RFP Checklist.**

6.2 Proposal Narrative

Evidence that the individual(s) submitting understands the scope and intention of the project and will work within the project guidelines as described under **Sections 2** and **3**. Evidence of a well-reasoned approach to designing the research agenda and the consultative process.

6.3 Project Personnel

Evidence that the individual or team submitting has the experience, expertise, research ability, and credentials to complete this project. Subcontracting any or all of this work to individuals not included in the proposal will not be permitted without prior written permission.

6.4 Project Plan and Schedule

Evidence that the individual (or team) submitting has a coherent, detailed, and robust work plan that adheres to the timeline in **Section 3.2.**

6.5 Project Budget

A clearly described and itemized budget as described in **Section 4.2.5.**

6.6 References

References from three individuals familiar with your and each individual on your team's qualifications and experience relevant to the purpose of this work.

7. Contract for Services and Payment Schedule

ACRL will prepare a letter of agreement with the contractor(s) that includes the specific responsibilities and timetable for the project. The Association will also clarify a schedule for payment that will be negotiated between the contractor(s) and ACRL. Subcontracting any or all of this work to individuals not included in the proposal will not be permitted without prior written permission.

8. Ownership of Materials

This project will be conducted as work for hire. The research agenda report and all materials developed to support it, under the terms of the project agreement, become the property of ACRL. ACRL reserves the non-exclusive rights to copy such material and to publish, disseminate, and otherwise use the materials developed under the terms of the agreement in print or electronically. ACRL will publish this work with a CC-BY-NC license as a free PDF download on the ACRL website and for sale in print in the ALA Store.

The contractor agrees that as a work for hire ACRL will have all rights to publish the work first and make use of the findings in many venues and products. The contractor will not have exclusive speaking, marketing, or consulting rights for the products, concepts, or techniques developed for this project. While ACRL holds the first right of publication, we are happy to work with the selected researcher(s) to publish subsequently in other venues, and after the report has been widely disseminated the researcher may incorporate findings from the research into his/her presentations and writings as long as clear attribution is given to ACRL.

9. Submission

Please submit a PDF (preferred) or MS Word version of your response to the RFP **by 4:00 p.m. CST, January 29, 2018, to:**

> Sophie Skinner
> Program Coordinator
> ACRL/ALA
> 50 E. Huron St.
> Chicago, IL 60611
> sskinner@ala.org
> 312-280-2512

A confirmation of receipt will be sent upon receipt of submission; if you do not receive this please call to ensure the proposal is not caught in a spam filter.

All proposals are confidential.

10. Notification

Applicants will be notified of their status no later than March 12, 2018.

For questions contact:

> Kara Malenfant
> Sr. Strategist for Special Initiatives
> ACRL/ALA
> 50 E. Huron St.
> Chicago, IL 60611
> kmalenfant@ala.org
> 312-280-2510

Appendix A: RFP Checklist

_____ Letter of application.

a. Describe the particular qualifications, knowledge, and experience you bring to this project.
b. Indicate ability and willingness to adhere to the timeline described in the **Section 3.2**.
c. Indicate availability to present at possible forums. (See details in **Section 3.2**.)
d. Provide a brief description of your (and, if applicable, your company's) experience doing research in the field of scholarly communication.
e. The letter of application must be signed by one or more individuals qualified to perform the work described. Individuals signing the letter must indicate position title. A contact person for further information must be identified.

_____Proposal narrative.

a. 1,000 to 1,500 words.
b. Describe plan to analyze background materials and significant literature.
c. Address synthesis of major ideas and themes to identify trends, effective and promising practices, and priority areas where outstanding research questions remain.
d. Describe design of an open process and steps to include meaningful consultation with representatives from historically underrepresented communities.
e. Describe potential challenges and how these would be addressed.
f. Identify all personnel to be included.

_____ Coherent and detailed work plan that adheres to the timeline.

_____ Budget with itemized detail.

_____ Letter of support from employer or faculty advisor, unless self-employed.

_____Curriculum Vitae (and additional CVs or résumés for subcontractors or members of the submitting team, if applicable).

_____ References (and additional references for each member of the submitting team if applicable).

APPENDIX 3: Methodology

The research process was designed to be highly consultative, bringing in a wide range and large number of voices from the library community to share thoughts on current problems and priority areas where research is needed. Feedback from the community of academic librarians was sought at every step; the ReSEC (ACRL's Research and Scholarly Environment Committee) advisory subcommittee was involved at key touchpoints throughout the work, and the researchers continuously synthesized what we were hearing to produce this final report.

The ReSEC advisory subcommittee served as both client and advisor throughout the process, reviewing and approving interview guides, survey questions, documentation to share with workshop attendees, and drafts of this report.

The research process involved the following data-gathering stages:

Literature review. A literature review focused on the current academic college and research library landscape for research and scholarly communications, with a particular focus on issues of social justice. See appendix 1 for a discussion of the social justice issues; see appendix 9 for an annotated list of recommended readings.

Community consultation. The research involved structured engagement with the community throughout the process, including

- **A community webinar,** to introduce the work underway and answer questions.
- **Expert interviews.** Interviews by phone were conducted with eight individuals at the start of the project. Early interviews were intended to provide context and leads for understanding pressing issues today. Once a draft had been produced, additional expert readers were invited to offer feedback on topics relevant to their areas of expertise; four readers provided such feedback.
- **Focus groups.** To maximize the chance to hear from certain traditionally underrepresented groups, we hosted seven focus groups, involving a total of thirty participants. Participants were invited via ACRL communications, announcements on relevant email discussion lists, and conferences. Sessions were run as virtual meetings, using the Zoom platform. Facilitation for each group followed a discussion guide. (See appendix 5.) The groups were formed to encourage engagement by special categories of participants, though many groups included participants who were not necessarily part of the stated target audience.
    - Three groups specifically included those from underrepresented cultural or ethnic communities. Because there are so many different library organizations and ACRL special interest groups, we felt we needed to have several of these groups to ensure we heard from as many voices as possible.
    - One group focused on those with expertise and experience in universal accessibility challenges.
    - One group focused on those at community colleges (i.e., two-year colleges).
    - One group focused on those from liberal arts colleges (i.e., four-year colleges).
    - One group focused on those from research-intensive universities (i.e., colleges and universities with graduate programs).
- **Workshops.** Several in-person events were run to gather feedback and engage the community. All invitations to events are included in appendix 6.
    - **Library Publishing Forum**, Minneapolis, MN. May 22, 2018. Lunchtime roundtable, thirty-five attendees.
    - **ACRL meeting at ALA**, New Orleans, LA. June 24, 2018. We presented the project in three separate settings:

    - ReSEC committee meeting update.
    - Scholarly Communications Discussion Group. Standing-room-only group of over fifty attendees.
    - Research Agenda on the Research Environment and Scholarly Communications System Working Session. This was intended as a large room discussion, but had very low attendance, which may have been due to counterprogramming, as well as the description of the session as "working session," which some may have thought meant it was not open to all.
- **Third National Joint Conference of Librarians of Color, JCLC 2018,** Albuquerque, NM. September 28, 2018. "Making Scholarly Communications and the Research Environment More Open, Inclusive, and Equitable: Roundtable to Review the Draft ACRL Research Agenda."
- **Community-wide online survey.** The survey was developed and deployed later in the workplan than originally intended, taking place while focus groups were already underway, rather than prior to their beginning. The aim of the survey was to surface respondents' priorities in areas of attention for a research agenda. Charts illustrating the survey responses are included in appendix 7, with additional survey analysis in appendix 8.
    - The survey was developed using SurveyMonkey and promoted through several channels, including ACRL mailing lists, social media related to scholarly communications, email discussion lists in the community, as well as the researchers' own networks.
    - The survey was open from Tuesday, June 26, through Friday, July 13, 2018. We received 832 responses; 362 respondents completed the entire survey. There was significant drop-off after question 3, at which point the questions became more complex.
- **Community consultation and editorial review.** A draft paper was shared with the ARCL community and opened for comments from December 11, 2018, through January11, 2019. Comments from that public period as well as a thorough review by members of the ReSEC advisory subcommittee were incorporated into the final report.

APPENDIX 4: List of Participants

Many gave generously of their time and thoughts—some several times over—throughout the process of consultation with the academic library community. Those who contributed in person are listed below.

Expert Interviews

- Perry Collins (Ball State)
- Raym Crow (Chain Bridge Group)
- Trevor Dawes (University of Delaware)
- Karen Estlund (Penn State)
- Ellen Finnie (Massachusetts Institute of Technology)
- Josh Greenberg (Sloan Foundation)
- April Hathcock (New York University)
- Adrian Ho (University of Kentucky)
- Harrison Inefuku (Iowa State)
- Bill Kasdorf (Apex Content and Media Solutions)
- Catherine Mitchell (California Digital Library)
- Michael Roy (Middlebury)

Focus Group Participants

- Nicky Agate (Columbia University)
- Emilie Algenio (Texas A&M)
- Nathasha Alvarez (East Los Angeles College)
- Rick Anderson (University of Utah)
- Pamela Andrews (University of North Texas)
- Jessica Brangiel (Swarthmore)
- Camille Callison (University of Manitoba)
- Lauren Collister (University of Pittsburgh)
- Nancy Colyar (Birmingham-Southern College)
- Jody Combs (Vanderbilt)
- Jenn Dandle (University of California San Diego)
- Morgan Davis (College of William and Mary)
- Sandra Enimil (Ohio State)
- Michele Gibney (Pacific University)
- Hal Hinderliter (Northern Illinois)
- Claudia Holland (Mississippi State)
- Valerie Horton (University of Minnesota)
- Reabeka King (CUNY—Kingsborough Community College)
- Debbie Krahmer (Colgate)
- Sara Kuhn (University of North Dakota)
- Maha Kumaran (University of Saskatchewan)
- Allison Langham-Putrow (University of Minnesota)
- Deborah Lee (Mississippi State)

- Monica Lopez (Cerritos College)
- Paige Mann (University of the Redlands)
- Shawn Martin (University of Indiana)
- Joyce Ogburn (Appalachian State)
- Eric Olson (ORCID)
- Amanda Page (Syracuse University)
- Chaitra Powell (UNC Chapel Hill)
- Rita Premo (Sonoma State)
- Charlotte Roh (University of San Francisco)
- Judy Ruttenberg (Association of Research Libraries)
- Allegra Swift (University of California San Diego)
- Malina Thiede (SUNY Plattsburgh)
- Sharell Walker (CUNY—Manhattan Community College)
- Sue Wiegand (Saint Mary's College)

Members of the ACRL Research and Scholarly Environment Committee (2018–2019)

- Yasmeen Shorish (Chair, July 1, 2018, to June 30, 2019)
- Nathan Frank Hall (Vice-Chair, July 1, 2018, to June 30, 2019; Member, July 1, 2017, to June 30, 2019)
- Wayne Bivens-Tatum (Member, July 1, 2017, to June 30, 2019)
- Paul Bracke (Member, July 1, 2017, to June 30, 2019)
- Tatiana Bryant (Member, July 1, 2018, to June 30, 2020)
- Jessica Clemons (Member, July 1, 2017, to June 30, 2019)
- Sandra L. DeGroote (Member, July 1, 2018, to June 30, 2020)
- Mel DeSart (Member, July 1, 2017, to June 30, 2019)
- Tim Dolan (Member, July 1, 2017, to June 30, 2019)
- Mary D. Galvin (Member, July 1, 2018, to June 30, 2020)
- Isaac Gilman (Member, July 1, 2018, to June 30, 2020)
- Steven R. Harris (Member, July 1, 2017, to June 30, 2019)
- Philip Herold (Member, July 1, 2017, to June 30, 2019)
- Pamella R. Lach (Member, July 1, 2018, to June 30, 2020)
- Allison Langham-Putrow (Member, July 1, 2018, to June 30, 2020)
- Yuan Li (Member, July 1, 2017, to June 30, 2019)
- Robert J. Nelson (Member, July 1, 2017, to June 30, 2019)
- Amy L. Nurnberger (Member, July 1, 2018, to June 30, 2020)
- Cynthia Mari Orozco (Member, July 1, 2018, to June 30, 2020)
- Lori J. Ostapowicz-Critz (Member, July 1, 2017, to June 30, 2019)
- Erin Elizabeth Owens (Member, July 1, 2018, to June 30, 2020)
- Michelle Reed (Member, July 1, 2017, to June 30, 2019)
- Charlotte Roh (Member, July 1, 2018, to June 30, 2020)
- William Shane Wallace (Member, July 1, 2018, to June 30, 2020)
- William Michael Cross (Ex-Officio Member, December 1, 2015, to June 30, 2019)
- Abigail H. Goben (Ex-Officio Member, July 1, 2017, to June 30, 2020)

- Beth McNeil (Board Liaison, July 1, 2017, to June 30, 2019)
- Kara Malenfant (Staff Liaison, July 1, 2018, to June 30, 2019)
- Erin Nevius (Interim Staff Liaison, April 1 to July 31, 2018)
- Chase Ollis (Staff Liaison, July 1, 2018, to June 30, 2019)

Library Publishing Forum Workshop

- Nicky Agate (Columbia University)
- Cheryl Ball (Wayne State)
- Marilyn Billings (University of Massachusetts Amherst)
- Robert Browder (Virginia Tech)
- Mahrya Burnett (University of Iowa)
- Sam Byrd (Virginia Commonwealth University)
- Perry Collins (Ball State)
- Lauren Collister (University of Pittsburgh)
- Sandra Enimil (Ohio State)
- Beth Fuget (University of Washington Press)
- Kaneisha Gaston Arhin (North Carolina Central University)
- Harriett Green (University of Illinois Urbana-Champaign)
- Jen Green (Dartmouth College)
- Dave Hansen (Duke University)
- Sarah Hare (Indiana University)
- Kevin Hawkins (University of North Texas)
- Matthew Hunter (Florida State University)
- Amanda Hurford (PALNI)
- Andy Keck (Luther Seminary)
- Shannon Kipphut-Smith (Rice University)
- James MacGregor (Simon Fraser University)
- Paige Mann (University of the Redlands)
- Sarah McKee (Emory University)
- Carrie Nelson (University of Wisconsin-Madison)
- Charlotte Roh (University of San Francisco)
- Alec Smecher (Simon Fraser University)
- Kevin Stranack (Simon Fraser University)
- Helen Szigeti (Society for Scholarly Publishing)
- Anita Walz (Virginia Tech)

Joint Conference of Librarians of Color Workshop

- José Aguiñaga (Glendale Community College)
- Frans Albarillo (CUNY—Brooklyn College)
- Rita Alfaro (Fort Worth Library)
- Jason Alston (University of Missouri–Kansas City)
- Chiuedu Amaefula (Indiana University)
- Tarida Anantachai (Syracuse University)

- Emma Antobam (CUNY—Bronx Community College)
- Olivia Baca (University of New Mexico)
- Michelle Baildon (Massachusetts Institute of Technology)
- Norda Bell (York University)
- Ruby Bell-Gam (UCLA)
- Janet Bishop (University of Minnesota)
- Kathy Bradshaw (Virginia Commonwealth University)
- Mark Clemente (Case Western Reserve)
- Jeremy Conley (Miami University [Ohio])
- Jessica Dai (West Virginia)
- Mary Ellen Davis (ACRL)
- William Felder (unaffiliated)
- Diana Floegel (Rutgers)
- Chelwea Gant (Bowling Green State)
- George Gottschalk (University of Illinois Urbana-Champaign)
- Rebecca Hankins (Texas A&M)
- April Hathcock (New York University)
- Harrison Inefuku (Iowa State)
- Sharon Ladenson (Michigan State)
- Andrea Malone (University of Houston)
- Rebecca Martin (Harvard)
- Tasha McClain (Louisiana State)
- Zoë McLaughlin (University of Michigan)
- Gloria Mims (Fulton County Library)
- Daisy Muralles (University of California Santa Barbara)
- Jharma Pascual (University of California Irvine)
- Mary Jane Petrowski (ACRL)
- Jennie Quiñónez (California State University at Northridge)
- Marie Radford (Rutgers)
- Maria Rios (University of South Carolina)
- Charlotte Roh (University of San Francisco)
- Lian Ruan (University of Illinois Urbana-Champaign)
- Ariana Santiago (University of Houston)
- Yasmeen Shorish (James Madison University)
- Kimberly Tate-Malone (Seattle Central College)
- Krystal Tribbett (University of California Irvine)
- Tinamarie Vella (CUNY Newmark J-School)
- Rachel Wexelbaum (St. Cloud State)
- Shirley Williams (Sharon Hill Public Library)
- Simone Yearwood (CUNY—Queens College)
- Joe Zhou (California State University at Sacramento)

Comments on Public Draft

In addition to the individuals listed below, several anonymous commenters provided useful feedback.

- Micah Altman (Massachusetts Institute of Technology)
- Rick Anderson (University of Utah)
- Andrea Baer (University of West Georgia)
- Sara Benson (University of Illinois at Urbana-Champaign)
- Elizabeth A. Brown (Binghamton University)
- Rebecca Bryant (Online Computer Library Center [OCLC])
- Tatiana Bryant (Adelphi University)
- Shawn Calhoun (University of San Francisco)
- Camille Callison (University of Manitoba, for the Indigenous Matters Committee of the Canadian Federation of Library Associations)
- Erin Carrillo (Virginia Commonwealth University)
- Raym Crow (Chain Bridge Group)
- Jessica Dai (West Virginia University)
- Jim DelRosso (Cornell University)
- Leslie Farmer (California State University—Long Beach)
- Lucy Fazzino (St. John's University [New York])
- Martin L. Garnar (University of Colorado—Colorado Springs, for the ALA Equity, Diversity, and Inclusion Implementation Working Group)
- Aliqae Geraci (Cornell University)
- April Hathcock (New York University)
- Kevin Hawkins (University of North Texas)
- Claudia Holland (George Mason University)
- Eugene Hsue (City of Philadelphia Law Department)
- Harrison Inefuku (Iowa State University)
- Allison Langham-Putrow (University of Minnesota)
- Paige Mann (University of Redlands)
- Sanjeet Mann (University of Redlands)
- Mark A. Matienzo (Stanford University)
- John Maxwell (Simon Fraser University)
- Siobhan McCarthy (Montclair State University)
- Catherine Mitchell (California Digital Library)
- Emma Molls (University of Minnesota)
- Allison Nolan (Indiana University)
- Amy Nurnberger (Massachusetts Institute of Technology)
- Megan O'Donnell (Iowa State University)
- Joyce Ogburn (Appalachian State University)
- Thomas Padilla (OCLC)
- Anali Perry (Arizona State University)
- Rita Premo (Sonoma State University)
- Lev Rickards (Santa Clara University)

- Oya Rieger (Ithaka S+R)
- Dorothea Salo (University of Wisconsin—Madison)
- Melanie Schlosser (Educopia Institute)
- Christy Shorey (University of Florida)
- Gail Steinhart (Cornell University)
- Steve Stratton (California State University—Channel Islands)
- Jennifer Anne Wood Stubbs (New York University)
- Chela Weber (OCLC)
- Rachel Wexelbaum (Saint Cloud State University)
- Ying Zhang (University of Central Florida, for the Chinese American Librarians Association)

APPENDIX 5: Focus Group Guide

This is a facilitator guide modeled on a ninety-minute focus group session.

Objectives

- Share overview of project.
- Gain feedback on priority topics.
- Surface additional key issues for the research agenda.

Agenda

1. Introduction (10 minutes)

- o Introductions and "rules of the road"
- o The goals of the project
- o Timeline and major milestones
- o What we will be doing here today
- o Offer an outline of the scope of our work (research environment and scholarly communications definition)

2. What do Open, Inclusive, Equitable mean to you? (30 mins)

The ACRL wants your help in identifying actionable steps that academic librarians can take to accelerate the transition to and build capacity for more open, inclusive, and equitable systems of scholarship. These are big ideas and can take on many meanings. We'd like to hear your thoughts first on what you think of when we say "open," "inclusive," and "equitable."

We are going to take each one in turn. There are no wrong answers!

So, when it comes to the research environment and scholarly communications, what does it mean for it to be "open"?

Then prompt: "Inclusive"? "Equitable"?

Prompts …of addressing inclusion/access:

- *underrepresented groups (people, culture)*
- *economic inequity (geographic, institutional)*
- *physical obstacles, barriers to access*

3. Review of topics (40 mins)

We'd like to get your take on some specific areas of the research environment and scholarly communications that we know are of significant interest. All play, or could play, a role in creating a scholarly communications system that is open, inclusive, and equitable. If you could change, reform, or otherwise improve the way things work today, which areas below would be most important to address?

Questions:

- o What would an ideal world look like?
- o What are the barriers right now? (Why don't we have that world?)
- o What concrete steps might be taken to get that world? What do you need to know to get there?

[Then] …Specifically, for you (in your setting)…

[Include topic list here—need to use a short list, with basic descriptions offered for each, to get the conversation started.]

4. Closing (10 minutes)

- o Summarize "what we heard"; get clarifications.
- o Next steps, including slide showing any future presentations.
- o Thank you!

APPENDIX 6: Invitations to Workshops

In-person events were held at the Library Publishing Forum in Minneapolis, at the American Library Association Annual Conference in New Orleans, and at the Third Joint Conference of Librarians of Color in Albuquerque. The text of the invitations to attend these events are included here.

Library Publishing Forum

Posted as part of LPF program

> Lunchtime Conversation
> Presenter: Nancy Maron, BlueSky to BluePrint
>
> The ACRL wants your help in identifying actionable steps that academic librarians can take to accelerate the transition to and build capacity for more open, inclusive, and equitable systems of scholarship. Rebecca Kennison and Nancy Maron have been hired by ACRL to undertake this work, working closely with their Research and Scholarly Environment Committee.
>
> The project (see full description here: http://www.ala.org/news/member-news/2018/04/acrl-selects-consultants-new-research-environment-and-scholarly-communication) involves community consultation to be sure that we understand the priorities of many different types of people involved in scholarly communications.
>
> This study will result in a report to be published in 2019 that captures effective current practices and outlines new directions for research and investigation to accelerate the transition to more open, inclusive, and equitable systems of scholarship.
>
> Please join Nancy Maron for a roundtable discussion to learn more about the project and to be sure we address the issues you care most about.

ACRL/ALA

(sent June 20, 2018, by Patricia Hswe, then-chair of ReSEC, to the ALA Connect list)

Subject line: Help shape the research agenda for scholarly communications!

Dear ALA Members,

The Research and Scholarly Environment Committee (ReSEC), a goal-area committee in ACRL, is sponsoring opportunities during Annual at which members are invited to contribute to shaping the Association's future research agenda for scholarly communications.

The first, a single-question poll, can actually be pursued right now! See: https://www.surveygizmo.com/s3/4425555/ACRL-Workshop-on-Research-Agenda.

The other opportunities are these sessions at Annual, both on Sunday:

Sunday, June 24, 2:30–3:30 PM | Scholarly Communications Discussion Group—Morial Convention Center, Rm 297

Sunday, June 24, 4–5:30 PM | Working Session—Morial Convention Center, Rm 388–389
The 2:30 session will be a facilitated discussion, while the format of the 4 PM slot will be break-out groups, with facilitators and note-takers. At both sessions, we are eager to capture the community's insight and suggestions for developing and advancing a new research agenda.

I hope you'll join us at one of the above gatherings at the convention center on Sunday!

All best,

Patricia

Patricia Hswe
Program Officer in Scholarly Communications
The Andrew W. Mellon Foundation

Joint Conference of Librarians of Color

(sent September 22, 2018, by Nancy Maron and Rebecca Kennison to the full list of registered attendees; follow-up responses were sent to individuals who RSVP'd.)

Subject line: Help shape ACRL research agenda at JCLC/Fri 4:30pm

Dear JCLC Community,

The Association of College and Research Libraries (ACRL) wants your help in identifying actionable steps that academic librarians can take to accelerate the transition to more open, inclusive, and equitable systems of scholarship. Please join us at JCLC:

Making Scholarly Communications and the Research Environment More Open, Inclusive, and Equitable: Round table to Review the Draft ACRL Research Agenda

Friday, September 28

4:30 PM–5:45 PM

Location: 19 Isleta & 21 Jemez

At this session, we will facilitate a large-forum discussion designed to elicit feedback on the six priority topics that we have identified. We are committed to making this research agenda as representative as possible, and the interests and needs of JCLC's constituent groups are a critical part of that representation.

As we work to complete a full first draft, we seek perspective from the JCLC community on whether the six areas we've identified resonate with you.

If you plan to join us, please reply to this email; we will forward you a short document describing the draft six areas in advance. Copies will also be available on site for participants who wish to drop in.

We look forward to seeing you there!

Rebecca Kennison

Nancy Maron

APPENDIX 7: Full Survey Results

Note: Responses were gathered via SurveyMonkey, data was exported, and charts and tables created in Excel. Several questions required further analysis. This, along with an explanation of method, is included in appendix 8.

The ACRL Research Agenda survey was open from Tuesday, June 26, 2018 through Friday, July 13, 2018. During this time, 832 participants started the survey; 362 completed it. The results are shown below.

Q1 OPEN ... refers to removing barriers to access, especially to the tools used to produce scholarly content and to the outputs of scholarly work.

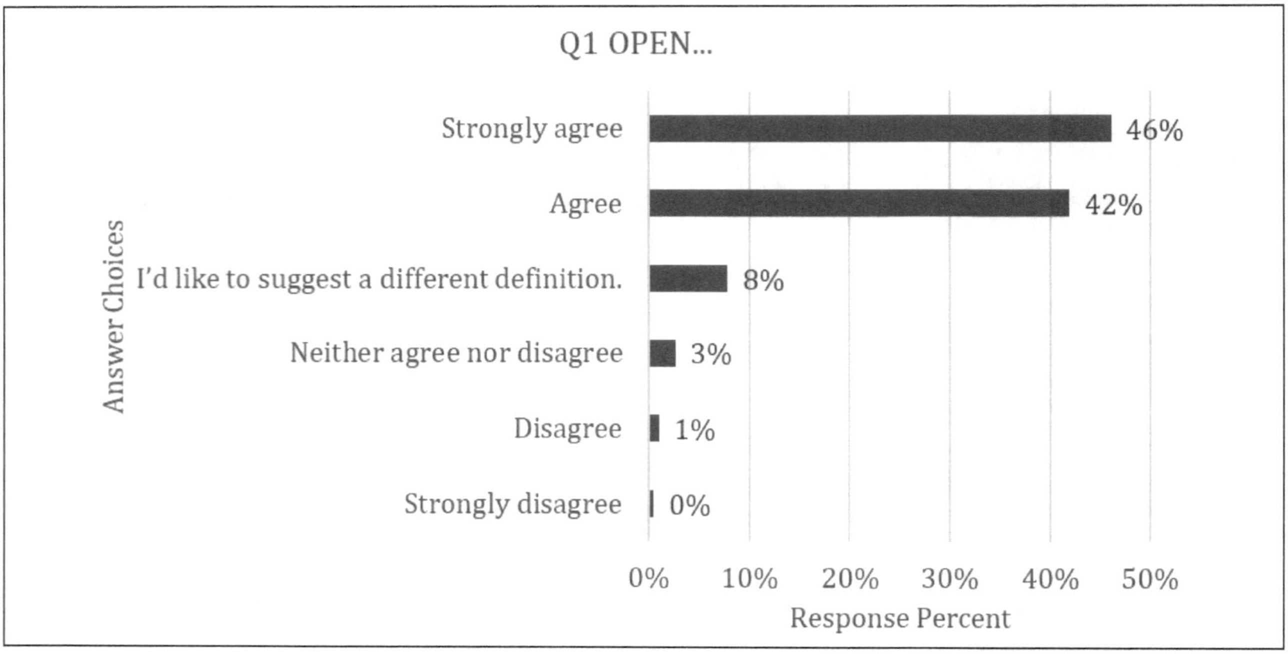

Chart 1. Responses to question 1 with answers shown highest percent to lowest.

Answer Choices	Response Percent	Response Count
Strongly agree	46%	384
Agree	42%	349
Neither agree nor disagree	3%	22
Disagree	1%	8
Strongly disagree	0%	4
I'd like to suggest a different definition.	8%	65
	Answered	832
	Skipped	0

Table 1. Responses to question 1 with answer choices shown in order presented on survey.

Q2 INCLUSIVE ... refers to (1) creating opportunities for greater participation in systems, institutions, and processes involved in creating, sharing, and consuming research and (2) removing barriers that can hinder such participation.

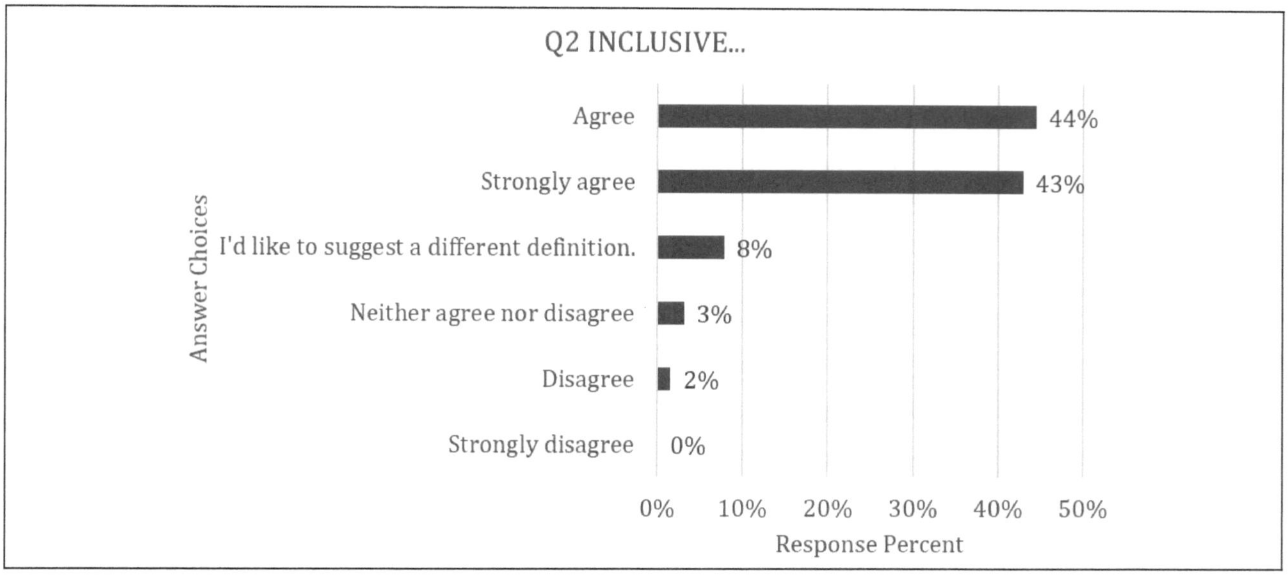

Chart 2. Responses to question 2 with answers shown highest percent to lowest.

Answer Choices	Response Percent	Response Count
Strongly agree	43%	357
Agree	44%	370
Neither agree nor disagree	3%	26
Disagree	2%	13
Strongly disagree	0%	1
I'd like to suggest a different definition.	8%	65
	Answered	832
	Skipped	0

Table 2. Responses to question 2 with answer choices shown in order presented on survey.

Q3 EQUITABLE …refers to ensuring that systems, institutions, and processes function in a way that demonstrates fairness, impartiality, and objectivity in all their practices.

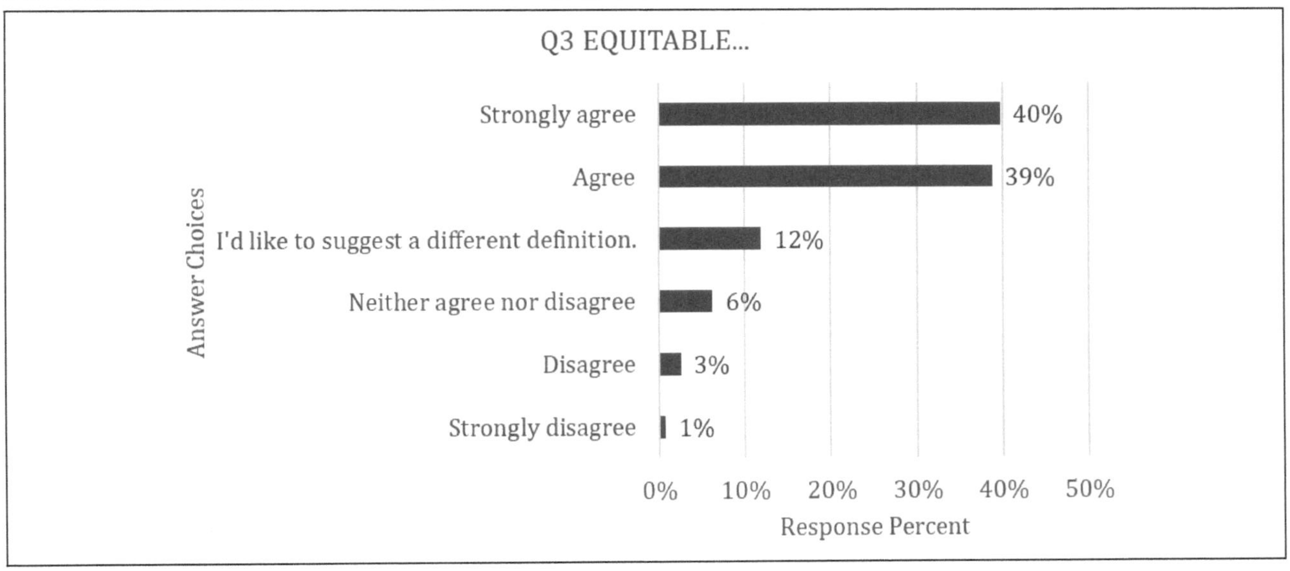

Chart 3. Responses to question 3 with answers shown highest percent to lowest.

Answer Choices	Response Percent	Response Count
Strongly agree	40%	331
Agree	39%	323
Neither agree nor disagree	6%	52
Disagree	3%	21
Strongly disagree	1%	6
I'd like to suggest a different definition.	12%	99
	Answered	832
	Skipped	0

Table 3. Responses to question 3 with answer choices shown in order presented on survey.

Q4 If you could change, reform, or otherwise improve the way things work today, in order to create a more open, inclusive, and equitable research environment, which areas below would be most important to address first? Please rank these five areas in order of importance, with 1 as most important and 5 as least important. To order the items you may use either the drag-and-drop function (by clicking and dragging on the far left) or use the dropdown.

Answer Choices	Rank 1	Rank 2	Rank 3	Rank 4	Rank 5	Score
The processes needed to create compelling research projects	10%	9%	15%	24%	42%	2.21
The ways in which the value or impact of scholarly work is assessed	30%	20%	20%	19%	12%	3.38
The forms and formats of production needed to produce works, from the most traditional (e.g., articles, monographs) to cutting-edge (e.g., multimodal projects)	8%	17%	26%	27%	22%	2.62
Increase in the distribution of and access to scholarly outputs of all forms	32%	29%	16%	13%	9%	3.63
Practices that ensure long-term access to past, current, and future work and that encourage inclusive collections	20%	25%	23%	17%	16%	3.16
					Answered	746
					Skipped	86

Table 4. Responses to question 4 as response percent with answer choices shown in order presented on survey.

Answer Choices	Rank 1	Rank 2	Rank 3	Rank 4	Rank 5	Score
The processes needed to create compelling research projects	74	66	113	179	314	2.21
The ways in which the value or impact of scholarly work is assessed	224	149	146	141	86	3.38
The forms and formats of production needed to produce works, from the most traditional (e.g., articles, monographs) to cutting-edge (e.g., multimodal projects)	59	127	196	200	164	2.62
Increase in the distribution of and access to scholarly outputs of all forms	242	218	121	99	66	3.63
Practices that ensure long-term access to past, current, and future work and that encourage inclusive collections	147	186	170	127	116	3.16
					Answered	746
					Skipped	86

Table 5. Responses to question 4 as response count with answer choices shown in order presented on survey.

Q5 What is needed to create compelling research projects and outputs? Rank your top 5, using 1 to indicate the most important. To order the items you may use either the drag-and-drop function (by clicking and dragging on the far left) or use the dropdown. Choose "Not in my top 5" for each item not ranked that highly; please note that you will need to check that box at the end of the process for each item you do not wish to rank.

Answer Choices	**Rank 1**	**Rank 2**	**Rank 3**	**Rank 4**	**Rank 5**	**Not in my top 5**	**Score**
Access to scholarly content (e.g., search and discovery, financial and physical constraints, intellectual property)	49%	14%	10%	7%	6%	10%	7.88
Availability of grant or institutional funding for new and innovative forms of research and investigation	13%	19%	17%	13%	6%	25%	6.89
Availability of grant or institutional funding for scholars and researchers from a wide range of backgrounds	15%	21%	19%	14%	10%	17%	6.98
Discovery of materials not written in English (e.g., other languages, non-written formats)	2%	7%	10%	14%	13%	44%	5.7
Publishing norms and publishing process in the Global South (especially where those might be different from those in the Global North)	2%	4%	4%	8%	10%	56%	5.05
Responsibility to vulnerable populations as a group (i.e., those not covered by institutional research board [IRB] approval)	3%	7%	6%	8%	12%	49%	5.47
Spaces, tools, and methods to share research (including data) in progress	6%	14%	13%	15%	14%	28%	6.1
Understanding of and respect for non-Western cultural practices (e.g., oral traditions)	5%	6%	9%	11%	13%	43%	5.7
Understanding of and transparency about cataloging and search/discovery algorithm biases	5%	8%	10%	9%	15%	41%	5.56
						Answered	382
						Skipped	450

Table 6. Responses to question 5 as response percent with answer choices shown in order presented on survey.

Answer Choices	**Rank 1**	**Rank 2**	**Rank 3**	**Rank 4**	**Rank 5**	**Not in my top 5**	**Score**
Access to scholarly content (e.g., search and discovery, financial and physical constraints, intellectual property)	188	55	39	25	23	38	7.88
Availability of grant or institutional funding for new and innovative forms of research and investigation	50	72	66	48	22	97	6.89
Availability of grant or institutional funding for scholars and researchers from a wide range of backgrounds	57	79	73	54	38	64	6.98
Discovery of materials not written in English (e.g., other languages, non-written formats)	7	25	40	52	49	168	5.7
Publishing norms and publishing process in the Global South (especially where those might be different from those in the Global North)	8	17	16	31	38	215	5.05
Responsibility to vulnerable populations as a group (i.e., those not covered by institutional research board [IRB] approval)	13	28	22	32	45	187	5.47

Answer Choices	Rank 1	Rank 2	Rank 3	Rank 4	Rank 5	Not in my top 5	Score
Spaces, tools, and methods to share research (including data) in progress	21	52	50	58	54	107	6.1
Understanding of and respect for non-Western cultural practices (e.g., oral traditions)	19	23	36	43	48	166	5.7
Understanding of and transparency about cataloging and search/discovery algorithm biases	18	30	37	35	58	156	5.56
						Answered	382
						Skipped	450

Table 7. Responses to question 5 as response count with answer choices shown in order presented on survey.

Q6 If you feel something is missing from the list above, what is It? Where you would have ranked it in your list (1-5)?

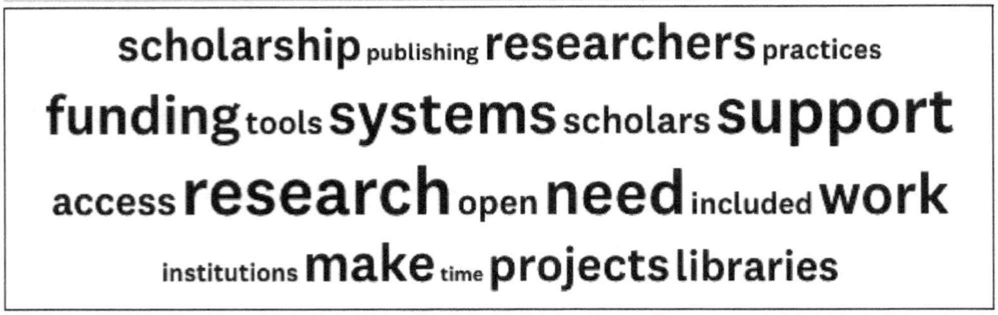

Figure 1. Word cloud of responses to question 6.

Total Responses = 63. Ranked 1: 41% (26); ranked 2: 25% (16); ranked 3: 16% (10); ranked 4: 8% (5); ranked 5: 9% (6).

Q7 Thinking about what you said was most important (ranked #1), what do we still need to know about that topic to develop a more open, inclusive, and equitable scholarly communications and research environment?

Figure 2. Word cloud of responses to question 7.

Total Responses = 210.

Q8 What are the most important issues to you concerning the ways in which the value or impact of scholarly work is (or should be) assessed? Rank your top 5, using 1 to indicate the most important. To order the items you may use either the drag-and-drop function (by clicking and dragging on the far left) or use the dropdown. Choose "Not in my top 5" for each item not ranked that highly; please note that you will need to check that box at the end of the process for each item you do not wish to rank.

Answer Choices	Rank 1	Rank 2	Rank 3	Rank 4	Rank 5	Not in my top 5	Score
Citation practices (e.g., who gets cited? who gets left out? why?)	4%	7%	4%	7%	6%	57%	9.04
Criteria for evaluation of research outputs (including definitions of what counts as "valuable" or "valued" scholarship, no matter where the research is produced)	34%	13%	10%	9%	8%	18%	11.2
Decision-making of libraries/archives in acquiring, collecting scholarly work	4%	6%	6%	4%	7%	56%	8.64
Decisions and determinations about who is designated as a collaborator	1%	3%	3%	5%	3%	68%	7.62
Determining quality beyond simple prestige proxy measures (e.g., affiliation, publishing venue, impact factor or h-factor)	14%	21%	13%	7%	9%	22%	10.48
"Invisible" or unrewarded labor in scholarly communications efforts and outputs (including by adjuncts, grad students)	4%	7%	9%	9%	9%	48%	9.29
New methods and metrics that better capture the value of emerging forms of scholarship created by scholars from a range of settings	6%	10%	11%	13%	7%	40%	9.73
Peer review procedures for evaluating work	6%	7%	7%	10%	9%	43%	9.17
The process of scholars and researchers in selecting and citing scholarly work	2%	2%	3%	4%	6%	60%	7.09
Pros and cons of alternative metrics ("altmetrics") (especially for those who are not white males)	1%	1%	2%	5%	5%	63%	6.36
Reward for "non-traditional" outputs (e.g., open educational resources [OER], open scholarship, datasets)	8%	12%	13%	13%	15%	26%	9.66
The role of publication in tenure and promotion	13%	6%	10%	8%	8%	38%	9.32
Valuing participation from beyond the academy	3%	5%	7%	6%	8%	52%	7.86
						Answered	382
						Skipped	450

Table 8. Responses to question 8 as response percent with answer choices shown in order presented on survey.

Answer Choices	Rank 1	Rank 2	Rank 3	Rank 4	Rank 5	Not in my top 5	Score
Citation practices (e.g., who gets cited? who gets left out? why?)	17	26	16	25	24	216	9.04
Criteria for evaluation of research outputs (including definitions of what counts as "valuable" or "valued" scholarship, no matter where the research is produced)	130	50	38	35	32	68	11.2
Decision-making of libraries/archives in acquiring, collecting scholarly work	14	23	24	14	28	212	8.64
Decisions and determinations about who is designated as a collaborator	4	10	12	19	10	261	7.62
Determining quality beyond simple prestige proxy measures (e.g., affiliation, publishing venue, impact factor or h-factor)	55	82	51	28	35	84	10.48

Answer Choices	Rank 1	Rank 2	Rank 3	Rank 4	Rank 5	Not in my top 5	Score
"Invisible" or unrewarded labor in scholarly communications efforts and outputs (including by adjuncts, grad students)	14	25	36	34	35	182	9.29
New methods and metrics that better capture the value of emerging forms of scholarship created by scholars from a range of settings	23	39	41	50	25	152	9.73
Peer review procedures for evaluating work	24	28	26	40	33	166	9.17
The process of scholars and researchers in selecting and citing scholarly work	7	8	11	17	21	231	7.09
Pros and cons of alternative metrics ("altmetrics") (especially for those who are not white males)	3	5	9	18	19	239	6.36
Reward for "non-traditional" outputs (e.g., open educational resources [OER], open scholarship, datasets)	31	46	51	48	57	98	9.66
The role of publication in tenure and promotion	48	22	40	31	30	147	9.32
Valuing participation from beyond the academy	12	18	27	22	29	200	7.86
						Answered	382
						Skipped	450

Table 9. Responses to question 8 as response count with answer choices shown in order presented on survey.

Q9 If you feel something is missing from the list above, what is It? Where you would have ranked it in your list (1-5)?

Figure 3. Word cloud of responses to question 9.

Total n = 15. Ranked 1: 47% (7); ranked 2: 7% (1); ranked 3: 27% (4); ranked 4: 13% (2); ranked 5: 7% (1).

Q10 Thinking about what you said was most important (ranked #1), what do we still need to know about that topic to develop a more open, inclusive, and equitable scholarly communications and research environment?

Figure 4. Word cloud of responses to question 10.

Total n = 169.

Q11 What elements of production are most needed to produce works that span the gamut from the most traditional to most cutting-edge research? Rank your top 5, using 1 to indicate the most important. To order the items you may use either the drag-and-drop function (by clicking and dragging on the far left) or use the dropdown. Choose "Not in my top 5" for each item not ranked that highly; please note that you will need to check that box at the end of the process for each item you do not wish to rank.

Answer Choices	Rank 1	Rank 2	Rank 3	Rank 4	Rank 5	Not in my top 5	Score
Data confidentiality, data integrity	17%	12%	10%	13%	12%	26%	6.6
Editing process in developing, shaping a new work	10%	12%	6%	10%	8%	42%	6.33
"Invisible" and unrewarded labor to make content available, reusable	8%	9%	9%	9%	12%	43%	6.2
Mechanisms for rewarding collaboration and contribution	11%	15%	16%	12%	13%	25%	6.56
Permissions, licensing, copyright	19%	12%	20%	13%	12%	20%	6.92
Process of layout, design, and formatting a new work	1%	5%	7%	7%	5%	57%	4.99
Selection of software/hardware (e.g., open source vs. proprietary)	5%	9%	7%	10%	10%	43%	5.52
Support for innovative formats	18%	12%	9%	12%	9%	28%	6.43
Technical process (coding, cataloging, metadata) of making new work digital-ready, discoverable, accessible	9%	13%	15%	13%	16%	23%	6.16
						Answered	382
						Skipped	450

Table 10. Responses to question 11 as response percent with answer choices shown in order presented on survey.

Answer Choices	Rank 1	Rank 2	Rank 3	Rank 4	Rank 5	Not in my top 5	Score
Data confidentiality, data integrity	66	46	39	49	45	100	6.6
Editing process in developing, shaping a new work	38	46	24	40	32	159	6.33
"Invisible" and unrewarded labor to make content available, reusable	32	36	36	33	45	165	6.2
Mechanisms for rewarding collaboration and contribution	43	57	60	44	51	97	6.56
Permissions, licensing, copyright	71	45	76	48	44	77	6.92
Process of layout, design, and formatting a new work	5	20	27	25	18	219	4.99
Selection of software/hardware (e.g., open source vs. proprietary)	20	34	26	40	39	165	5.52
Support for innovative formats	68	44	34	46	35	107	6.43
Technical process (coding, cataloging, metadata) of making new work digital-ready, discoverable, accessible	36	51	56	49	61	87	6.16
						Answered	382
						Skipped	450

Table 11. Responses to question 11 as response count with answer choices shown in order presented on survey.

Q12 If you feel something is missing from the list above, what is It? Where you would have ranked it in your list (1-5)?

Figure 5. Word cloud of responses to question 12.

Total n = 18. Ranked 1: 50.00% (9); ranked 2: 16.67% (3); ranked 3: 16.67% (3); ranked 4: 11.11% (2); ranked 5: 5.56% (1).

Q13 Thinking about what you said was most important (ranked #1), what do we still need to know about that topic to develop a more open, inclusive, and equitable scholarly communications and research environment?

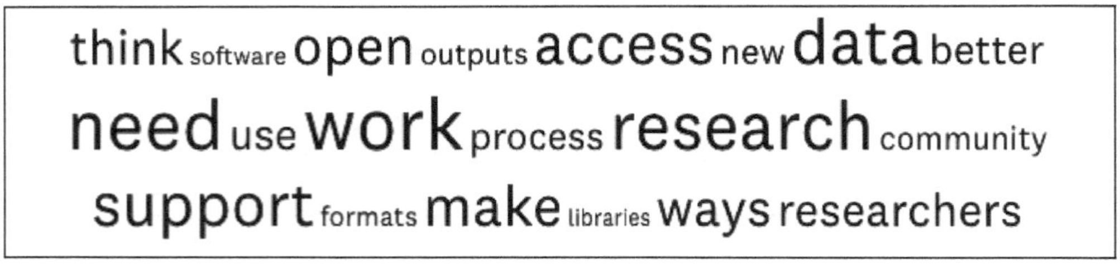

Figure 6. Word cloud of responses to question 13.

Total n = 144.

Q14 What issues are most important to affecting or influencing increased distribution and access to scholarly outputs of all forms? Rank your top 5, using 1 to indicate the most important. To order the items you may use either the drag-and-drop function (by clicking and dragging on the far left) or use the dropdown. Choose "Not in my top 5" for each item not ranked that highly; please note that you will need to check that box at the end of the process for each item you do not wish to rank.

Answer Choices	**Rank 1**	**Rank 2**	**Rank 3**	**Rank 4**	**Rank 5**	**Not in my top 5**	**Score**
Accessibility and universal design	23%	14%	13%	13%	9%	23%	9.07
The digital divide and information inequality	21%	19%	10%	11%	8%	25%	9.07
Discovery (e.g., what do scholars and researchers [including developers, librarians, students] need to be able to identify the software, content, data, etc., they need to do their best work?)	16%	21%	18%	8%	10%	21%	9.06
Intellectual property (who owns what? who can use what? for what?)	16%	14%	18%	13%	10%	22%	8.77
Open sharing platforms (both pros and cons) (e.g., institutional repositories, discipline-specific "preprint" servers, commercial platforms like ResearchGate)	8%	11%	14%	17%	14%	25%	8.21
"Piracy" of content (e.g., Sci-Hub, #icanhazpdf)	0%	2%	2%	3%	5%	68%	5.7
Pressures on scholars and researchers to self-promote (especially via social media)	1%	2%	4%	5%	4%	66%	6.06

Public engagement, public scholarship, advocacy, activism (e.g., how are those beyond the academy being served? what role could/should libraries play in extending the audience for scholarship beyond the walls of the academy?)	7%	7%	7%	10%	12%	42%	7.39
Tactics for distribution, practices for sharing and collaboration	4%	4%	8%	8%	11%	49%	6.98
Technical infrastructure	4%	3%	4%	9%	8%	50%	6.29
User privacy	1%	1%	1%	2%	7%	65%	4.35
						Answered	382
						Skipped	450

Table 12. Responses to question 14 as response percent with answer choices shown in order presented on survey.

Answer Choices	**Rank 1**	**Rank 2**	**Rank 3**	**Rank 4**	**Rank 5**	**Not in my top 5**	**Score**
Accessibility and universal design	86	55	49	50	33	88	9.07
The digital divide and information inequality	79	72	39	43	29	96	9.07
Discovery (e.g., what do scholars and researchers [including developers, librarians, students] need to be able to identify the software, content, data, etc., they need to do their best work?)	61	81	70	31	37	82	9.06
Intellectual property (who owns what? who can use what? for what?)	60	54	69	48	37	84	8.77
Open sharing platforms (both pros and cons) (e.g., institutional repositories, discipline-specific "preprint" servers, commercial platforms like ResearchGate)	31	43	55	64	55	96	8.21
"Piracy" of content (e.g., Sci-Hub, #icanhazpdf)	1	9	6	13	18	260	5.7
Pressures on scholars and researchers to self-promote (especially via social media)	4	8	14	18	17	251	6.06
Public engagement, public scholarship, advocacy, activism (e.g., how are those beyond the academy being served? what role could/should libraries play in extending the audience for scholarship beyond the walls of the academy?)	26	25	28	37	47	159	7.39
Tactics for distribution, practices for sharing and collaboration	15	16	30	29	42	187	6.98
Technical infrastructure	15	13	17	36	32	191	6.29
User privacy	2	4	3	9	28	249	4.35
						Answered	382
						Skipped	450

Table 13. Responses to question 14 as response count with answer choices shown in order presented on survey.

Q15 If you feel something is missing from the list above, what is It? Where you would have ranked it in your list (1-5)?

Figure 7. Word cloud of responses to question 15.

Total n = 8. Ranked 1: 75% (6); ranked 2: 0% (0); ranked 3: 13% (1); ranked 4: 13% (1); ranked 5: 0% (0).

Q16 Thinking about what you said was most important (ranked #1), what do we still need to know about that topic to develop a more open, inclusive, and equitable scholarly communications and research environment?

Figure 8. Word cloud of responses to question 16.

Total n = 129.

Q17 What practices are most important to ensure long-term access to all works—past, present, and future—and to develop and make accessible collections that are inclusive? Rank your top 5, using 1 to indicate the most important. To order the items you may use either the drag-and-drop function (by clicking and dragging on the far left) or use the dropdown. Choose "Not in my top 5" for each item not ranked that highly; please note that you will need to check that box at the end of the process for each item you do not wish to rank.

Answer Choices	Rank 1	Rank 2	Rank 3	Rank 4	Rank 5	Not in my top 5	Score
Access to materials (to whom? for what purpose? via what modalities?)	30%	11%	12%	8%	8%	24%	7.21
Addressing technology challenges	16%	13%	11%	8%	13%	29%	6.59
Collection practices (especially in terms of representation)	10%	14%	11%	9%	9%	38%	6.5
Collection priorities (especially in terms of representation)	7%	15%	12%	14%	7%	36%	6.43
Digitization priorities (especially in terms of representation)	6%	8%	15%	14%	15%	30%	5.92
Labor that goes into making content viable and usable in the long term	7%	8%	10%	12%	9%	40%	5.78
Long-term commitments (including data format migration)	10%	11%	14%	13%	12%	26%	6.08
Preservation practices	9%	10%	9%	11%	10%	35%	5.89
Preservation priorities	4%	10%	7%	11%	14%	36%	5.27
						Answered	382
						Skipped	450

Table 14. Responses to question 17 as response percent with answer choices shown in order presented on survey.

Answer Choices	Rank 1	Rank 2	Rank 3	Rank 4	Rank 5	Not in my top 5	Score
Access to materials (to whom? for what purpose? via what modalities?)	116	41	44	29	32	91	7.21
Addressing technology challenges	62	50	41	32	50	109	6.59
Collection practices (especially in terms of representation)	37	52	42	35	34	145	6.5
Collection priorities (especially in terms of representation)	28	58	44	52	28	138	6.43
Digitization priorities (especially in terms of representation)	23	30	57	52	59	114	5.92
Labor that goes into making content viable and usable in the long term	25	31	38	44	34	153	5.78
Long-term commitments (including data format migration)	39	41	53	51	44	99	6.08
Preservation practices	36	38	34	42	40	135	5.89
Preservation priorities	14	39	27	41	54	139	5.27
						Answered	382
						Skipped	450

Table 15. Responses to question 17 as response count with answer choices shown in order presented on survey.

Q18 If you feel something is missing from the list above, what is It? Where you would have ranked it in your list (1-5)?

Figure 9. Word cloud of responses to question 18.

Total n = 16. Ranked 1: 69% (11); ranked 2: 0% (0); ranked 3: 25% (4); ranked 4: 0% (0); ranked 5: 6% (1).

Q19 Thinking about what you said was most important (ranked #1), what do we still need to know about that topic to develop a more open, inclusive, and equitable scholarly communications and research environment?

Figure 10. Word cloud of responses to question 19.

Total n = 106.

Q20 Cultural Change in Scholarly Communications, Academic Libraries, and Higher Education. Please indicate how important you feel each issue is to creating a system that is more open, inclusive, and equitable.

Answer Choices	Urgent	Very important	Somewhat important	Not particularly important	Unimportant	Don't know
Defining the value of libraries in scholarly communications and the research environment	27%	48%	20%	1%	2%	1%
Diversity and inclusion	38%	44%	14%	3%	0%	1%
Hiring policies and practices	26%	40%	28%	4%	2%	1%
The intersection of digital/information literacy and scholarly communications	22%	45%	30%	2%	0%	1%
Labor issues	18%	31%	34%	11%	2%	4%
Leadership	30%	39%	24%	5%	0%	2%
Promotion policies and practices (incl. tenure and promotion criteria)	35%	34%	25%	3%	1%	1%
Reimagining the neoliberal university	17%	17%	26%	17%	9%	14%
Responsibility to vulnerable populations vs. academic freedom	23%	34%	28%	7%	2%	6%
Retention and promotion, especially of underrepresented minorities	35%	38%	20%	4%	1%	2%
Social justice issues (other than diversity and inclusion)	27%	36%	21%	7%	4%	4%
Whiteness of the academy, libraries, publishing industry	32%	32%	21%	7%	4%	5%
					Answered	366
					Skipped	466

Table 16. Responses to question 20 as response percent with answer choices shown in order presented on survey.

Answer Choices	Urgent	Very important	Somewhat important	Not particularly important	Unimportant	Don't know
Defining the value of libraries in scholarly communications and the research environment	99	176	74	4	7	5
Diversity and inclusion	138	161	52	10	1	3
Hiring policies and practices	94	143	99	14	6	4
The intersection of digital/information literacy and scholarly communications	81	166	108	7	0	4
Labor issues	65	113	125	40	8	13
Leadership	109	142	88	19	0	6
Promotion policies and practices (incl. tenure and promotion criteria)	129	123	93	12	3	5
Reimagining the neoliberal university	62	63	95	63	33	50

Answer Choices	Urgent	Very important	Somewhat important	Not particularly important	Unimportant	Don't know
Responsibility to vulnerable populations vs. academic freedom	84	122	103	25	7	23
Retention and promotion, especially of underrepresented minorities	127	138	73	14	5	8
Social justice issues (other than diversity and inclusion)	100	132	75	26	15	16
Whiteness of the academy, libraries, publishing industry	115	115	78	24	15	17
					Answered	366
					Skipped	466

Table 17. Responses to question 20 as response count with answer choices shown in order presented on survey.

Something URGENT you think is missing? Check that here and tell us what that is in the text box below.

If you chose URGENT for any item, please tell us specifically what needs to change and what we still need to know to make this happen.

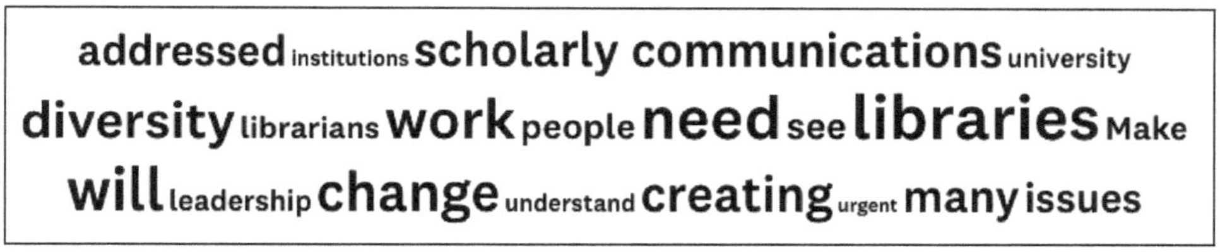

Figure 11. Word cloud of open-ended responses to question 20.

Comments n = 50.

Q21 Financial and Organizational Models. Please indicate how important you feel each issue is to creating a system that is more open, inclusive, and equitable.

Answer Choices	Urgent	Very important	Somewhat important	Not particularly important	Unimportant	Don't know
"Academy-owned" infrastructure	24%	36%	24%	7%	0%	9%
Community-supported initiatives	22%	53%	19%	4%	1%	3%
Economics of scholarly publishing	47%	41%	10%	1%	0%	1%
Global South-specific viewpoints (e.g., decolonialized models)	22%	37%	26%	5%	1%	9%
Infrastructure that supports scholarly communications	33%	51%	13%	2%	0%	2%
Organizational models that support scholarly communications	32%	50%	15%	1%	0%	2%
Support models for open initiatives	37%	46%	12%	1%	0%	2%
					Answered	366
					Skipped	466

Table 18. Responses to question 21 as response percent with answer choices shown in order presented on survey.

Answer Choices	Urgent	Very important	Somewhat important	Not particularly important	Unimportant	Don't know
"Academy-owned" infrastructure	89	132	87	24	1	31
Community-supported initiatives	79	192	68	13	2	10
Economics of scholarly publishing	172	149	37	5	0	2
Global South-specific viewpoints (e.g., decolonialized models)	79	133	94	18	5	34
Infrastructure that supports scholarly communications	118	185	46	7	0	7
Organizational models that support scholarly communications	116	183	54	3	1	8
Support models for open initiatives	136	169	45	4	1	9
					Answered	366
					Skipped	466

Table 19. Responses to question 21 as response count with answer choices shown in order presented on survey.

Something URGENT you think is missing? Check that here and tell us what that is in the text box below.

If you chose URGENT for any item, please tell us specifically what needs to change and what we still need to know to make this happen.

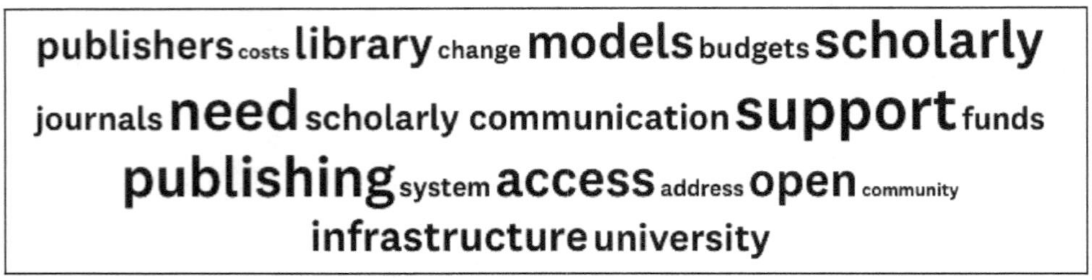

Figure 12. Word cloud of open-ended responses to question 21.

Comments n = 36.

Q22 I am a member of ACRL.

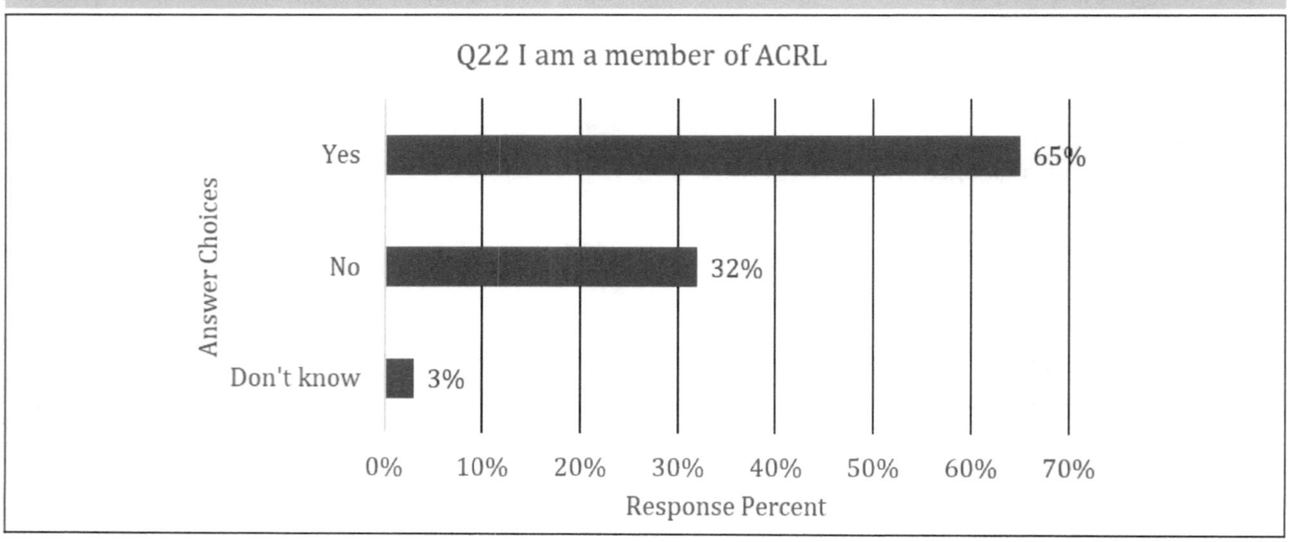

Chart 4. Responses to question 22 with answers shown highest percent to lowest.

Answer Choices	Response Percent	Response Count
Yes	65%	234
No	32%	117
Don't know	3%	11
	Answered	362
	Skipped	470

Table 20. Responses to question 22 with answer choices shown in order presented on survey.

Q23 I am a(n)... (Please check only one.)

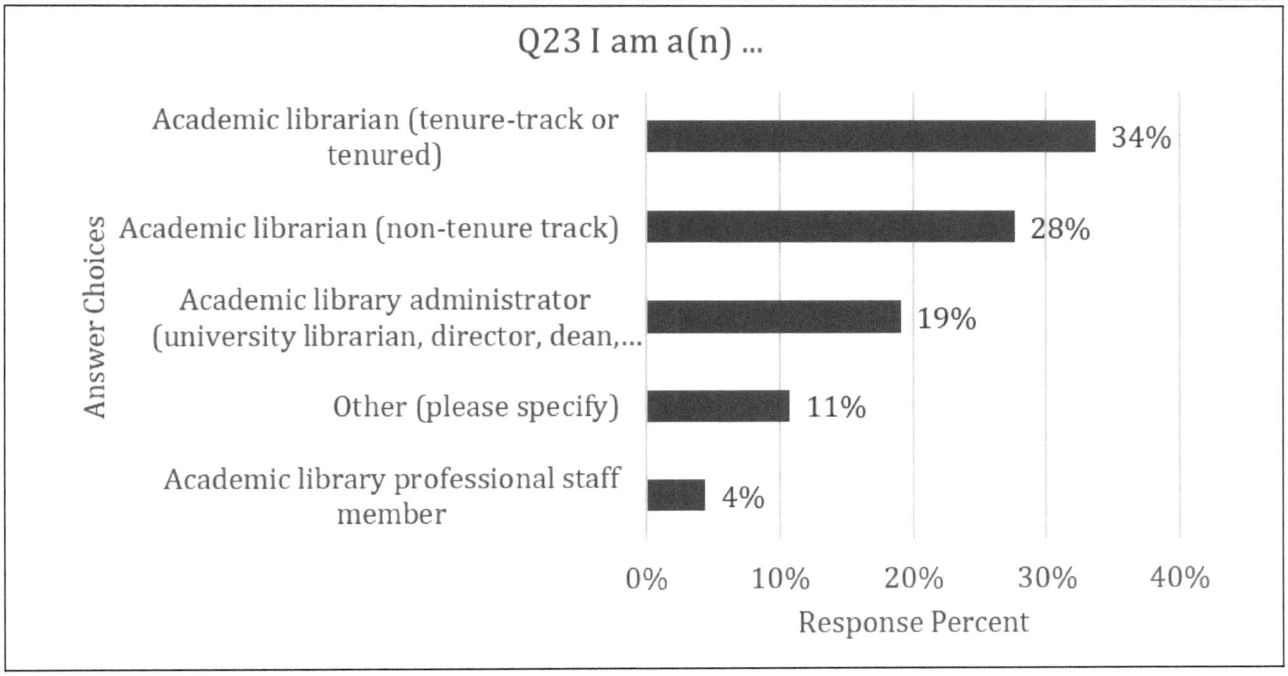

Chart 5. Responses to question 23 with answers shown highest percent to lowest.

Answer Choices	Response Percent	Response Number
Academic library administrator (university librarian, director, dean, AUL, etc.)	19%	69
Academic librarian (tenure-track or tenured)	34%	122
Academic librarian (non-tenure track)	28%	100
Academic library professional staff member	4%	16
Health sciences library administrator	0%	1
Health sciences librarian (tenure-track or tenured)	1%	3
Health sciences librarian (non-tenure track)	1%	4
Health sciences library professional staff member	0%	0
Library administrator (at other than an academic or health sciences library)	1%	2
Librarian (at other than an academic or health sciences library)	1%	2
Library professional staff (at other than an academic or health sciences library)	1%	3

Answer Choices	Response Percent	Response Number
Professional staff member at a library membership organization (e.g., ALA, ARL, GWLA, SPARC)	0%	1
Other (please specify)	11%	39
	Answered	362
	Skipped	470

Table 21. Responses to question 23 with answer choices shown in order presented on survey.

Other (n = 39): Academic library consortium staff (2); consultant (1); Library student or other grad student (10); Professor or other faculty (17); Publisher (3); Public librarian (3); Retired (2); Unemployed (1).

Q24 The job title that most closely aligns with what I do daily is ...(Please check only one.)

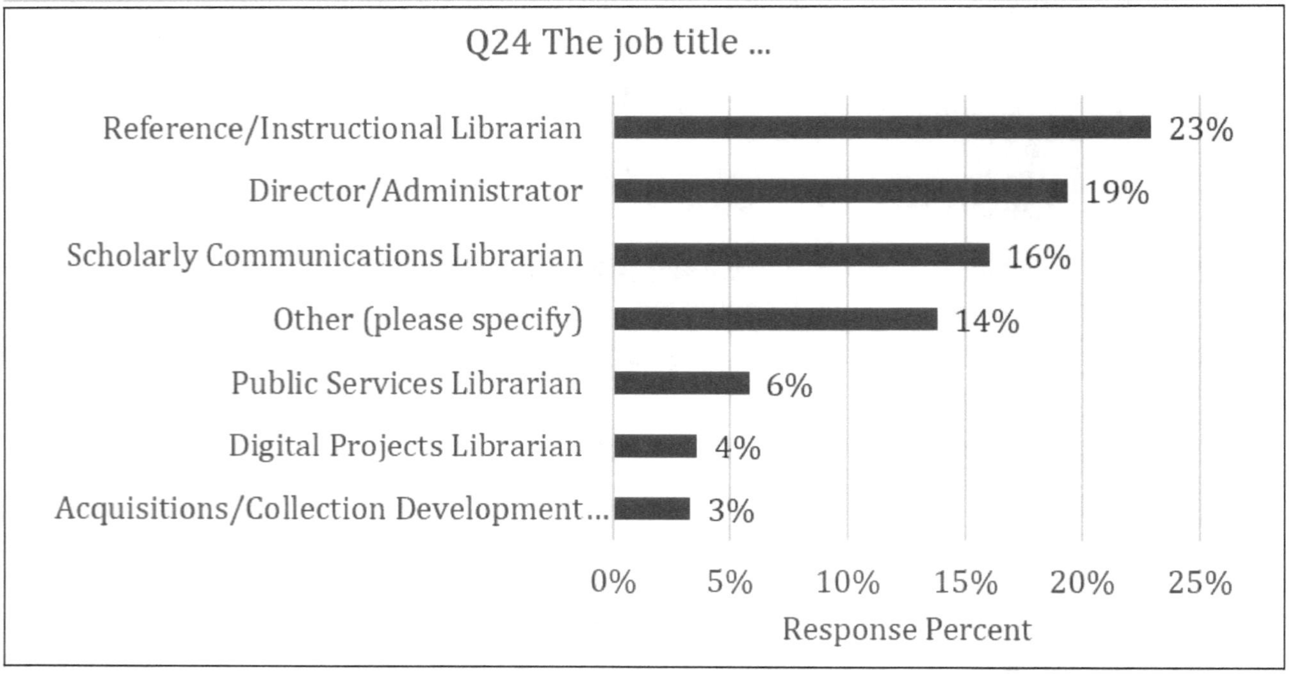

Chart 6. Responses to question 24 with answers shown highest percent to lowest.

Answer Choices	Response Percent	Response Count
Director/Administrator	19%	70
Scholarly Communications Librarian	16%	58
Data Management/Data Services Librarian	2%	9
Acquisitions/Collection Development Librarian	3%	12
Technical Services/Metadata Librarian	2%	6
Public Services Librarian	6%	21
Reference/Instructional Librarian	23%	83
Digital Projects Librarian	4%	13
Educational Media Librarian	0%	1
Digital/Electronic Resources Librarian	2%	9
Special Collections/Archives/Rare Books Librarian	1%	5

Answer Choices	Response Percent	Response Count
Preservation Librarian	1%	3
Access Services Librarian	1%	5
Library Systems/Information Technology Librarian	2%	7
Project Manager	1%	3
Library Support Staff	2%	7
Other (please specify)	14%	50
	Answered	362
	Skipped	470

Table 22. Responses to question 24 with answer choices shown in order presented on survey.

Other (n = 50): Access services and scholarly communications librarian (1); Area studies librarian (1); Assessment librarian (1); Assistant director/department head (4); Branch librarian (1); Consultant (1); Copyright librarian (2); Digital scholarship librarian (4); Executive director (1); Grad student (4); Grants and awards librarian (1); Library assistant (2); Open access librarian (1); Professor or other faculty (15); Publisher (2); Retired (2); Subject liaison librarian (6); Undergraduate librarian (1).

Q25 I am at a(n) ...

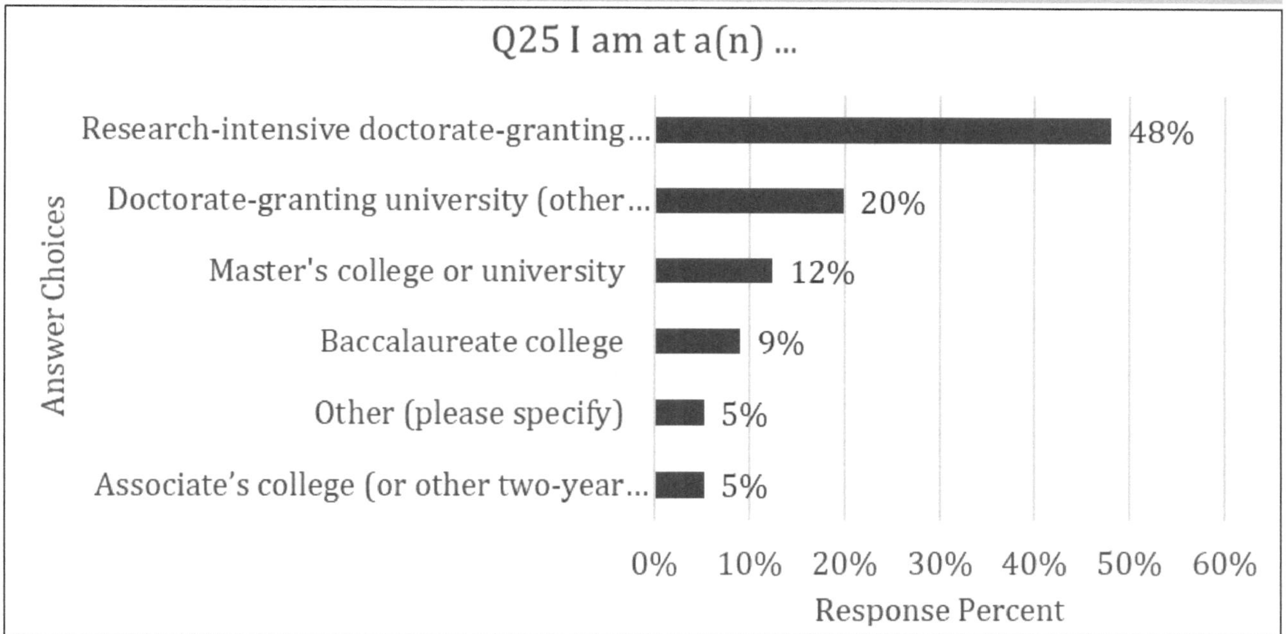

Chart 7. Responses to question 25 with answers shown highest percent to lowest.

Answer Choices	Response Percent	Response Count
Research-intensive doctorate-granting university	48%	174
Doctorate-granting university (other than research intensive)	20%	72
Master's college or university	12%	45
Baccalaureate college	9%	33
Associate's college (or other two-year college)	5%	19
Other (please specify)	5%	19
	Answered	362
	Skipped	470

Table 23. Responses to question 25 with answer choices shown in order presented on survey.

Other (n = 19): Academic library consortium (4); National library (1); Publishing company (1); Research institute (2); Retired (2); Seminary (2); Special collections library (non-academic) (1); Teaching-intensive college or university (5); Technology institute (1).

Q26 My institution or organization is a...

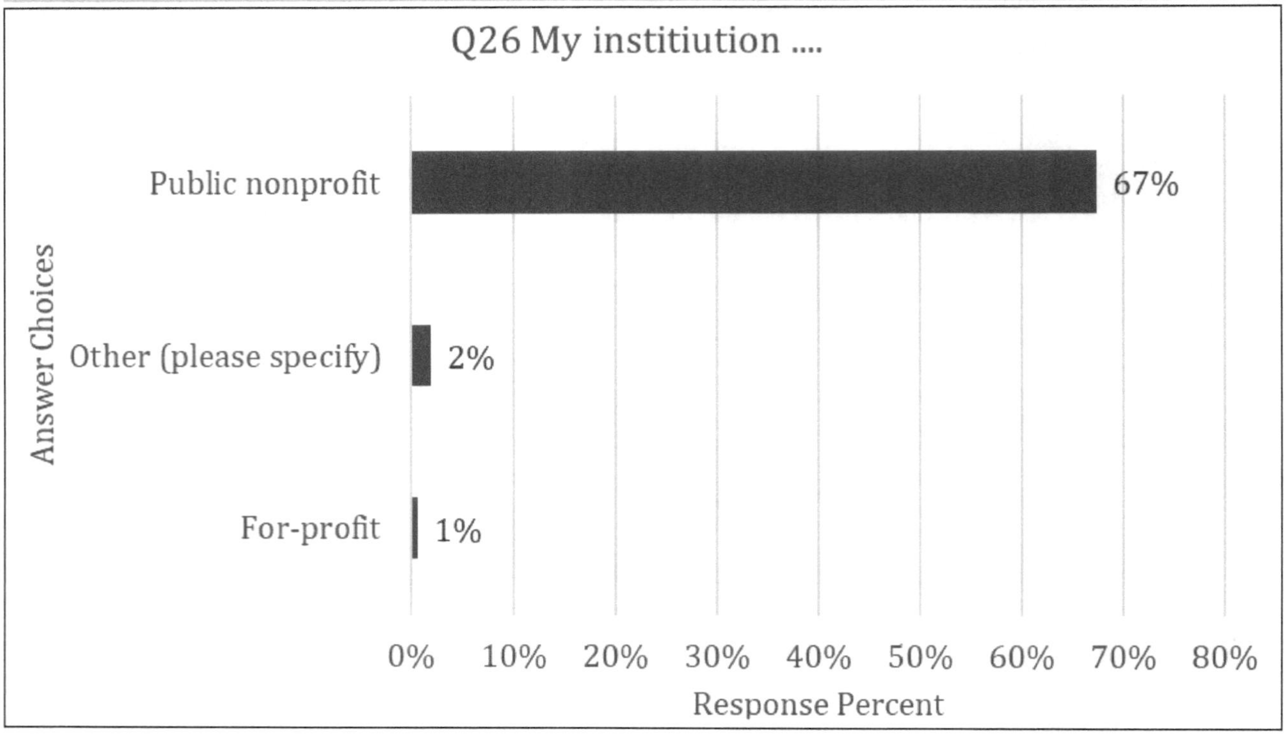

Chart 8. Responses to question 26 with answers shown highest percent to lowest.

Answer Choices	Response Percent	Response Count
Public nonprofit	67%	244
Private nonprofit	30%	109
For-profit	1%	2
Other (please specify)	2%	7
	Answered	362
	Skipped	470

Table 24 Responses to question 26 with answer choices shown in order presented on survey.

Other (n = 7): Blended public and private (5); Consulting firm (1); Retired (1).

Q27 What size is your academic institution?

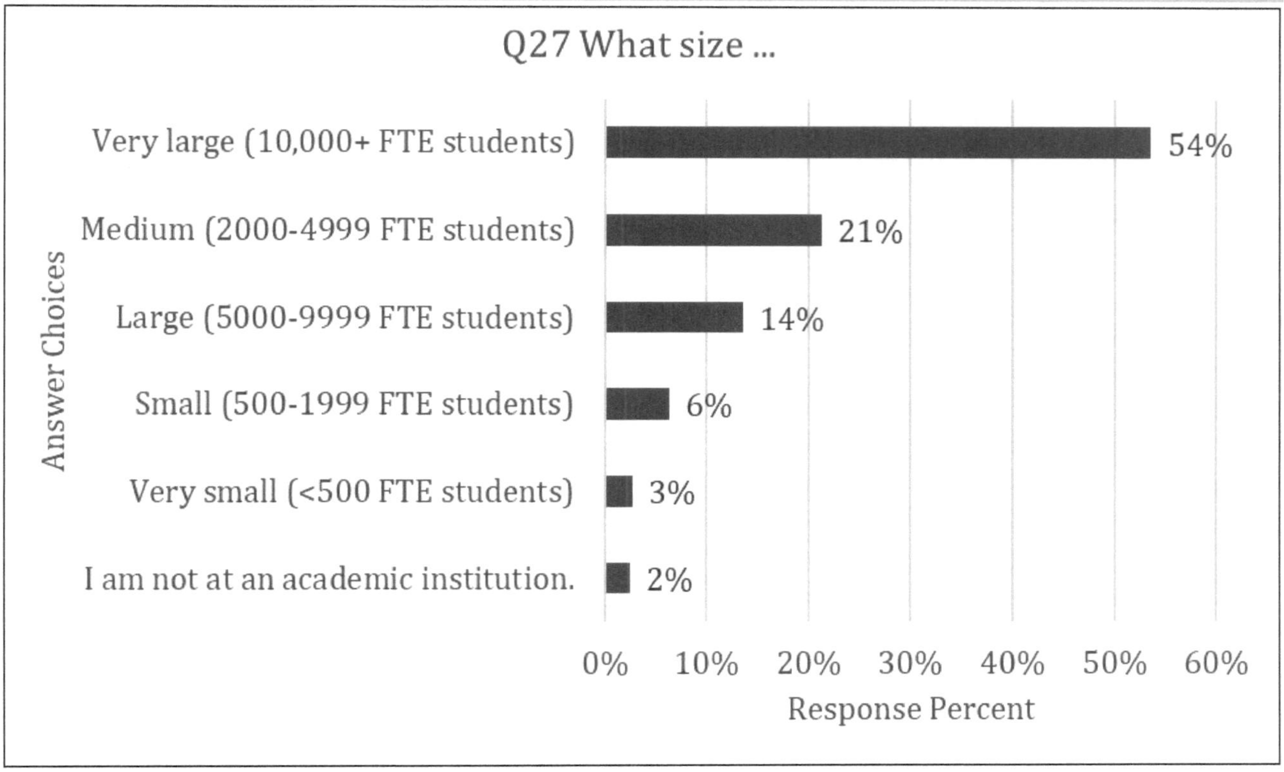

Chart 9. Responses to question 27 with answers shown highest percent to lowest.

Answer Choices	Response Percent	Response Count
Very small (<500 FTE students)	3%	10
Small (500-1999 FTE students)	6%	23
Medium (2000-4999 FTE students)	21%	77
Large (5000-9999 FTE students)	14%	49
Very large (10,000+ FTE students)	54%	194
I am not at an academic institution.	2%	9
	Answered	362
	Skipped	470

Table 25. Responses to question 27 with answer choices shown in order presented on survey.

Q28 My institution or organization is located in ...

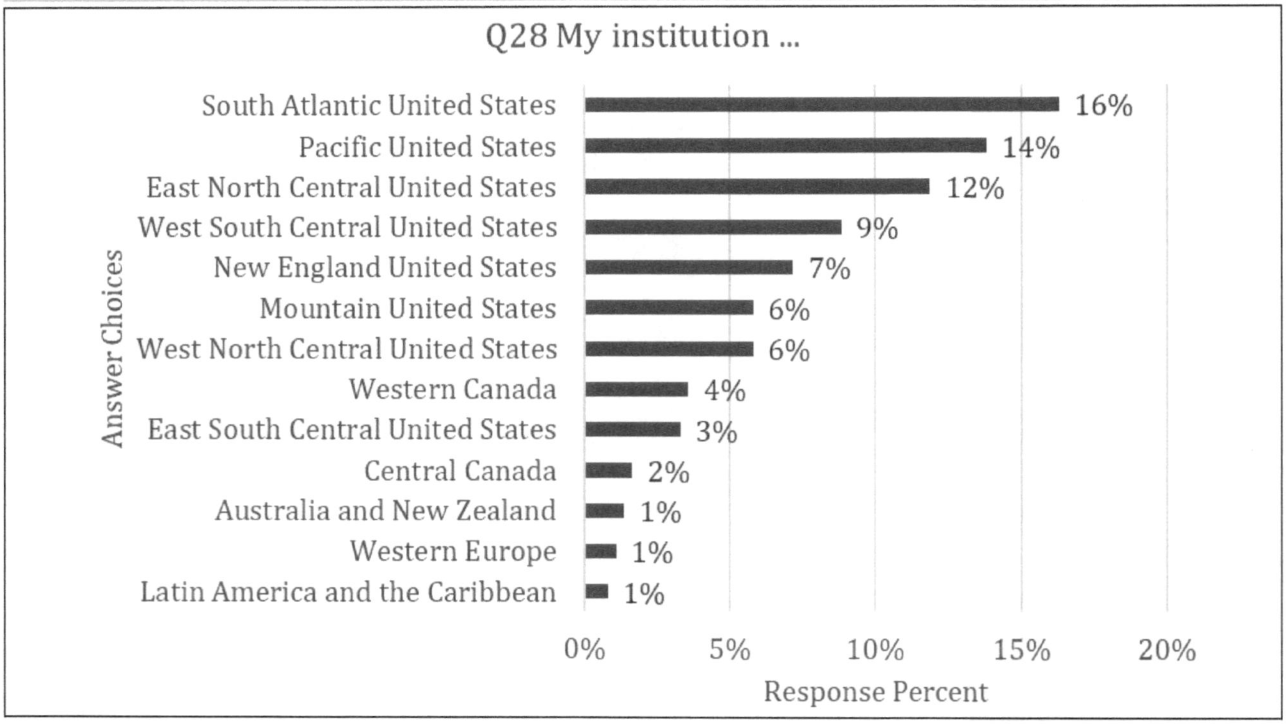

Chart 10. Responses to question 28 with answers shown highest percent to lowest.

Answer Choices	Response Percent	Response Count
New England United States (Connecticut, Maine, Massachusetts, New Hampshire, Rhode Island, and Vermont)	7%	26
Mid-Atlantic United States (New Jersey, New York, and Pennsylvania)	17%	61
South Atlantic United States (Delaware, Florida, Georgia, Maryland, North Carolina, South Carolina, Virginia, District of Columbia, and West Virginia)	16%	59
East North Central United States (Illinois, Indiana, Michigan, Ohio, and Wisconsin)	12%	43
West North Central United States (Iowa, Kansas, Minnesota, Missouri, Nebraska, North Dakota, and South Dakota)	6%	21
East South Central United States (Alabama, Kentucky, Mississippi, and Tennessee)	3%	12
West South Central United States (Arkansas, Louisiana, Oklahoma, and Texas)	9%	32
Mountain United States (Arizona, Colorado, Idaho, Montana, Nevada, New Mexico, Utah, and Wyoming)	6%	21
Pacific United States (Alaska, California, Hawaii, Oregon, and Washington)	14%	50
United States Territory (Puerto Rico, Guam, Northern Mariana Islands, the U.S. Virgin Islands, and American Samoa)	0%	1
Western Canada (Alberta, British Columbia, Manitoba, Saskatchewan)	4%	13
Central Canada (Ontario, Quebec)	2%	6
Atlantic Canada (New Brunswick, Newfoundland and Labrador, Prince Edward Island, Nova Scotia)	0%	0
Northern Canada (Northwest Territories, Nunavut, Yukon)	0%	0
Latin America and the Caribbean	1%	3
Western Europe	1%	4

Answer Choices	Response Percent	Response Count
Eastern Europe	0%	0
Northern Africa	0%	0
Sub-Saharan Africa	0%	0
Southern Africa	1%	3
The Middle East	0%	1
Central Asia	0%	0
Southern Asia	0%	0
Eastern Asia	0%	1
Southeastern Asia	0%	0
Australia and New Zealand	1%	5
Oceania (other than Australia and New Zealand)	0%	0
	Answered	362
	Skipped	470

Table 26. Responses to question 28 with answer choices shown in order presented on survey.

Q29 I identify as:

Answers	Response Percent	Response Count
Female	65%	195
Male	22%	67
woman	4%	12
F	3%	9

Table 27. Responses to question 29: gender.

Answers	Response Percent	Response Count
While	67%	194
Caucasian	11%	32
Asian	3%	9
African American	3%	8
American	2%	7
Hispanic	2%	6
Black	2%	5
Latina	2%	5
non-Hispanic	1%	4
European	1%	3

Table 28. Responses to question 29: race/ethnicity.

Q30 We welcome any further thoughts you'd like to share with us.

Q31 Would you be willing for us to contact you to discuss these issues in more depth?

Q32 If you indicated we could contact you, please provide the following information.

APPENDIX 8: Additional Survey Analysis*

Author's Note on Methodology:

In the online survey, in Question 4, respondents were asked to comment on five (5) broad areas first, encompassing the scholarly communications lifecycle including:

- Processes needed to create compelling research projects
- Forms and formats of production
- Practices that ensure long-term access to past, current, and future work
- Ways in which the value or impact of scholarly work is assessed
- Increase in the distribution and access to scholarly outputs

Then, for each of those areas, respondents were asked to evaluate, in terms of importance, several subtopics (Q5, Q8, Q11, Q14, Q17). For those ranking questions, the following weighting method* was used:

> Each rank is assigned a score that reflects its importance in the ranking process. The score is the opposite of the rank, since a lower rank means a higher score. Responses that are not in the top 5 are disregarded.
>
> So:
> Rank 1 = 5 points
> Rank 2 = 4 Points
> Rank 3 = 3 Points
> Rank 4 = 2 Points
> Rank 5 = 1 Point
>
> The weight (W), or point score, is multiplied by the number of respondents for each rank (X), and all of these values are summed. This sum total is then divided by the total number of respondents.
>
> (X1*W1)+(X2*W2)+(X3*W3)+(X4*W4)+(X5*W5) / Total Responses = Weighted Average
>
> To give an example from the question below—take the item "processes needed to create compelling research projects":
>
> In this case X1 = 74, X2 = 66, X3 = 113, X4 = 179, and X5 = 314. And the total responses = 746 (total responses will include those who did not place this topic in the top 5 at all, although there are no examples of that in this particular question).
>
> With the number above: ((74*5) + (66*4) + (113*3) + (179*2) + (314*1)) / 746 = **2.21**
>
> "Total top 3" is simply the sum of responses ranked either 1, 2, or 3 for a given category. The bar charts are plotted in descending order of this measure. Similarly, "Total top 5" is the sum of responses ranked either 1,2,3,4 or 5 for a given category.

* The charts in this section were developed by research associate Rohan N. Shah.

Question 4

If you could change, reform, or otherwise improve the way things work today, in order to create a more open, inclusive, and equitable research environment, which areas below would be most important to address first?

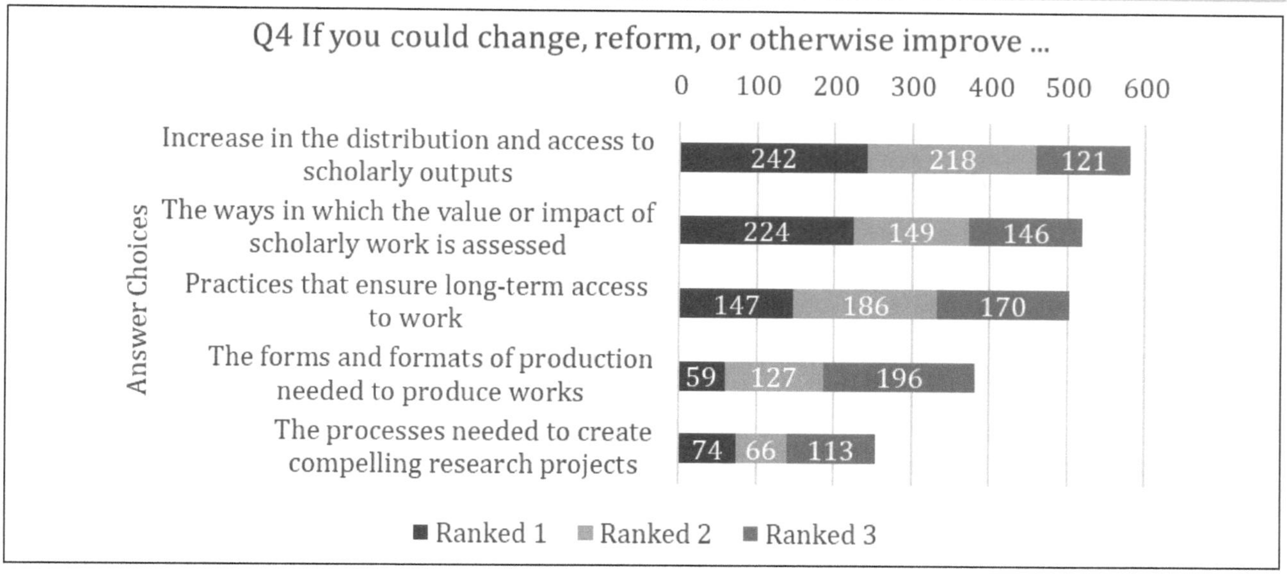

Chart 11. Responses to question 4 with answers shown by total of top 3 ranking scores, highest to lowest.

Answer Choices	Rank 1	Rank 2	Rank 3	Rank 4	Rank 5	Total Top 5	Weight	Total Top 3	Respondents
The processes needed to create compelling research projects	74	66	113	179	314	746	2.21	253	746
The ways in which the value or impact of scholarly work is assessed	224	149	146	141	86	746	3.38	519	746
The forms and formats of production needed to produce works…	59	127	196	200	164	746	2.62	382	746
Increase in the distribution of and access to scholarly outputs of all forms	242	218	121	99	66	746	3.63	581	746
Practices that ensure long-term access to past, current, and future work and that encourage inclusive collections	147	186	170	127	116	746	3.16	503	746

Table 29. Responses to question 4 as response count with answer choices shown in order presented on survey.

Takeaways:

- "The ways in which the value of scholarly work is assessed" and "increase in the distribution of scholarly output of all forms" were the most highly ranked choices. Together they account for 62.5% of the #1 rankings.
- "Practices that ensure long-term access" accounted for a number of top 3 rankings—503 in total. Only 16 less than "The ways in which the value of scholarly work is assessed."

- A very high number of respondents, 42%, ranked "processes needed to create compelling research projects" 5th—suggesting especially low importance.

Question 5

What is needed to create compelling research projects and outputs?

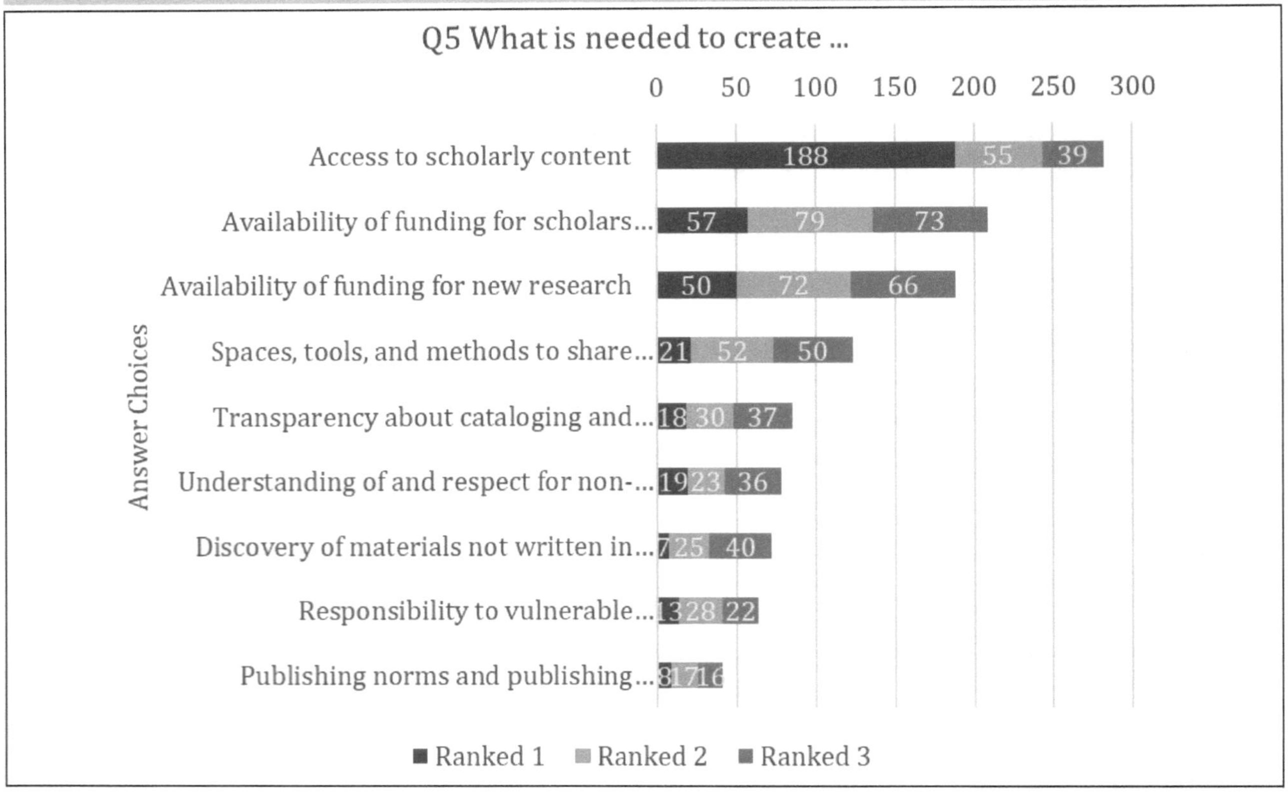

Chart 12. Responses to question 5 with answers shown by total of top 3 ranking scores, highest to lowest.

Answer Choices	Rank 1	Rank 2	Rank 3	Rank 4	Rank 5	Total Top 5	Weight	Total Top 3	Percent Not in Top 5	Respondents
Access to scholarly content	188	55	39	25	23	330	4.09	282.00	13.61	382
Availability of funding for innovative research	50	72	66	48	22	258	3.31	188.00	32.46	382
Availability of funding for researchers from a wide range of backgrounds	57	79	73	54	38	301	3.21	209.00	21.20	382
Discovery of materials not written in English	7	25	40	52	49	173	2.36	72.00	54.71	382
Publishing norms and publishing process in the Global South	8	17	16	31	38	110	2.33	41.00	71.20	382
Responsibility to vulnerable populations as a group	13	28	22	32	45	140	2.51	63.00	63.35	382

Answer Choices	Rank 1	Rank 2	Rank 3	Rank 4	Rank 5	Total Top 5	Weight	Total Top 3	Percent Not in Top 5	Respondents
Spaces, tools, and methods to share research	21	52	50	58	54	235	2.69	123.00	38.48	382
Understanding of and respect for non-Western cultural practices	19	23	36	43	48	169	2.54	78.00	55.76	382
Understanding about cataloging and search biases	18	30	37	35	58	178	2.52	85.00	53.40	382

Table 30. Responses to question 5 as response count with answer choices shown in order presented on survey.

Takeaways:

- Access to scholarly content is by far the most highly ranked answer to this question with the most respondents placing it in their top 3, and a large subset of those respondents naming it the highest ranked.
- More than 70% of respondents did not place publishing norms in the Global South in their top 5.
- Access to scholarly content, Availability of funding for research, availability of funding for diverse researcher background, and spaces tools methods were the only 4 responses where more than 50% of respondents placed it in their top 5.

Question 8

What are the most important issues to you concerning the ways in which the value or impact of scholarly work is (or should be) assessed?

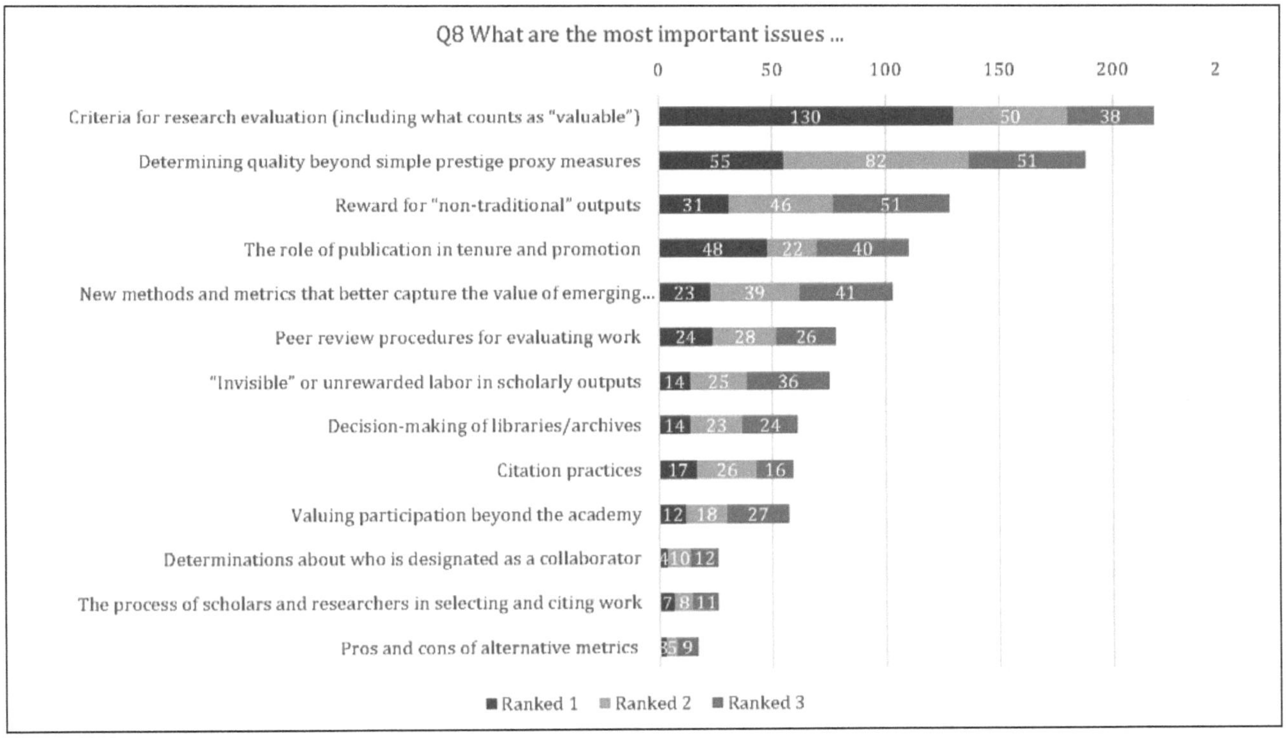

Chart 13. Responses to question 8 with answers shown by total of top 3 ranking scores, highest to lowest.

Answer Choices	Rank 1	Rank 2	Rank 3	Rank 4	Rank 5	Total Top 5	Weight	Total Top 3	Not in Top 5 (%)	Respondents
Citation practices	17	26	16	25	24	108	2.88	59	71.73	382
Criteria for evaluation of research	130	50	38	35	32	285	3.74	218	25.39	382
Decision-making of libraries/archives	14	23	24	14	28	103	2.82	61	73.04	382
Determinations about who is designated as a collaborator	4	10	12	19	10	55	2.62	26	85.60	382
Determining quality beyond simple prestige proxy measures	55	82	51	28	35	251	3.37	188	34.29	382
"Invisible" or unrewarded labor in scholarly outputs	14	25	36	34	35	144	2.65	75	62.30	382
New methods and metrics that better capture the value of emerging scholarship	23	39	41	50	25	178	2.92	103	53.40	382
Peer review procedures for evaluating work	24	28	26	40	33	151	2.80	78	60.47	382
The process of scholars and researchers in selecting and citing work	7	8	11	17	21	64	2.42	26	83.25	382
Pros and cons of alternative metrics	3	5	9	18	19	54	2.17	17	85.86	382
Reward for "non-traditional" outputs	31	46	51	48	57	233	2.77	128	39.01	382
The role of publication in tenure and promotion	48	22	40	31	30	171	3.16	110	55.24	382
Valuing participation beyond the academy	12	18	27	22	29	108	2.65	57	71.73	382

Table 31. Responses to question 8 as response count with answer choices shown in order presented on survey.

Takeaways:

- "Criteria for research evaluation" accounts for the vast majority of number 1 rankings. 130 respondents ranked it 1, more than twice the number of the second most frequently cited topic.
- "Determining quality beyond simple proxies" was the topic most frequently cited as 2, and also has the second most top 3 rankings, clearly establishing it as the second most popular response.
- More than 85% of respondents did not include "pros and cons of altmetrics" in their top 5, only 3 respondents ranked it number 1.

Consolidated Chart for Q8

For Question #8, the number of answer choices suggested the need to cluster some responses into broader categories for the purposes of analysis. Topics consolidated into larger categories in the following way, with the topic listed in CAPITAL letters encompassing those listed:

> **CITATIONS:** "Citation practices" and "The process of scholars and researchers in selecting and citing work"
>
> **RESEARCH VALUE:** "Criteria for evaluation of research (including definitions of what counts as "valuable")," "Reward for "non-traditional" outputs," and "Valuing participation beyond the academy"
>
> **LABOR PRACTICES:** "Determinations about who is designated as a collaborator," ""Invisible" or unrewarded labor in scholarly outputs," and "Peer review procedures for evaluating work"
>
> **INSTITUTIONAL DECISIONS:** "Decision-making of libraries/archives" and "the role of publication in tenure and promotion"
>
> **NEW METRICS:** "Pros and cons of alternative metrics," "Determining quality beyond simple prestige proxy measures," and "New methods and metrics that better capture the value of emerging scholarship"

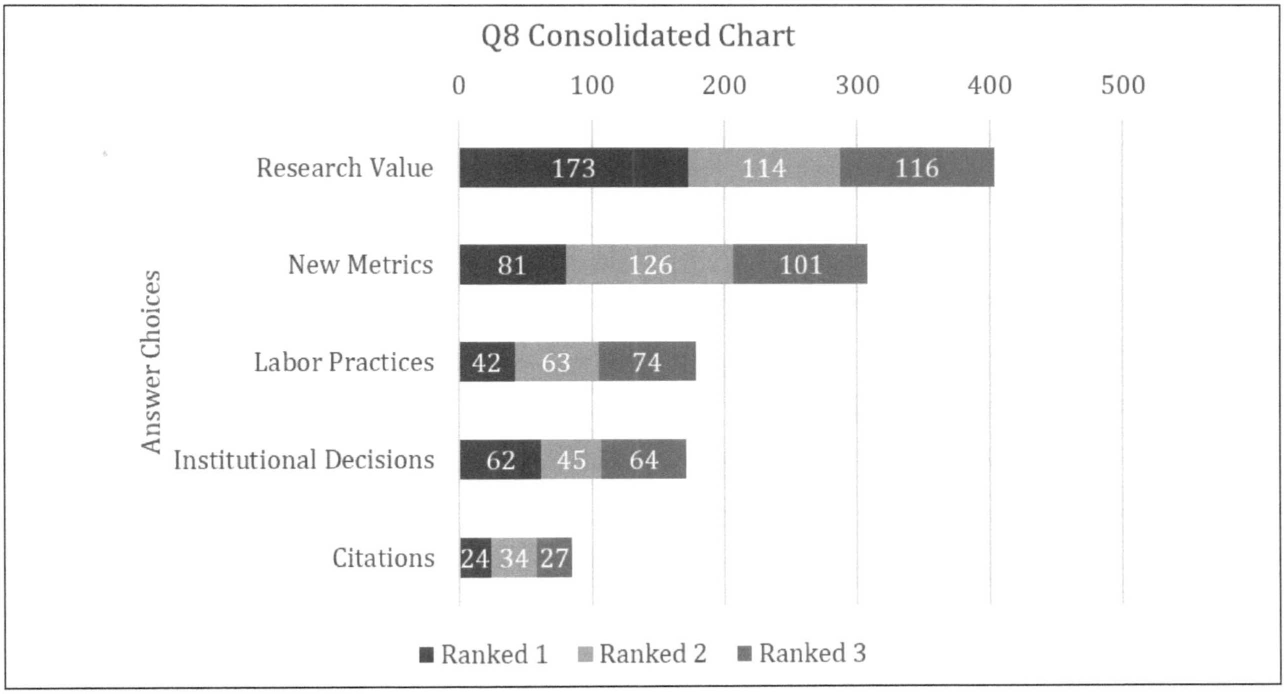

Chart 14. Consolidated responses to question 8.

> **Question 11**
> *What elements of production are most needed to produce works that span the gamut from the most traditional to most cutting-edge research?*

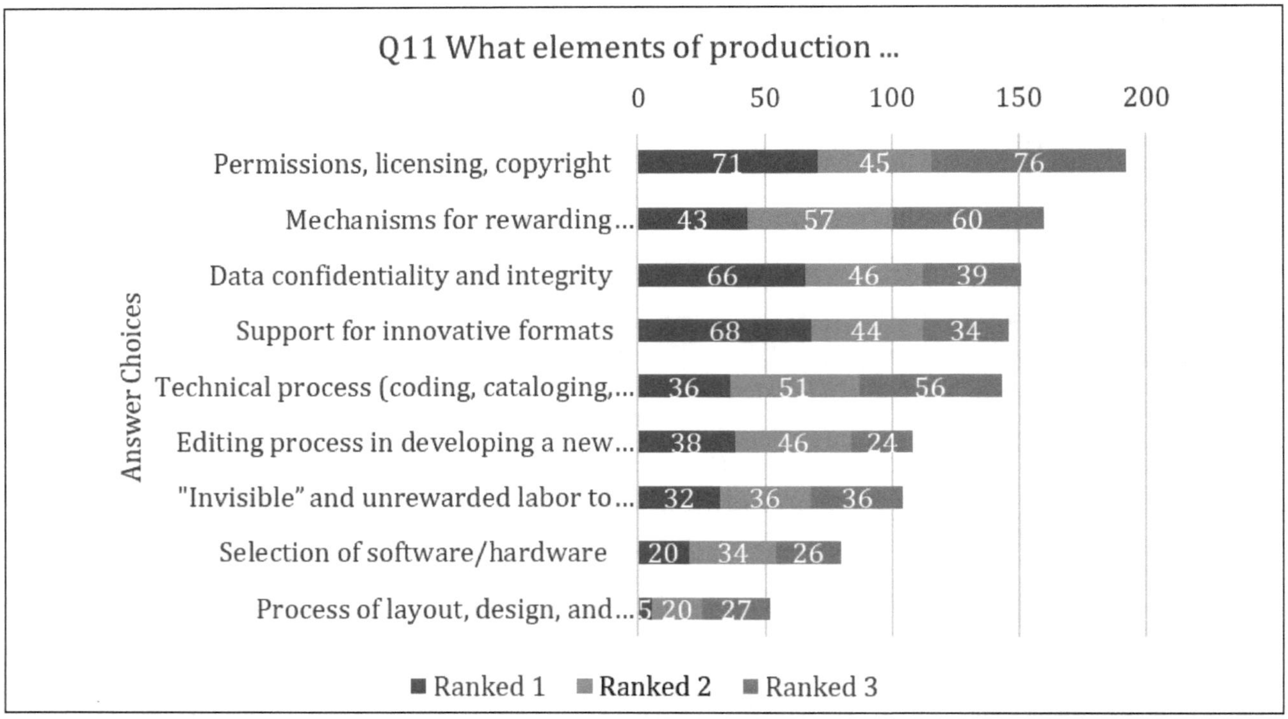

Chart 15. Responses to question 11 with answers shown by total of top 3 ranking scores, highest to lowest.

Answer Choices	Rank 1	Rank 2	Rank 3	Rank 4	Rank 5	Total Top 5	Weight	Total Top 3	Not in Top 5 (%)	Respondents
Data confidentiality and integrity	66	46	39	49	45	245	3.16	151	35.86	382
Editing process in developing a new work	38	46	24	40	32	180	3.1	108	52.88	382
"Invisible" and unrewarded labor	32	36	36	33	45	182	2.87	104	52.36	382
Mechanisms for rewarding collaboration and contribution	43	57	60	44	51	255	2.99	160	33.25	382
Permissions, licensing, copyright	71	45	76	48	44	284	3.18	192	25.65	382
Process of layout, design, and formatting a new work	5	20	27	25	18	95	2.67	52	75.13	382
Selection of software/hardware	20	34	26	40	39	159	2.72	80	58.38	382
Support for innovative formats	68	44	34	46	35	227	3.28	146	40.58	382
Technical process	36	51	56	49	61	253	2.81	143	33.77	382

Table 32. Responses to question 11 as response count with answer choices shown in order presented on survey.

Takeaways:

- While "Permissions, licensing, and copyright" emerges as the top category in the bar chart (based on the sum of top 3), it is important to note that "data confidentiality and agreement" and "support for innovative formats" have very similar numbers of rankings if one only looks at sum of the top 2 rankings.
- "Mechanisms for rewarding calculation" is the second item in the bar chart, but respondents most frequently ranked it 3rd, and so it may be less important than the above items.
- "Process of layout, design, and formatting" was the least popular topic among respondents—75.1% left it out of the top 5.

Question 14

What issues are most important to affecting or influencing increased distribution and access to scholarly outputs of all forms?

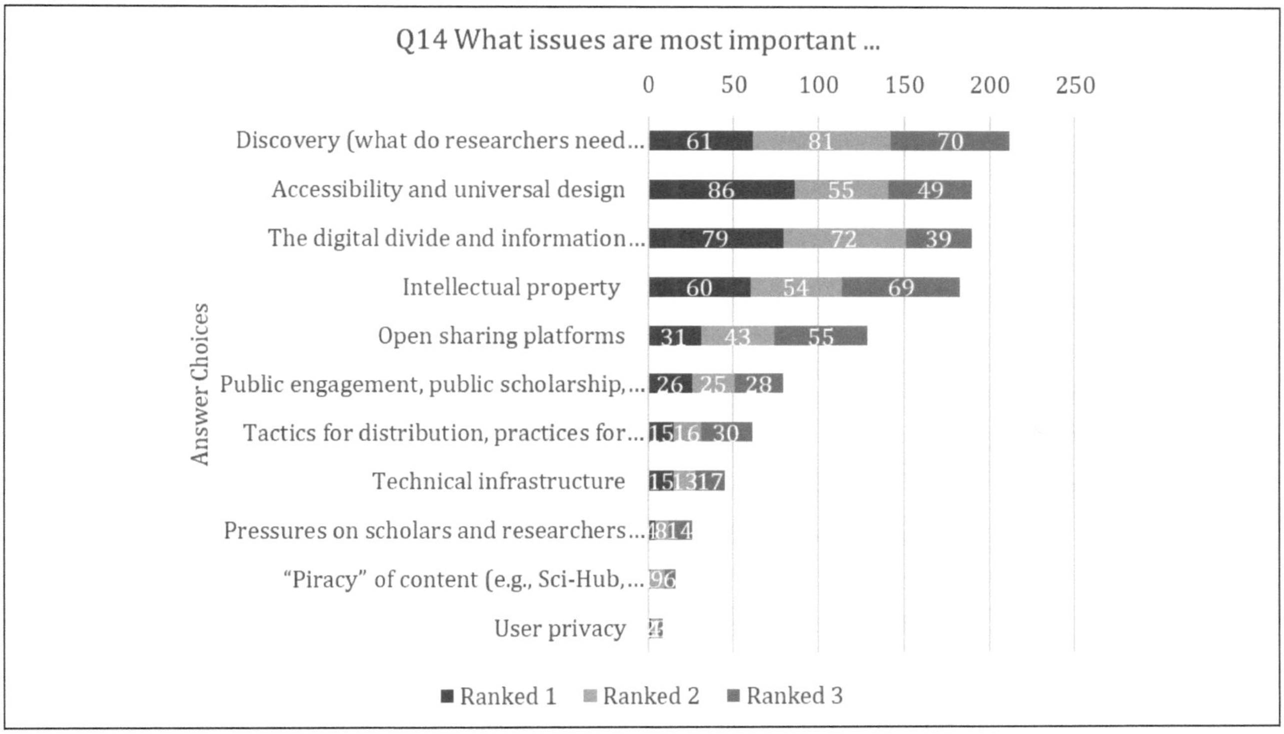

Chart 16. Responses to question 14 with answers shown by total of top 3 ranking scores, highest to lowest.

Answer Choices	Rank 1	Rank 2	Rank 3	Rank 4	Rank 5	Total Top 5	Weight	Total Top 3	Not in Top 5 (%)	Respondents
Accessibility and universal design	86	55	49	50	33	273	3.41	190	28.53	382
The digital divide and information inequality	79	72	39	43	29	262	3.49	190	31.41	382
Discovery	61	81	70	31	37	280	3.35	212	26.70	382
Intellectual property	60	54	69	48	37	268	3.19	183	29.84	382
Open sharing platforms	31	43	55	64	55	248	2.72	129	35.08	382
"Piracy" of content (e.g., Sci-Hub, #icanhazpdf)	1	9	6	13	18	47	2.19	16	87.70	382

Pressures on scholars and researchers to self-promote (especially via social media)	4	8	14	18	17	61	2.41	26	84.03	382
Public engagement, public scholarship, advocacy, activism	26	25	28	37	47	163	2.67	79	57.33	382
Tactics for distribution, practices for sharing and collaboration	15	16	30	29	42	132	2.49	61	65.45	382
Technical infrastructure	15	13	17	36	32	113	2.50	45	70.42	382
User privacy	2	4	3	9	28	46	1.76	9	87.96	382

Table 33. Responses to question 14 as response count with answer choices shown in order presented on survey.

Takeaways

- Although "discovery" had the highest top 3 total—and is therefore top of the bar chart—it is important to note that both "accessibility and universal design" and "digital divide and information inequality" garnered more number 1 rankings from respondents.
- If one was to only look at rank 1 and rank 2 (and ignore 3), then "digital divide and information inequality" would be the top ranked topic.
- The top 4 items account were clearly prioritized by respondents over the rest; there is a large gulf.
- Together, "user privacy" and "piracy" only received 3 number 1 rankings.

Question 17

What practices are most important to ensure long-term access to all works—past, present, and future—and to develop and make accessible collections that are inclusive?

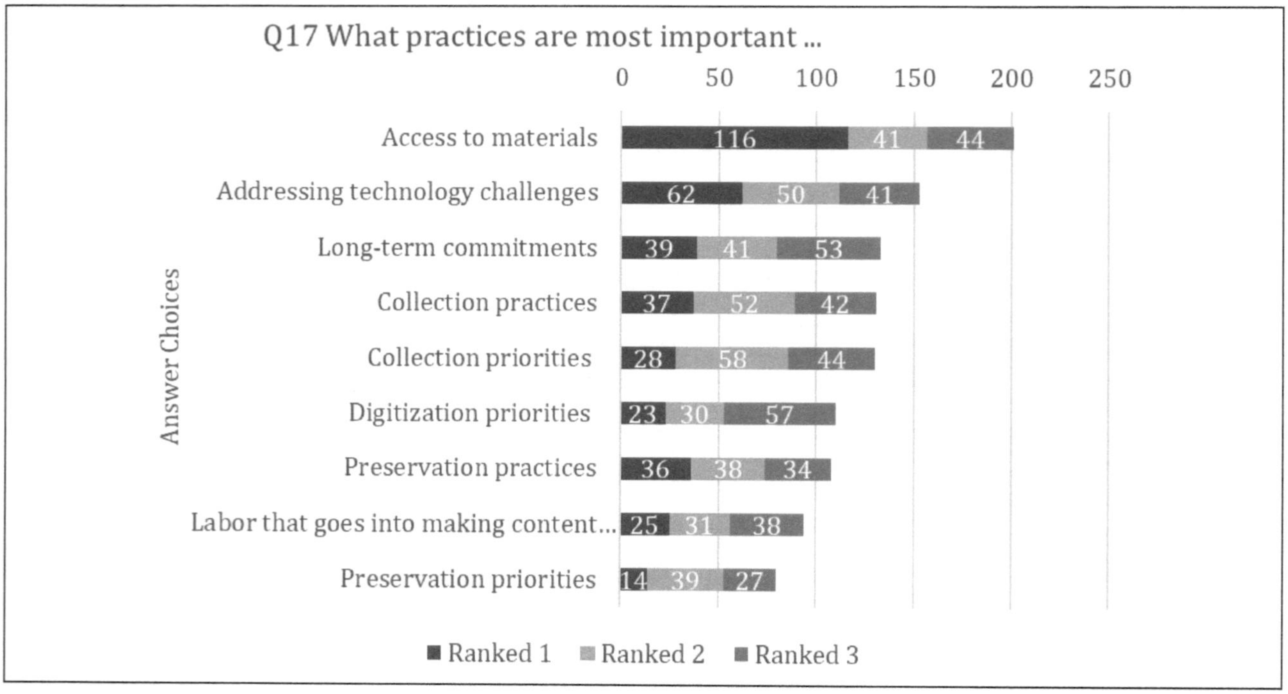

Chart 17. Responses to question 17 with answers shown by total of top 3 ranking scores, highest to lowest.

Answer Choices	Rank 1	Rank 2	Rank 3	Rank 4	Rank 5	Total Top 5	Weight	Total Top 3	Not in Top 5 (%)	Respondents
Access to materials	116	41	44	29	32	262	3.69	201	31.41	382
Addressing technology challenges	62	50	41	32	50	235	3.18	153	38.48	382
Collection practices	37	52	42	35	34	200	3.12	131	47.64	382
Collection priorities	28	58	44	52	28	210	3.03	130	45.03	382
Digitization priorities (especially in terms of representation)	23	30	57	52	59	221	2.57	110	42.15	382
Labor that goes into making content viable and usable in the long term	25	31	38	44	34	172	2.82	94	54.97	382
Long-term commitments (including data format migration)	39	41	53	51	44	228	2.91	133	40.31	382
Preservation practices	36	38	34	42	40	190	2.94	108	50.26	382
Preservation priorities	14	39	27	41	54	175	2.53	80	54.19	382

Table 34. Responses to question 17 as response count with answer choices shown in order presented on survey.

Takeaways:

- "Access to materials" is clearly the most important topic according to respondents. It received almost twice as many 1st rankings as the next most important item, "addressing technology challenges."
- The remaining topics in this category are fairly evenly divided. The difference in top 3 rankings between item 2 ("addressing technological challenges") and the last item ("preservation priorities") is only 73. For a sense of context, the difference between 2nd and last for Q. 14 was much higher—181.

Question 20

Cultural Change in Scholarly Communications, Academic Libraries, and Higher Education: Please indicate how important you feel each issue is to creating a system that is more open, inclusive, and equitable.

Note on methodology for calculating weight:
Unlike the ranking method used in earlier questions, Q20 and Q21 ask survey participants to choose a level of urgency, from "urgent" to "unimportant." In order to construct the graphs below and to assign weights, a numerical score was assigned to each designation that matches the schema above. So:

Urgent (U) = 5 points
Very Important (VI) = 4 points
Somewhat Important (SI) = 3 points
Not Particularly Important (NPI)= 2 points
Unimportant (U) = 1 point

"Don't know" responses have been disregarded for the purposes of analysis. After this, the same method was used to calculate weight and top 3 sums as was used in the earlier questions.

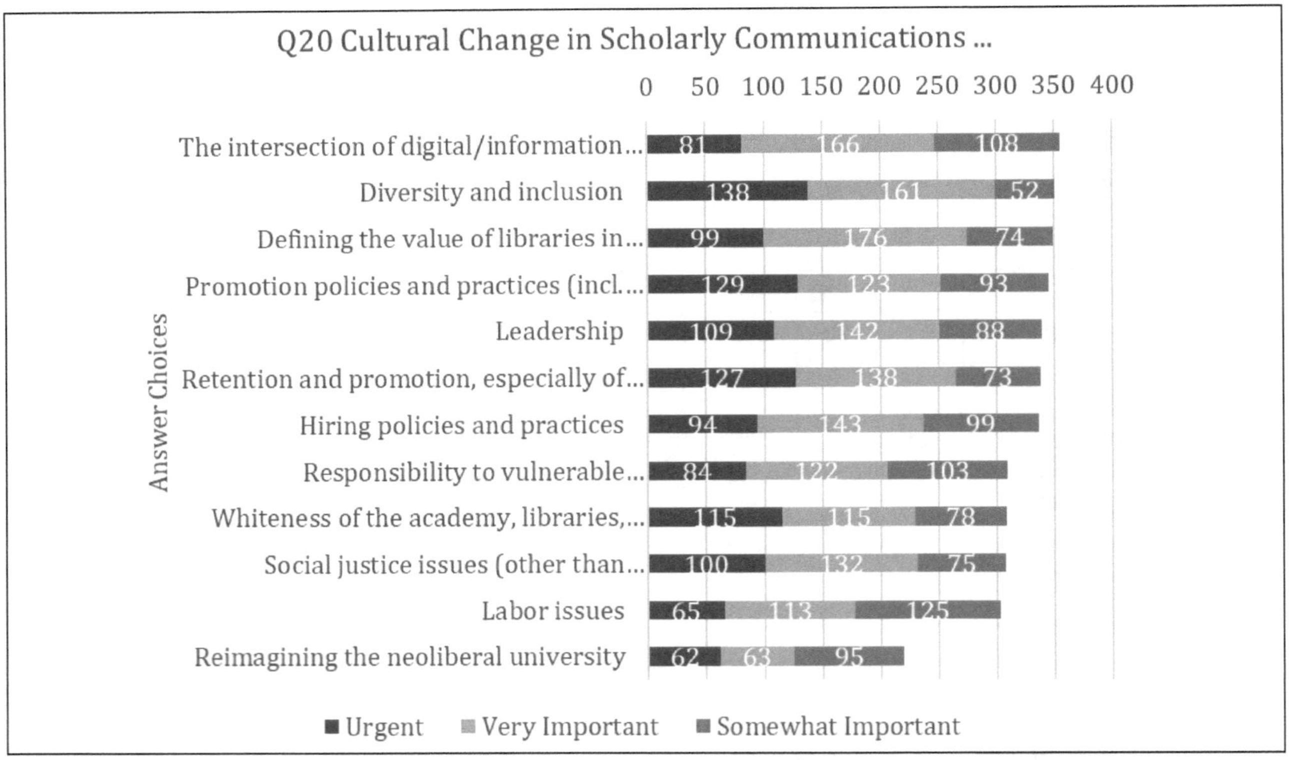

Chart 18. Responses to question 20 with answers shown by total of top 3 ranking scores, shown highest to lowest.

Answer Choices	U (5)	VI (4)	SI (3)	NPI (2)	U (1)	Total Ranked	Weight	Total Top 3	Not in Top 5 (%)	Respondents
Defining the value of libraries in scholarly communications and the research environment	99	176	74	4	7	360	3.99	349	1.37	365
Diversity and inclusion	138	161	52	10	1	362	4.17	351	0.82	365
Hiring policies and practices	94	143	99	14	6	356	3.86	336	1.11	360
The intersection of digital/ information literacy and scholarly communications	81	166	108	7	0	362	3.89	355	1.09	366
Labor issues	65	113	125	40	8	351	3.53	303	3.57	364
Leadership	109	142	88	19	0	358	3.95	339	1.65	364
Promotion policies and practices (incl. tenure and promotion criteria)	129	123	93	12	3	360	4.01	345	1.37	365
Reimagining the neoliberal university	62	63	95	63	33	316	3.18	220	13.66	366
Responsibility to vulnerable populations vs. academic freedom	84	122	103	25	7	341	3.74	309	6.32	364
Retention and promotion, especially of underrepresented minorities	127	138	73	14	5	357	4.03	338	2.19	365
Social justice issues (other than diversity and inclusion)	100	132	75	26	15	348	3.79	307	4.40	364
Whiteness of the academy, libraries, publishing industry	115	115	78	24	15	347	3.84	308	4.67	364

Table 35. Responses to question 20 as calculated weights with answer choices shown in order presented on survey.

Takeaways:

- Almost all of the options given were considered important in some regard. Even the lowest ranked response—"reimagining the neoliberal university"—was considered to be "urgent," "very important," or "somewhat important" by 60% of respondents, and the second lowest response—"Labor issues"—by 83%.
- The top 3 issues, "intersection of digital issues," "diversity and inclusion," and "defining the value of libraries" were very similarly ranked. The sum of their top 3 scores were separated by just 6.

Question 21

Financial and Organizational Models: Please indicate how important you feel each issue is to creating a system that is more open, inclusive, and equitable.

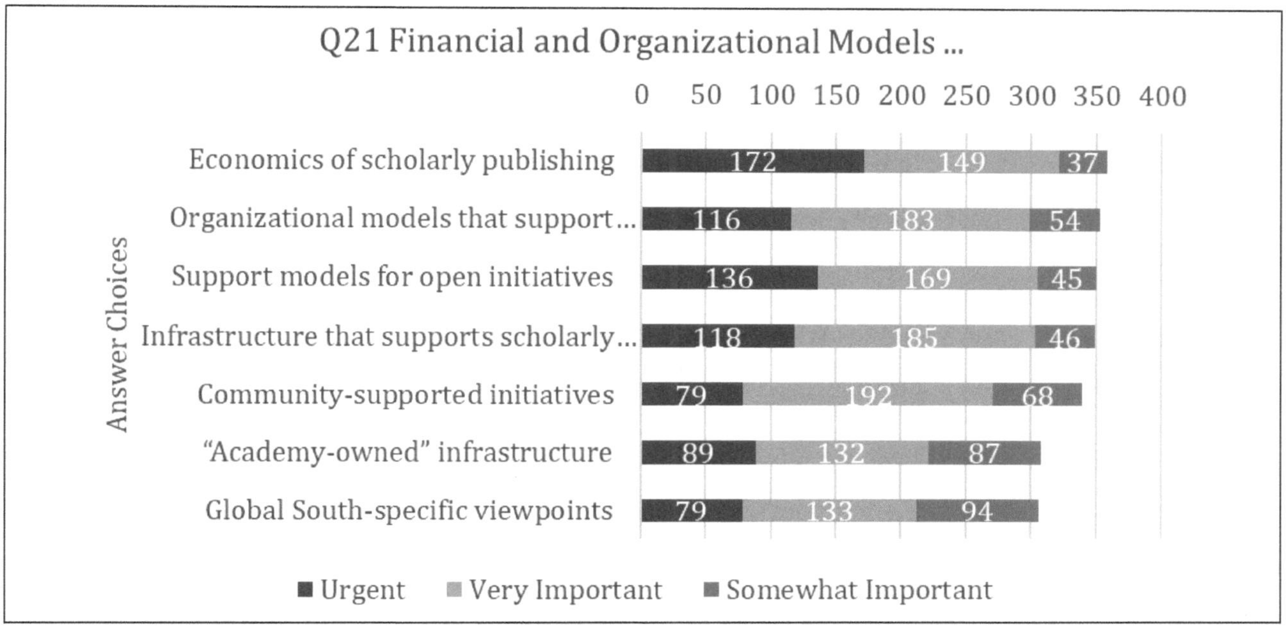

Chart 19. Responses to question 21 with answers shown by total of top 3 ranking scores, highest to lowest.

Answer Choices	U (5)	VI (4)	SI (3)	NPI (2)	U (1)	Total Ranked	Weight	Total Top 3	Respondents
"Academy-owned" infrastructure	89	132	87	24	1	333	3.85	308	364
Community-supported initiatives	79	192	68	13	2	354	3.94	339	364
Economics of scholarly publishing	172	149	37	5	0	363	4.34	358	365
Global South-specific viewpoints	79	133	94	18	5	329	3.80	306	363
Infrastructure that supports scholarly communications	118	185	46	7	0	356	4.16	349	363
Organizational models that support scholarly communications	116	183	54	3	1	357	4.15	353	365
Support models for open initiatives	136	169	45	4	1	355	4.23	350	364

Table 36. Responses to question 21 as calculated weights with answer choices shown in order presented on survey.

Takeaways:

- As with the above question, almost every subject was considered important. The lowest item in this question, "Global-South specific viewpoints," still had 84.3% of respondents mark it as either "urgent," "very important," or "somewhat important."
- Although its top 3 score is similar to the items below it, "economics of scholarly publishing" was comfortably the category which most respondents marked "urgent" most frequently—172 times, in comparison with the next most important item, "support models for open initiatives," which was marked urgent 136 times.
- Although further down the list, "community support initiatives" was marked "very important" by 192 respondents—the most for any category.

APPENDIX 9: Recommended Readings*

PEOPLE

Embracing Diversity and Inclusion

Alabi, Jaena. "To Be Seen and Heard: Realizing the Benefits of Diversity and Responding to the Needs of Minority Academic Librarians." Presentation, Mississippi Library Association Annual Conference, Natchez, MS, October 21, 2015.

> Alabi explains that "diversity" in hiring does not mean just hiring people of color or women, but setting specific goals of inclusion and then meeting them. Those goals necessarily must be sourced from the needs of librarians of diverse background and, once met, will demonstrably strengthen the library as a whole.

Alexander, David L. "American Indian Studies, Multiculturalism, and the Academic Library." *College and Research Libraries* 74, no. 1 (2013): 60–68.

> This article lays out a framework for how the nascent but growing field of American Indian studies is a case study for how libraries can both increase the multiculturalism of their collections and better serve their minority students.

American Library Association. "Diversity Counts: 2009–2010 Update." September 18, 2012. http://www.ala.org/aboutala/offices/diversity/diversitycounts/2009-2010update.

> In 2006, the ALA and the research firm Decision Demographics worked together to conduct Diversity Counts, a comprehensive study of the field in terms of diversity of race, age, gender, and disability status. This is an update to that study and an updated call to action to address the inequality and gaps in diversity the study has identified.

Anaya, Toni, and Charlene Maxey-Harris. *Diversity and Inclusion: SPEC Kit 356*. Washington, DC: Association of Research Libraries, 2017. https://doi.org/10.29242/spec.356.

> This 2017 update to a 2010 survey on diversity and inclusion of ARL member institutions gathers mission statements, values statements, descriptions of mentoring programs, and other representative documents from sixty-eight institutions (about 55 percent of ARL's membership). While diversity in hiring in libraries has increased, the results of the survey show the necessity of better training and educational opportunities in communities of color, better outreach efforts, and changes in the promotion and assessment process.

Association of College and Research Libraries (ACRL) Scholarly Communications Committee. *Establishing a Research Agenda for Scholarly Communication: A Call for Community Engagement*. Chicago: Association of College and Research Libraries 2007.

Association of College and Research Libraries (ACRL) Working Group on Intersections of Scholarly Communication and Information Literacy. *Intersections of Scholarly Communication and Information Literacy:*

* The annotations in this section were written by Penelope Weber.

Creating Strategic Collaborations for a Changing Academic Environment. Chicago: Association of College and Research Libraries, 2013.

The work set out in these two ACRL reports from 2007 and 2013 provides the basis for the current report, focusing on the changing digital infrastructure of ACRL work and possible responses to it. Especially relevant are subsections 3–5 of the report from 2007, focusing on shifting scholarly activities and their recognition, and subsection 1 of the 2013 report, identifying early efforts in OA and speculating on their impact on academic publishing.

Baffoe, Michael, Lewis Asimeng-Boahene, and Buster C. Ogbuagu. "Their Way or No Way: 'Whiteness' as Agent for Marginalizing and Silencing Minority Voices in Academic Research and Publication." *European Journal of Sustainable Development* 3, no. 1 (2014): 13–32.

Baffoe and colleagues argue that the academy is built on whiteness and white privilege, and while there is a lot of scholarship on how academics of color work within that space, this article argues, there is little critical examination of whiteness as an active mechanism rather than a passive canvas. The university as an institution and by extension the publishing industry are inherently white constructs, and resistance to the open-access movements has its roots in the maintenance of consolidated power over knowledge.

Baildon, Michelle, Dana Hamlin, Czeslaw Jankowski, Rhonda Kauffman, Julia Lanigan, Michelle Miller, Jessica Venlet, and Ann Marie Willer. "Creating a Social Justice Mindset: Diversity, Inclusion, and Social Justice in the Collections Directorate of the MIT Libraries." Collections Directorate of the MIT Libraries, February 9, 2017. https://dspace.mit.edu/handle/1721.1/108771.

This report from the MIT Collections Directorate Diversity, Inclusion, and Social Justice Task Force includes a working definition of the differences between diversity, inclusion, and social justice and provides steps forward in three major areas: economics (responses to neoliberalism, corporatization, and the commercialization of publishing), systems of oppression and privilege, and values or ethics and the concept of neutrality.

Brown, Jessie, and Martin Kurzweil. *Funding Socioeconomic Diversity at High Performing Colleges and Universities.* New York: Ithaka S+R, 2017. http://www.sr.ithaka.org/publications/funding-socioeconomic-diversity-at-high-performing-colleges-and-universities/.

This report profiles five top-performing four-year colleges and universities that have made strides recently to better serve the financial needs of their underprivileged student populations, comparing the funding, leadership, data, and community strategies necessary to do so.

Downing, Karen E. "The Relationship between Social Identity and Role Performance among Academic Librarians." PhD diss., University of Michigan, 2009.

Downing identifies librarians as the main purveyors of information literacy in the academy and subsequently highlights the problem of the overwhelming whiteness of library faculty, examining how intersecting social identities shape library and information work.

Fontenot, Mitch. "Diversity: A Task Force: Survey of the Literature and Some Possible Trends for Academic Libraries." *Louisiana Libraries* 73, no. 1 (2010): 8–11.

This article reviews different strategies for developing diversity programming in academic libraries and offers suggestions for how Lousiana's own academic libraries can best serve the needs of their diverse community.

Ford, Emily, Wendi Arant Kaspar, and Peggy Seiden. "Diversity of ACRL Publications, Editorial Board Demographics: A Report from ACRL's Publications Coordinating Committee." *College and Research Libraries* 78, no. 10 (2017): 548–51.

This article presents a survey of the demographics of the ACRL editorial boards, including age, gender, race, geographic location, professional and institutional affiliation, length of professional and editorial experience, and faculty and tenure status, in order to promote diversity in their publishing environment.

Freeman, Rodney E. "A Snapshot of Indiana's Librarians Leading in Diversity Fellowship Participants after the Program Has Concluded." *Indiana Libraries* 33, no. 1 (2014): 12–15.

From 2008 to 2012, the Indiana's Librarians Leading in Diversity program recruited, educated, and funded thirty-one minority librarians. Two years later, this report surveyed seven of those graduates who have found career success in their fields on their experiences in a still white-dominated academic library space.

Gazula, Suhasini. "Diversity in Academic Librarianship: A New Zealand Perspective." *New Zealand Library and Information Management Journal* 55, no. 2 (2015): 23–29.

Gazula gives an overview of diversity efforts in New Zealand libraries and reflects on the difficulties facing libraries serving diverse communities, especially immigrant and Indigenous communities, as well as the power libraries have as centers of information literacy in the twenty-first century.

Greco, Albert N., Robert M. Wharton, and Amy Brand. "Demographics of Scholarly Publishing and Communication Professionals." *Learned Publishing* 29, no. 2 (2016): 97–101.

This article is a survey of academic publishing employees to determine demographics, including race, gender, years in the profession, and level of education. The authors advocate regular surveys in order to evaluate efforts for further diversity.

Hathcock, April. "White Librarianship in Blackface: Diversity Initiatives in LIS." *In the Library with the Lead Pipe*, October 7, 2015. https://bit.ly/1Pj087V.

This article says that diversity efforts as they currently stand unduly burden the individuals they are intended to help, placing the onus of mentorship and other unrewarded labors on academic librarians of color and asking that applicants academic library positions meet standards of white, middle-class life in order to be hired. In order to actually confront the whiteness of academic libraries, librarians must attract and retain applicants from truly diverse backgrounds, not people of color able to accurately "play at whiteness."

Honma, Todd. “Trippin’ over the Color Line: The Invisibility of Race in Library and Information Studies.” *InterActions: UCLA Journal of Education and Information Studies* 1 (2005): article 2. http://escholarship.org/uc/item/4nj0w1mp.

Honma argues that library scholarship and information studies cannot continue to treat the subject of race as outside the “objective” work of inquiry and presents a critique of LIS that works to include the voices of multiple marginalized groups and acknowledges intersecting identities, oppressions, and privileges.

Jaeger, Paul T., Nicole A. Cooke, Cecilia Feltis, Michelle Hamiel, Fiona Jardine, and Katie Shilton. “The Virtuous Circle Revisited: Injecting Diversity, Inclusion, Rights, Justice, and Equity into LIS from Education to Advocacy.” *Library Quarterly* 85, no. 2 (2015): 150–71.

Jaeger and colleagues present a number of case studies from LIS education programs centered around diversity, inclusion, rights, justice, and equity in order to argue that effective inclusion efforts in the field of LIS need to combine interventions in education and advocacy, not treat them as separate concepts.

Kim, Kyung-Sun, and Sei-Ching Joanna Sin. “Increasing Ethnic Diversity in LIS: Strategies Suggested by Librarians of Color.” *Library Quarterly* 78, no. 2 (2008): 153–77.

This article is a 2008 survey and set of recommendations for effective recruitment and retention of library school students of color.

Kumaran, Maha. “Succession Planning Process That Includes Visible Minority Librarians.” *Library Management* 36, no. 6–7 (2015): 434–47.

This 2015 study of librarians of color (“visible minorities”) at senior positions in academic libraries is accompanied by a set of recommendations around inclusion in the process of succession planning.

Lyon, Becky J., Kathel Dunn, and Sally Sinn. “Leveraging Partnerships to Develop a Strong and Diverse Workforce.” *Journal of Library Administration* 51, no. 2 (2011): 231–41.

This article examines diversity efforts in academic health science libraries in order to better integrate libraries with campus organizations, research institutions, and clinical settings and diversify the workforce across the health science field.

Mathuews, Katy. “Moving beyond Diversity to Social Justice: A Call to Action for Academic Libraries.” *Progressive Librarian* 44 (2016): 6–27.

Mathuews explores how libraries can shift their focus from shallow diversity efforts to an effective agenda for social justice and how doing so means hewing more closely to the ideals academic libraries are based on in their role in the system of knowledge production, dissemination, and preservation.

Pearson, George, and Heidi Lowry. “Hating Hate Speech: Debating Freedom and Tolerance in the Chicago IFRT Program.” *Intellectual Freedom Round Table Report* 46, no. 2 (2000): 1–3.

Pearson and Lowry explain that an absolutist interpretation of freedom of speech allows hate speech, which critical race theory understands to be a primary tool of white supremacy and cisheteronormativity, thus actually infringing on the other freedoms of historically oppressed minorities.

Pickens, Chanelle, and Ashleigh D. Coren. "Diversity Residency Programs: Strategies for a Collaborative Approach to Development." *Collaborative Librarianship* 9, no. 2 (2017): 104–8.

Pickens and Coren offer suggestions for diversity and inclusion residency programs in libraries from the point of view of second-year residents, stressing the importance of ongoing evaluation and assessment of the program, robust diversity training for program administrators, well-coordinated onboarding, support for mentors and advocates, and an articulation of vision for both the library as a whole and the resident librarians.

Riley-Reid, Trevar. "Breaking Down Barriers: Making It Easier for Academic Librarians of Color to Stay." *Journal of Academic Librarianship* 43, no. 5 (September 2017): 392–96. https://doi.org/10.1016/j.acalib.2017.06.017.

There are many barriers to the retention of people of color in academic library spaces. Riley-Reid offers suggestions for how to get past both explicit racist barriers and implicit bias, including mentorship, reframing from "diversity" to "antiracism," and other work to shift cultural norms.

Schonfeld, Roger C., and Liam Sweeney. *Inclusion, Diversity, and Equity: Members of the Association of Research Libraries: Employee Demographics and Director Perspectives.* New York: Andrew W. Mellon Foundation, 2017. https://sr.ithaka.org/publications/inclusion-diversity-and-equity-arl/.

The Mellon Foundation commissioned Ithaka S+R to gather data about employee diversity in academic libraries at four-year universities and colleges in the United States. This study surveyed deans and directors on the diversity of their own libraries and that of the larger library community.

Semenza, Jenny Lynne, Regina Koury, and Sandra Shropshire. "Diversity at Work in Academic Libraries, 2010–2015: An Annotated Bibliography." *Collection Building* 36, no. 3 (2017): 89–95.

This annotated bibliography gathers literature concerned with diversity and inclusion initiatives within academic libraries up through 2015, with sources from Google Scholar and multidisciplinary databases.

Society of College, National and University Libraries (SCONUL). *Research Project: BAME Staff Experiences of Academic Libraries.* London: SCONUL, May 17, 2018. https://www.sconul.ac.uk/sites/default/files/documents/Research%20Project%20-%20BAME%20staff%20experiences%20of%20academic%20libraries.pdf.

In this document, SCONUL solicits commissioned research into the experiences of BAME (black, Asian, and minority ethnic) staff at UK academic libraries, with the aim of developing focus groups and analysis drawn from one-on-one interviews.

Swanson, Juleah, Ione Damasco, Isabel Gonzalez-Smith, Dracine Hodges, Todd Honma, and Azusa Tanaka. "Why Diversity Matters: A Roundtable Discussion on Racial and Ethnic Diversity in Librarianship." *In the*

Library with the Lead Pipe, July 29, 2015. http://www.inthelibrarywiththeleadpipe.org/2015/why-diversity-matters-a-roundtable-discussion-on-racial-and-ethnic-diversity-in-librarianship/.

This roundtable discussion returns to why librarians put diversity efforts in place, examining why diversity matters through "whiteness theory," identity theory, and the reinvention of the library as a structure no longer reliant on the homogeneity of people and ideas.

Vinopal, Jennifer. "The Quest for Diversity in Library Staffing: From Awareness to Action." *In the Library with the Lead Pipe*, January 13, 2016. http://www.inthelibrarywiththeleadpipe.org/2016/quest-for-diversity/.

Vinopal identifies issues with data collection around diversity, including confirmation bias, sourcing data from white librarians rather than librarians of color, and assumptions baked into the survey questions. Implicit bias must be acknowledged and prevented in order to actually understand, and thus increase the effectiveness of, diversity efforts in academic libraries.

Improving the Working Lives of People Engaged in Scholarly Communications

Andrews, Nicola. "Reflections on Resistance, Decolonization, and the Historical Trauma of Libraries and Academia." In *The Politics of Theory and the Practice of Critical Librarianship*, edited by Karen P. Nicholson and Maura Seale, 181–92. Sacramento: Library Juice Press, 2018.

Māori scholar Nicola Andrews gives a personal account of the ways in which libraries can uphold and reinforce colonialist traditions and narratives and outlines possible change through Indigenous frameworks such as Historical Trauma Therapy; the inclusion of contemporary works by Indigenous scholars alongside older, exoticizing anthropological work in their collections; and intentional consultation with the Indigenous communities they serve.

Brook, Freeda, Dave Ellenwood, and Althea Eannace Lazzaro. "In Pursuit of Antiracist Social Justice: Denaturalizing Whiteness in the Academic Library." *Library Trends* 64, no. 2 (2015): 246–84.

Efforts for "diversity" that focus only around hiring haven't been successful in the library and information worlds because the work must instead be genuinely antiracist. This article explores three important areas for antiracist interventions: physical space, staffing, and methods and values.

Chou, Rose L., and Annie Pho. "Intersectionality at the Reference Desk: Lived Experiences of Women of Color Librarians." In *The Feminist Reference Desk: Concepts, Critiques, and Conversations*, edited by Maria T. Accardi, 225–52. Sacramento: Library Juice Press, 2017.

Through qualitative interviews, two Asian American librarians conducted a study of the experiences of women of color working at the reference desks across America, dividing the stories of their participants into categories: labor ("diversity labor" and the judgment and isolation that go along with it); perceptions of competence and authority (microaggressions borne while teaching, providing reference services, or managing library staff); questions of personal identity, appearance, and sexual harassment; and finally self-care (how librarians of color can take care of themselves and each other in the white-dominated workplace). The study shows the way systems of oppression interact in library spaces and illustrates why diverse hiring practices are only one step toward creating an antiracist, antisexist environment.

Damasco, Ione T., and Dracine Hodges. "Tenure and Promotion Experiences of Academic Librarians of Color." *College and Research Libraries* 73, no. 3 (2012): 279–301.

Reported in this article, an online survey of academic librarians of color asked participants questions around promotion and tenure, professional activities and productivity, and job satisfaction. The results include recommendations that review boards and library administrators consistently evaluate and update their promotion processes and policies, understand whether any mentorship or peer support groups for junior faculty are effective or only making busy work for senior librarians of color, and other checks on "diversity" labor.

Galvan, Angela. "Soliciting Performance, Hiding Bias: Whiteness and Librarianship." *In the Library with the Lead Pipe*, June 3, 2015. http://tinyurl.com/ycoe9fmf.

Galvan examines the invisible bias not only in librarianship but also in the structures of the professional hiring process, highlighting the ways in which whiteness reinforces itself in library structures prior to, during, and after hiring librarians of color.

Kumaran, Maha. *Leadership in Libraries: A Focus on Ethnic-Minority Librarians.* Oxford: Chandos, 2012.

Kumaran offers advice on communication, transitions, and cultural norms and differences to minority and immigrant librarians interested in library leadership and connects their needs to the literature of leadership theory in library studies.

Matthew, Patricia A. "Tweeting Diversity: Race and Tenure in the Age of Social Media." In *Written/Unwritten: Diversity and the Hidden Truths of Tenure*, edited by Patricia A. Matthew, 241–60. Chapel Hill: University of North Carolina Press, 2016.

In this conclusion to the 2016 anthology *Written/Unwritten: Diversity and the Hidden Truths of Tenure,* Matthew engages with the risks and possibilities inherent in the use of social media, especially Twitter, as a black female academic. She uses as a case study the ways in which Twitter has shaped the career of Tressie McMillan Cottom, then a doctoral candidate.

Society for Scholarly Publishing. "On Being Excluded: Testimonies by People of Color in Scholarly Publishing." *Scholarly Kitchen* (blog), April 4, 2018. https://scholarlykitchen.sspnet.org/2018/04/04/excluded-testimonies-people-color-scholarly-publishing/.

This blog post is an anonymous collection of stories of workplace harassment, microaggressions, and exclusion in scholarly publishing from people of color. It includes an excellent chart that explains the problem with simply encouraging diverse hiring as opposed to active antiracism efforts.

Thornton, Joyce K. "African American Female Librarians: A Study of Job Satisfaction." *Journal of Library Administration* 33, no. 1–2 (2001): 141–64.

This survey collates responses from ninety-eight African American female librarians across a variety of ages, years of experience, and years at current institution on questions of isolation and discrimination in the workplace, as well as overall job satisfaction.

Increasing Awareness Concerning Creators' Rights

Association of European Research Libraries (LIBER). *The Hague Declaration*. December 10, 2014. https://thehaguedeclaration.com/.

The Hague Declaration lays out a vision, five principles, and a road map for action for how to treat intellectual property, research activity, property law, and individual rights online. Researchers, businesses, policy makers, and institutions across the European Union signed on to these ground rules and agreed to participate in implementing next steps toward ethical research practice.

Ferber, Abby. "Faculty under Attack." *Humboldt Journal of Social Relations* 39, no. 1 (2017): 37–42.

Ferber explains the ways the corporatization of academia, the rise of social media, and the politicization of concepts of "free speech" and "academic freedom" have led to an increasingly dangerous and toxic environment for female and minority academics. She relates her own experience alongside the experiences of five other women, examining how their intersecting identities changed the nature of the harassment.

Gilman, Isaac. "Responsibilities and Rights: Balancing the Institutional Imperative for Open Access with Authors' Self-Determination." In *Making Institutional Repositories Work*, edited by Burton B. Callicott, David Scherer, and Andrew Wesolek, 69–85. West Lafayette, IN: Purdue University Press, 2015.

Gilman argues that creating open-access institutional repositories is not only a solution to various publishing concerns but is also a moral imperative, to be balanced in an ethical sense with the rights of academics to determine how and where to share their work.

Jones, Paul. "Digital Labour in the Academic Context: Challenges for Academic Staff Associations." *Ephemera* 10, no. 3/4 (2010): 537–39.

The Canadian Association of University Teachers (CAUT) presented this talk at the Digital Labour: Workers, Authors, Citizens conference, describing new challenges to academic freedom on three fronts: teaching, scholarly communication, and copyright law.

Library Publishing Coalition. "An Ethical Framework for Library Publishing," version 1.0. San Francisco: Educopia, 2018. https://doi.org/10.5703/1288284316777

The Library Publishing Coalition (LPC) released this ethical framework in July 2018. Primary concerns are publishing practice; accessibility; diversity, equity, and inclusion; privacy and analytics; and academic and intellectual freedom. It offers a set of recommendations for ethical practice in each of these areas, some from the point of view of an individual, others for institutions as actors, and a set of recommended readings for each.

Lor, Peter Johan, and Johannes Britz. "Knowledge Production from an African Perspective: International Information Flows and Intellectual Property." *International Information and Library Review* 37, no. 2 (2005): 61–76.

Lor and Britz contend that intellectual property should be a moral issue, not a legal one, and that its legal definition has contributed to eddies and blockages in the flow of academic knowledge. They examine information flow in three directions (North-South, South-North, and South-South) from the perspective of an African scholar.

CONTENT

Rethinking What "Counts"

Academic College and Research Libraries. "Altmetrics and Library Outreach." "ACRL Liaisons to Professional Associations: Major Issues, Talking Points, and Resources." July 21, 2017. https://acrl.libguides.com/c.php?g=452958&p=3094032.

This LibGuide provides an overview of the main topics in alternative metrics and examples of platforms offering nonstandard metrics services for use in conversation with professional associations and other practitioners and administrators involved in assessment and evaluation.

Ainley, Kirsten, Ida Danewid, and Joanne Yao. "Challenging the Gender Citation Gap: What Journals Can Do." *International Affairs Blog*, Medium, August 22, 2017. https://medium.com/international-affairs-blog/challenging-the-gender-citation-gap-what-journals-can-do-f79e0b831055.

Ainley and colleagues review the literature on the gender citation gap in the top international relations journals and the implications thereof, suggesting action items, including stressing equitable citation in submission guidelines, diversifying the content published and the pool of reviewers relied on, creating presubmission mentorships for authors from underrepresented communities, and working to set the agenda around gender equity in publishing.

Archambault, Éric, Étienne Vignola-Gagne, Grégoire Côté, Vincent Larivière, and Yves Gingras. "Benchmarking Scientific Output in the Social Sciences and Humanities: The Limits of Existing Databases." *Scientometrics* 68, no. 3 (2006): 329–42.

This paper compares the Thomson Scientific and the Ulrich databases of journals on the basis of linguistic coverage to argue that relying on Thomson Scientific alone for bibliometric benchmarking skews the results toward English-language and thus often Global North scholarship.

Aviles, Frank P., and Ivonne S. Ramirez. "Evaluating the Internationality of Scholarly Communications in Information Science Publications." Poster presentation, iConference 2015, Newport Beach Marriott Hotel and Spa, Newport Beach, CA, March 24–27, 2015.

Aviles and Ramirez examine the geographic diversity of ten top LIS journals based on seven indicators: authorship, editorial and advisory board membership, peer-review participation, peer review evaluation criteria, distribution, citations, and citation impact.

Benedictus, Rinze, Frank Miedema, and Mark W. J. Ferguson. "Fewer Numbers, Better Science." *Nature News* 538, no. 7626 (2016): 453.

This essay argues that bibliometrics based on citation counts and publication numbers lead to a valuing of numbers rather than real impact on patient care in the health sciences. It gives two examples of new evaluation methods for research programs that take into account a fuller breadth of activity for health science scholars.

Bernal, Isabel. "Open Access and the Changing Landscape of Research Impact Indicators: New Roles for Repositories." *Publications* 1, no. 2 (2013): 56–77.

Bernal interrogates the link between open-access movements in publication and the reworking of evaluation metrics based on citations, using the Spanish National Research Council's work on its DIGITAL. CSIC repository.

Bornmann, Lutz. "Do Altmetrics Point to the Broader Impact of Research? An Overview of Benefits and Disadvantages of Altmetrics." *Journal of Informetrics* 8, no. 4 (2014): 895–903.

Bornmann gives an overview of altmetric efforts as of 2014, identifying problem areas such as social media "gaming," and argues that like traditional impact metrics, altmetrics should serve as only a part of the evaluation process, being paired with expert peer review for funding or tenure purposes.

Bornmann, Lutz, and Hans-Dieter Daniel. "What Do Citation Counts Measure? A Review of Studies on Citing Behavior." *Journal of Documentation* 64, no. 1 (2008): 45–80.

This paper collects approximately thirty studies of citation behavior by scholars in the sciences from the early 1960s to mid-2005, examining how citation practices have changed and what behaviors still persist. Additionally, Bornmann and Daniel argue, these studies show that citation practices are not and never have been solely about recognizing excellence in peer scholarship, and this fact should be taken into account in current conversations around metrics and evaluation.

Burrows, Roger. "Living with the H-Index? Metric Assemblages in the Contemporary Academy." *Sociological Review* 60, no. 2 (2012): 355–72.

This paper argues that the current system of citation metrics, workload models, costing data, research and teaching assessments, and commercial rankings for universities in the UK increasingly combine to reinforce capitalist market logic within the academic system, rather than functioning as a system of excellence and accountability.

Chou, Chuing Prudence, Hsiao Fang Lin, and Yun-ju Chiu. "The Impact of SSCI and SCI on Taiwan's Academy: An Outcry for Fair Play." *Asia Pacific Education Review* 14, no. 1 (2013): 23–31.

In response to the rise of global university rankings, the Ministry of Education in Taiwan instituted the Social Science Citation Index (SSCI) to accompany the Science Citation Index (SCI) in the STEM fields. This article explores the negative consequences of privileging citation metrics over other measures of excellence in the social sciences and includes a petition calling for more nuanced and culturally responsive criteria for evaluating scholarship.

Collini, Stefan. *What Are Universities For?* New York: Penguin, 2012.

Collini argues that both financial gain and immediate social impact are damaging metrics by which to evaluate universities and that, particularly in the case of humanities disciplines, education has a slow, complex, but absolutely vital effect on the overall good of the public.

Connell, Ruth Sara. "Promotion and Tenure Procedures: A Study of U.S. Academic Libraries." *Library Leadership and Management* 32, no. 4 (2018): article 7296. https://journals.tdl.org/llm/index.php/llm/article/view/7296.

This study of promotion and tenure for academic librarians from 200 institutions of higher education included questions on such topics as who performs reviews; whether review committees are library-specific, campus-wide, or include external reviewers; and what documentation guides the review process. Institutions studied included both public and private universities of varying sizes.

Corrall, Sheila, Mary Anne Kennan, and Waseem Afzal. "Bibliometrics and Research Data Management Services: Emerging Trends in Library Support for Research." *Library Trends* 61, no. 3 (2013): 636–74.

This study expands efforts to understand bibliometric and data-support activities beyond North America, surveying 140 academic libraries across Australia, New Zealand, Ireland, and the UK. National pressures to assess the quality of research have pushed librarians to adopt performance-based tools and measures at a higher rate, and data management and collection follow quickly behind.

de Rijcke, Sarah, Paul F. Wouters, Alex D. Rushforth, Thomas P. Franssen, and Björn Hammarfelt. "Evaluation Practices and Effects of Indicator Use—A Literature Review." *Research Evaluation* 25, no. 2 (2016): 161–69.

Part of a larger review commissioned by the Higher Education Funding Council for England (HEFCE) to inform its assessment of the role of metrics in evaluation, this article condenses the major themes in metrics literature into three categories: the effects of evaluation exercises on scholarship, the "gaming" of indicators, and strategic responses by scientific communities to the requirements of evaluation. However, it also notes the difficulty of a full literature review of such a heterogeneous collection of sources and styles of evidence.

Duff, Wendy M., Andrew Flinn, Karen Emily Suurtamm, and David A. Wallace. "Social Justice Impact of Archives: A Preliminary Investigation." *Archival Science* 13, no. 4 (2013): 317–48.

Duff and colleagues articulate a framework of social justice action and examine how archives, archivists, and archival repositories are contributing both positively and negatively to the furthering of social justice goals.

Duffy, Brooke Erin, and Jefferson D. Pooley. "'Facebook for Academics': The Convergence of Self-Branding and Social Media Logic on Academia.edu." *Social Media and Society* 3, no. 1 (2017): 1–11.

This article contends that Academia.edu functions similarly to other social networks, both in terms of the platform gathering data on its users for corporate use and in terms of the constant self-curation and self-monitoring it encourages, which limits experimentation and necessary risktaking in scholarly work and selects for a specific kind of scholar.

Edwards, Marc A., and Siddhartha Roy. "Academic Research in the 21st Century: Maintaining Scientific Integrity in a Climate of Perverse Incentives and Hypercompetition." *Environmental Engineering Science* 34, no. 1 (2017): 51–61.

Perverse economy and metric-driven incentives for research, Edwards and Roy argue, lead to unethical behavior by scientists and the eventual possibility that the entire scientific endeavor becomes corrupt and its contributions to knowledge false and meaningless. In order for research to be turned to the public good, federal and private funding agents need to incentivize ethical behavior and de-emphasize publication numbers.

Fitzpatrick, Kathleen, and Rebecca Kennison. "Altmetrics in Humanities and Social Sciences." White paper, October 30, 2017. http://dx.doi.org/10.17613/M6MW28D5J.

Through interviews, a focus group of deans at three different institutions, and a series of surveys, this study focuses on how metrics, and data around faculty publication and scholarly activity in general, are actually used by administrators and how stakeholders at a variety of levels feel about current evaluative practices. The discussion culminates in descriptions of two projects based on the need for more robust qualitative understandings of research: the Quality and Relevance in the Humanities (QRiH) project and the Humane Metrics in Humanities and Social Sciences (HuMetricsHSS) initiative.

Flaherty, Colleen. "Refusing to Be Measured." *Inside Higher Ed*, May 11, 2016. https://www.insidehighered.com/news/2016/05/11/rutgers-graduate-school-faculty-takes-stand-against-academic-analytics.

This *Inside Higher Ed* piece describes the resolution taken by Rutgers faculty in May 2016 demanding that administrators not use Academic Analytics in tenure and promotion or resource allocation, citing incorrect data, a lack of nuanced understanding of the work of academia, and invasion of privacy.

Gruber, Thorsten. "Academic Sell Out: How an Obsession with Metrics and Rankings Is Damaging Academia." *Journal of Marketing for Higher Education* 24, no. 2 (2014): 165–77.

Gruber gives an overview of the problems of current metrics, both journal impact factor and citation index, and argues that entirely anonymous review—where no one, including the journal editors, knows any identifying information about the author of an article—should be combined with open-access journals in order to ensure nonbiased, quality scholarship available to the greatest number of constituents.

Hammarfelt, Björn. "Using Altmetrics for Assessing Research Impact in the Humanities." *Scientometrics* 101, no. 2 (2014): 1419–30.

This paper examines the altmetric coverage and impact of humanities articles and books published by Swedish universities during 2012 in order to understand if and how altmetric coverage of humanities work differs from altmetric coverage of STEM fields, or if altmetric and traditional metric coverage of humanities work differ.

Haustein, Stefanie, and Vincent Larivière. "The Use of Bibliometrics for Assessing Research: Possibilities, Limitations and Adverse Effects." In *Incentives and Performance: Governance of Research Organizations*, edited by Isabell Welpe, Jutta Wollersheim, Stefanie Ringelhan, and Margit Osterloh, 121–39. New York: Springer, 2015.

This chapter gives a historical overview of bibliometric methods, from development to application and subsequent mis- and overuse, laying out the ways they shape scholarly behavior rather than the other way around.

Heller, Margaret, and Franny Gaede. "Measuring Altruistic Impact: A Model for Understanding the Social Justice of Open Access." *Journal of Librarianship and Scholarly Communication* 4 (2016): eP2132. https://doi.org/10.7710/2162-3309.2132.

Heller and Gaede use web analytics, rather than citations or download counts, to measure access to social justice–focused scholarship in institutional repositories, especially from lower-resourced countries. They conclude that opening access to social justice content improves the ranking of that content in search results and advocate using this as an entry point to talking to social justice scholars who may not already be interested in open access.

Herther, Nancy K. "Citation Analysis and Discoverability: A Critical Challenge for Disability Studies." *Disability and Society* 30, no. 1 (2015): 130–52.

Herther, in an attempt to do a comprehensive study of disability studies, discovered instead a lack of indexing and metadata that would allow traditional citation analysis, forcing her to rely mostly on dissertation work rather than journal articles and books and showing a foundational importance of dissertation work to the ongoing legitimization of disability studies as a field.

Hicks, Diana. 2012. "Performance-Based University Research Funding Systems." *Research Policy* 41, no. 2 (2012): 251–61.

Hicks gives an overview of performance-based university research funding systems (PRFSs), national systems of research evaluation that combine peer review and metrics, finding them able to accommodate differences between fields, but allows that the emphasis on "excellence" might compromise diversity and equity.

Hoecht, Andreas. "Quality Assurance in UK Higher Education: Issues of Trust, Control, Professional Autonomy and Accountability." *Higher Education* 51, no. 4 (2006): 541–63.

Hoecht argues that the shift to an audit-based quality control in recent years of evaluation in higher education has high opportunity costs and negative effects on the culture of trust and professional autonomy in academia.

Hug, Sven E., Michael Ochsner, and Hans-Dieter Daniel. "Criteria for Assessing Research Quality in the Humanities: A Delphi Study among Scholars of English Literature, German Literature and Art History." *Research Evaluation* 22, no. 5 (2013): 369–83.

Hug and colleagues have compared research and evaluation criteria across three disciplines in order to understand the mismatch between evaluators and scholars and to formulate solutions to bridge the gap and allow for accurate and holistic evaluation of research.

Jackson, J. Kasi, Melissa Latimer, and Rachel Stoiko. "The Dynamic between Knowledge Production and Faculty Evaluation: Perceptions of the Promotion and Tenure Process across Disciplines." *Innovative Higher Education* 42, no. 3 (2017): 193–205.

This study compares various job satisfaction factors (collegiality, college commitment to field, work-life integration, mentoring) with satisfaction with promotion, tenure, and expectation among academic faculty in both high- and low-consensus disciplines, finding that faculty with high job satisfaction were more likely to agree with the criteria by which they were evaluated.

Kousha, Kayvan, and Mike Thelwall. "Can Amazon.com Reviews Help to Assess the Wider Impacts of Books?" *Journal of the Association for Information Science and Technology* 67, no. 3 (2016): 566–81.

This article explores the possibility of supplementing citation count with metrics derived from Amazon.com reviews of academic texts in order to better measure impact. It recommends that an evaluation of books aimed at a wide audience rather than just intended to be read within academia should take into consideration the sales numbers and reviews on public sites like Amazon.

Larivière, Vincent, Chaoqun Ni, Yves Gingras, Blaise Cronin, and Cassidy R. Sugimoto. "Bibliometrics: Global Gender Disparities in Science." *Nature* 204 (2013): 211–13.

This article presents a cross-disciplinary, global bibliometric analysis of gender and research output, including collaboration and scientific impact, and offers a set of recommendations for bridging the gender gap, including programs for international collaborations between female researchers.

Laudel, Grit, and Jochen Gläser. "Tensions between Evaluations and Communication Practices." *Journal of Higher Education Policy and Management* 28, no. 3 (2006): 289–95.

Laudel and Gläser point out the discrepancy between communication channels used by Australian National University faculty and those understood and taken into account by evaluation systems either by academia itself or by funding institutions. They argue that those systems, if they remain unchanged, could change—and perhaps limit—the behaviors of faculty themselves.

Ma, Lai, and Michael Ladisch. "Scholarly Communication and Practices in the World of Metrics: An Exploratory Study." *Proceedings of the Association for Information Science and Technology* 53, no. 1 (2016): 1–4.

This study explores the use of and attitudes toward metrics in research evaluation, but also in self-monitoring and evaluations of self-worth as a researcher.

Manzari, Laura. "Library and Information Science Journal Prestige as Assessed by Library and Information Science Faculty." *Library Quarterly* 83, no. 1 (2013): 42–60.

This survey asked full-time faculty in ALA-accredited programs to rank journals by two criteria: most important to their teaching and to the field at large, and most prestigious to be published in for purposes of tenure and promotion. Manzari recommends that journal prestige/contribution to the field should be evaluated alongside impact factor when disciplinary journals are ranked.

Moher, David, Florian Naudet, Ioana A. Cristea, Frank Miedema, John P. A. Ioannidis, and Steven N. Goodman. "Assessing Scientists for Hiring, Promotion, and Tenure." *PLoS Biology* 16, no. 3 (2018): article 2004089. https://doi.org/10.1371/journal.pbio.2004089.

This report from a convening of twenty-two experts in clinical and life sciences outlines six principles for the assessment of scientists, their research, and policy implications. It offers a set of best practices in order to not overly rely on the current system of evaluation, which the authors argue is misaligned to the needs and goals of the science it is measuring.

Mott, Carrie, and Daniel Cockayne. "Citation Matters: Mobilizing the Politics of Citation toward a Practice of 'Conscientious Engagement.'" *Gender, Place and Culture* 24, no. 7 (2017): 954–73.

This article discusses the issues with citation metrics as they are currently used, but argues that, if undertaken intentionally and with a critical theoretical lens, citation itself can further social justice goals and shape the scholarly record moving forward into something more inclusive, diverse, and anticolonial.

Nederhof, Anton J. "Bibliometric Monitoring of Research Performance in the Social Sciences and the Humanities: A Review." *Scientometrics* 66, no. 1 (2006): 81–100.

This paper compares publication and citation behavior in the sciences versus that in the social sciences and humanities and discusses possibilities for bibliometric systems to evaluate academic performance in each set of fields.

Odell, Jere D., Heather L. Coates, and Kristi L. Palmer. "Rewarding Open Access Scholarship in Promotion and Tenure: Driving Institutional Change." *College and Research Libraries News* 77, no. 7 (2016): 322–25.

Odell and colleagues describe their strategy to include open access in promotion and tenure at Indiana University-Purdue University Indianapolis. They combined top-down policy approaches with education and outreach from the library sector, creating direct links between the mission of the university and the open-access movement.

Pontille, David, and Didier Torny. "The Controversial Policies of Journal Ratings: Evaluating Social Sciences and Humanities." *Research Evaluation* 19, no. 5 (2010): 347–60.

This article discusses three versions of national journal ratings, exploring the inherent tension in systems designed to be both political reputational tools and unbiased scientific assessment structures.

Priem, Jason, Dario Taraborelli, Paul Groth, and Cameron Neylon. *Altmetrics: A Manifesto* website, October 26, 2010. http://altmetrics.org/manifesto.

This "manifesto" argues that the complete story of the impact of any given work cannot be known strictly through traditional bibliometrics (i.e., citations in peer-reviewed work) but must be contextualized by "alternative metrics" such as references to the work in social media, in reference management systems, in the news media, and so on.

Ray, Victor. "The Racial Exclusions in Scholarly Citations." *Inside Higher Ed*, April 27, 2018. https://www.insidehighered.com/advice/2018/04/27/racial-exclusions-scholarly-citations-opinion.

This piece breaks down the myriad ways citation practice in the social sciences reproduces social and racial inequalities, reinforces an overwhelmingly white canon, and cannot be viewed as a neutral or equalizing measure of quality and indicator of worth.

Roemer, Robin Chin, and Rachel Borchardt. "Institutional Altmetrics and Academic Libraries." *Information Standards Quarterly* 25, no. 2 (2013): 14–19.

This article gives an overview of the ways bibliometrics have been used in libraries historically and explores the possibility of and challenges to developing systematic, aggregate-level altmetrics to put in place at the institutional level.

Roh, Charlotte. "Inequalities in Publishing." *Urban Library Journal* 22, no. 2 (2016): article 2. https://academicworks.cuny.edu/ulj/vol22/iss2/2/.

This article is a brown bag presentation Roh gave to the Graduate Students of Color Association at the University of Massachusetts Amherst, breaking down the publishing process and its importance to promotion and tenure for faculty, moving through statistics and demographics within academic publishing, and ending with a list of actions that librarians can take to change the unbalanced, white-dominated status quo.

Roh, Charlotte. "Library Publishing and Diversity Values: Changing Scholarly Publishing through Policy and Scholarly Communication Education." *College and Research Libraries* 77, no. 2 (2016): 82–85.

Homogeneity in positions of power in publishing means homogeneity of scholarship published, a privileging of white male voices, and an embedding of traditional oppressive systems of value and access. Roh highlights several projects within scholarly communication working actively to change the demographics of publishing and establish more equitable models.

Roh, Charlotte. "Scholarly Communication in a Time of Change: Considering the Impact of Bias, Diversity, and Traditional Publishing Structures as Scholarly Communication Moves to New Platforms and Systems." Presentation, California Academic and Research Libraries Conference: Academic Libraries in Times of Change, Redwood City, CA, April 14, 2018.

This transcribed talk focuses on bias in publishing through the lens of Elsevier and its gendered pay gap, women in STEM fields, and the impact of a white, male-dominated publishing landscape on type of scholarship published.

Roh, Charlotte. "Scholarly Publishing, Information Literacy, and Social Justice." Presentation, University of San Diego Digital Initiatives Symposium, San Diego, CA, May 2, 2017.

This presentation is a version of the talk "Inequalities in Publishing," listed above, this one aimed at libraries themselves rather than graduate students of color. It includes several takeaways centered around whether or not a library has a diversity statement, how involved librarians are in awareness and training for diversity and inclusion, and self-reflection questions about scholarly communication as tools for social as well as economic injustice.

Roh, Charlotte, Emily Drabinski, and Harrison W. Inefuku. "Scholarly Communication as a Tool for Social Justice and Diversity." Presentation, National Diversity in Libraries Conference, University of California Los Angeles, Los Angeles, CA, August 12, 2016.

This panel discussed how scholarly communication and LIS publishing can challenge institutional academic norms around race, gender, and sexuality, and how, in order to do so, new, radical journals must be created with specific social justice aims and goalposts.

Roh, Charlotte, and Harrison W. Inefuku. "Scholarly Communication and Diversity." Presentation, Association for Library Collections and Technical Services 2017 Midwinter Symposium, Atlanta, GA, January 20, 2017.

Roh and Inefuku emphasize the student population's reaction to the lack of diversity among their faculty, citing antiracist student protests across fifty-one campuses in 2015, and explore the geographic distribution and Global North domination of top-ranked academic journals.

Sánchez Peñas, Celia, and Peter Willett. "Brief Communication: Gender Differences in Publication and Citation Counts in Librarianship and Information Science Research." *Journal of Information Science* 32, no. 5 (2006): 480–85.

Sánchez Peñas and Willet compare the citation counts and publication numbers of male and female academics within LIS, finding that while male academics are published more often, they are not cited meaningfully more often.

Scott, Nick. "Altmetrics Are the Central Way of Measuring Communication in the Digital Age but What Do They Miss?" *LSE Impact Blog*, December 17, 2012. https://blogs.lse.ac.uk/impactofsocialsciences/2012/12/17/scott-altmetrics-central-digital-whats-missing/.

Scott argues that altmetrics, like citation counts and publication numbers, fail to take into account the full range of scholarly activity and outputs in the working academic's portfolio and need to be expanded to encompass other kinds of sharing and impact.

Thelwall, Mike, and Maria M. Delgado. "Arts and Humanities Research Evaluation: No Metrics Please, Just Data." *Journal of Documentation* 71, no. 4 (2015): 817–33.

This article surveys citation-based evaluation in order to make the case against systematic metrics as a whole, arguing instead for contextual evaluation of research based on the outputs according to each scholar. It points to the ways evaluation functions in the performing arts as a case study in using "environmental" (contextual) data for assessing quality.

Tremblay, Crystal. "Recognizing Excellence in Community Engaged Scholarship at the University of Victoria: Peer Review Guidelines for Faculty Promotion and Tenure and Impact Rubric." Working paper, May 23, 2017. http://hdl.handle.net/1828/8165.

This working paper provides peer-review guidelines for promotion and tenure in Community Engaged Scholarship (CES), a research and impact framework recognizing civic engagement and service, community-based participatory research, and community-engaged learning across a variety of disciplines. It includes a table of possible indicators of impact area, context, scholarship, and significance, stretching from influence on professional practice and curricula enrichment to knowledge mobilization and degree of collaboration.

Vesper, Inga. "Peer Reviewers Unmasked: Largest Global Survey Reveals Trends." Nature News, September 7, 2018. https://doi.org/10.1038/d41586-018-06602-y.

This study of peer review breaks down the numbers of reviewer fatigue and geographic distribution of submissions versus reviews, noting that the Global South's lower review numbers are due to fewer requests for scholars there to review, not lack of time or enthusiasm to do so.

Willmott, Hugh. "Journal List Fetishism and the Perversion of Scholarship: Reactivity and the ABS List." *Organization* 18, no. 4 (2011): 429–42.

Journal impact lists, this article argues, limit the breadth of topic, perspective, and methodology—which would otherwise enrich a field of scholarship—and reinforce a Western-dominated publishing landscape.

Creating More Representative and Open Collections

Almeida, Nora. "Open Educational Resources and Rhetorical Paradox in the Neoliberal Univers(ity)." *Journal of Critical Library and Information Studies* 1, no 1 (2017): article 16, https://theidealis.org/open-educational-resources-and-rhetorical-paradox-in-the-neoliberal-university/.

In order to properly accomplish the goals of "openness," what "open" means cannot be applied in an indiscriminate, top-down manner; instead, the definition of openness must be determined by conversation within communities served by the educational resources being developed.

Baildon, Michelle. "Extending the Social Justice Mindset: Implications for Scholarly Communication." *College and Research Libraries News* 79, no. 4 (2018): 176–79. https://doi.org/10.5860/crln.79.4.176.

This article discusses the Diversity, Inclusion, and Social Justice (DISJ) Task Force, convened by the Collections Directorate of the MIT Libraries, which concluded that while the open-access movement has the potential to further social justice goals, the interplay between Global North and Global South academia must be understood as properly complex. Efforts must be made to not only increase access to scholarship produced in the North, but also to increase participation, consumption, and citation of Global South scholars and scholarship.

Barwick, Linda, and Nicholas Thieberger. "Libraries in Paradise: New Technologies and Ethnographic Repositories." In *Libr@ries: Changing Information Space and Practice*, edited by Cushla Kapitzke and Bertram C. Bruce, 133–49. Mahwah, NJ: Lawrence Erlbaum, 2006.

> Barwick and Thieberger outline the importance of audiovisual ethnographic field recordings as tools that allow cultural heritage communities to access their own histories. They describe the work of PARADISEC (the Pacific and Regional Archive for Digital Sources) to preserve and facilitate access to these records.

Bastian, Jeannette A. "The Records of Memory, the Archives of Identity: Celebrations, Texts and Archival Sensibilities." *Archival Science* 13, no. 2–3 (2013): 121–31.

> Bastian critiques the concept of "post-colonial archives," pointing out the term was coined by academics rather than archivists, and examines the relationship between narratives and counternarratives of colonial memory in various communities in the Caribbean.

Bear, Suzy. "Building Libraries One Book at a Time." In *Aboriginal and Visible Minority Librarians: Oral Histories from Canada*, edited by Deborah Lee and Mahalakshmi Kumaran, 1–16. Lanham, MD: Rowman and Littlefield, 2014.

> Bear describes her professional career, starting with running a one-person library at the First Nations University of Canada and growing into supporting a whole network of community and institutional libraries serving First Nations students. She outlines the considerations necessary in building that library up from a historical collection to a contemporary teaching resource and community center with minimal funding.

Bowdoin, Natalia Taylor. "Open Access, African Scholarly Publishing, and Cultural Rights: An Exploratory Usage and Accessibility Study." *Library Philosophy and Practice* (2011): article 619, http://digitalcommons.unl.edu/libphilprac/619.

> Information workers are not neutral parties, and, historically, libraries have been sites of paternalistic and colonial action in Sub-Saharan Africa. Bowdoin argues that converting publication of African academia to OA will not inherently undo this positionality, and can, without critical care, continue to perpetuate it. However, such conversion also is an opportunity to shift information flow between the Global South and the Global North by allowing scholars and citizens to exert their cultural rights (as defined by the UN) through providing them with the information necessary to either participate in existing cultural norms and traditions or create new ones.

Branum, Candise, and J. Turner Masland. "Critical Library Management: Administrating for Equity." *Oregon Library Association Quarterly* 23, no. 2 (2017): 28–36.

> Branum and Masland argue that libraries are at base community resources. In order to best serve their communities, librarians and information workers have a responsibility to understand and engage with critical theory and implement critical approaches to information work and collections into their management styles. This includes creating new social justice–oriented frameworks, policies, and mission statements on both the institutional and departmental levels, being vocal in support of marginalized groups, and listening and learning when called out on their mistakes.

Buschsbaum, Julianne. "Academic Libraries and the Remaking of the Canon: Implications for Collection Development Librarians." *Library Philosophy and Practice* (2009): article 266, http://digitalcommons.unl.edu/libphilprac/266/.

The concept of a universal—or even discipline-specific—literary canon presupposes a nonexistent "objective" truth about literary and aesthetic quality, but dispensing with a canon altogether would mean a lack of shared vocabulary for a community and no framework from which library collections could work at all. This article poses the guiding question "For whose society should we collect?" and explores how to expand and rework canons to best serve their diverse communities.

Callison, Camille. "Indigenous Peoples' New Canoe." In *Aboriginal and Visible Minority Librarians: Oral Histories from Canada*, edited by Deborah Lee and Mahalakshmi Kumaran, 135–46. Lanham, MD: Rowman and Littlefield, 2014.

Callison argues that archives and libraries that serve Indigenous communities have an opportunity and a responsibility to be a "new canoe," carrying collective memories to future generations. In order to do so, they must be organized according to Indigenous ways of knowing.

Fleischmann, Kenneth R. "Digital Libraries with Embedded Values: Combining Insights from LIS and Science and Technology Studies." *Library Quarterly* 77, no. 4 (2007): 409–27.

Fleischmann advocates for empirical and theoretical approaches to LIS and STS being combined in order to understand digital libraries critically and tease out the values embedded therein, rather than accepting them as neutral repositories of objective information.

Gilliland, Anne. "Neutrality, Social Justice and the Obligations of Archival Education and Educators in the Twenty-First Century." *Archival Science* 11, no. 3–4 (2011): 193–209.

Gilliland argues that neutrality and objectivity are often considered the most desirable stances for information centers, but for archives and other institutions concerned with the politics of memory, what is perceived as "neutrality" may be a political position in itself and one that often has a negative effect on the community served by the archive.

Harris, Verne. "The Archival Sliver: Power, Memory, and Archives in South Africa." *Archival Science* 2, no. 1–2 (2002): 63–86.

Harris tracks themes of race, power, and public records through archives and archivists in South Africa's transition from apartheid to democracy and appeals to archivists to engage in the realities of how collective memory shapes, reflects, and expresses structural inequalities.

Hathcock, April. "Making the Local Global: The Colonialism of Scholarly Communication." *At the Intersection* (blog), September 27, 2016. https://bit.ly/2dsgotJ.

Hathcock argues that scholarly communication discussions, even those based on creating scholarly "commons" and other concepts that should be inherently anticolonialist, are conducted in colonialist ways, centering and treating issues in the Global North as default concerns and sidelining the critically important issues facing scholars from the Global South—many of which stem from the colonization/North-centrism of knowledge in the first place.

Inefuku, Harrison W., and Charlotte Roh. "Agents of Diversity and Social Justice: Librarians and Scholarly Communication." In *Open Access and the Future of Scholarly Communication: Policy and Infrastructure*, edited by Kevin L. Smith and Katherine A. Dickson, 107–27. Lanham, MD: Rowman and Littlefield, 2016.

Scholarly communication is the means by which scholarly knowledge, produced by academics, is encoded and distributed. Inefuku and Row argue that the academic library, as the increasingly central actor in scholarly communication, has an opportunity to diversify the scholarly narrative, pushing back on the "master narrative" of traditional methodologies and voices and furthering goals of social justice.

Jimerson, Randall C. "Archives for All: Professional Responsibility and Social Justice." *American Archivist* 70, no. 2 (2007): 252–81.

Jimerson distinguishes between neutrality and objectivity, arguing that while archives can and should strive to be objective, they cannot and should not be neutral. Instead, archivists should adopt a social conscience for their profession, committing to actively engaging in their communities and in the public as a whole to uphold social justice ideals.

Mbembe, Achille. "Decolonizing Knowledge and the Question of the Archive." Wits Institute for Social and Economic Research, University of the Witwatersrand, Johannesburg, South Africa, May 2, 2015. http://wiser.wits.ac.za/system/files/Achille%20Mbembe%20-%20Decolonizing%20Knowledge%20and%20the%20Question%20of%20the%20Archive.pdf.

Written as the basis of a series of lectures at the Wits Institute for Social and Economic Research, this piece speaks to the decolonization of knowledge as a project to decolonize the physical spaces of the South African university and demythologize whiteness as the foundational logic of those spaces.

Pickover, Michele. "Patrimony, Power and Politics: Selecting, Constructing and Preserving Digital Heritage Content in South Africa and Africa." Presentation, International Federation of Library Associations and Institutions World Library and Information Congress 2014 (Libraries, Citizens, Societies: Confluence for Knowledge), Lyon Convention Centre, Lyon, France, August 19, 2014.

In order to illustrate archives not as neutral spaces but as both actors and subjects in the historical record, Pickover examines a number of memory preservation and heritage initiatives in Africa and South Africa, interrogating the ways they fit within a shifting postcolonial and postapartheid cultural narrative.

Quinn, Brian. "Collection Development and the Psychology of Bias." *Library Quarterly* 82, no. 3 (2012): 277–304.

In order to confront bias in collections activity, it must be understood as more than conscious prejudicial action, but as a complex combination of conscious and unconscious thought. By marrying psychological research on bias and a literature review on the subject of bias in library studies, Quinn arrives at a set of suggestions for better understanding the bias at work in collections, including implicit association tests, mindfulness practice, and forming implementation strategies.

Reidsma, Matthew. "Algorithmic Bias in Library Discovery Systems." Matthew Reidsrow website, March 11, 2016. https://matthew.reidsrow.com/articles/173.

Working off of scholarship in algorithmic bias in general search engines like Google, Reidsma explores library discovery algorithms, interrogating their blackbox nature and their reliance on "relevancy," asking who the assumed audience for that relevance might be.

Tuhiwai Smith, Linda. "Imagining Our Own Approaches." *Cataloging and Classification Quarterly* 53, no. 5–6 (2015): 473–74.

This introduction lays out how Western systems of knowledge have deconstructed and devalued Indigenous knowledge while benefiting from it and proposes the formulation of new systems of classification, cataloguing, and collections to repatriate Indigenous knowledge.

Williams, Virginia Kay, and Nancy Deyoe. "Controversy and Diversity: LGBTQ Titles in Academic Library Youth Collections." *Library Resources and Technical Services* 59, no. 2 (2015): 62–71.

This article reviews the literature on collections of LGBTQ youth literature in academic libraries and describes a study conducted to assess their size and quality across the United States. It ends with suggestions for libraries to conduct their own assessments and calls for increased robustness in LGBTQ topic areas in academic libraries in general.

SYSTEMS

Supporting Technological Infrastructure That Is Sustainable

de Reuver, Mark, Carsten Sørensen, and Rahul C. Basole. "The Digital Platform: A Research Agenda." *Journal of Information Technology* 33, no. 2 (2018): 124–35. https://doi.org/10.1057/s41265-016-0033-3.

Digital platforms have emerged from commercial rather than academic research quarters and should be studied critically. De Reuver and colleagues lay out a research agenda based on six initial questions: (1) Are platforms here to stay? (2) How should platforms be designed? (3) How do digital platforms transform industries? (4) How can data-driven approaches inform digital platform research? (5) How should researchers develop theory for digital platforms? (6) How do digital platforms affect everyday life?

De Smedt, Koenraad, Franciska de Jong, Bente Maegaard, Darja Fišer, and Dieter Van Uytvanck. "Towards an Open Science Infrastructure for the Digital Humanities: The Case of CLARIN." In *Proceedings of the Digital Humanities in the Nordic Countries 3rd Conference, Helsinki, Finland, March 7–9, 2018*, edited by Eetu Mäkelä, Mikko Tolonen, and Jouni Tuominen, 139–51. *CEUR Workshop Proceedings* 2084 (2018), paper 11. http://ceur-ws.org/Vol-2084/paper11.pdf.

CLARIN, the European research infrastructure for language resources, has grown from nine members in 2012 to nineteen. De Smedt and colleagues examine its successes and argue for its adoption as a model for an infrastructure and a meeting ground for digital humanities scholars to have access to resources and tools.

Henfridsson, Ola, and Bendik Bygstad. "The Generative Mechanisms of Digital Infrastructure Evolution." *MIS Quarterly* 37, no. 3 (2013): 907–31.

Through a case study of a Scandinavian airline and a survey of forty-one digital infrastructure cases, Henfridsson and Bygstad break down changes in digital infrastructure into three stages—adoption, innovation, and scaling—and present an argument for understanding all three of these stages and their transformative whole through the lens of critical realism.

Manoff, Marlene. "Human and Machine Entanglement in the Digital Archive: Academic Libraries and Socio-technical Change." *portal: Libraries and the Academy* 15, no. 3 (2015): 513–30.

Manoff advocates an interdisciplinary approach to understanding the effects of digital tools and repositories on scholarly knowledge, borrowing from models from science studies used for understanding how tools have historically shaped the production, dissemination, and preservation of research.

Marrall, Rebecca M. "Teaching the Digital Divide: Connecting Students to Community, Knowledge, and Service Learning." *Library Philosophy and Practice* (June 2014): article 1126. http://digitalcommons.unl.edu/libphilprac/1126/.

Marrall breaks down her experience of teaching a service-learning course on the "digital divide" in an American context, identifying the planning and communication challenges of combining practice and theory in academia.

Neylon, Cameron. "Sustaining Scholarly Infrastructures through Collective Action: The Lessons That Olson Can Teach Us." *KULA: Knowledge Creation, Dissemination, and Preservation Studies* 1, no. 1 (2017). https://doi.org/10.5334/kula.7.

Using Mancur Olson's work on the "free-loader" problem, Neylon examines the infrastructure of information sharing in order to understand the interlocking factors new, more "open" infrastructure will have to take into account: political sustainability, community size, and financial interest.

Padilla, Thomas, and Vicky Steeves. "Data Librarianship: A Path and an Ethic—A Conversation." *Data Praxis* (blog), dh+lib, April 4, 2018. https://acrl.ala.org/dh/2018/04/04/repro/.

Padilla interviews Steeves about her dual librarian/data science center appointment and the perspective it gives her on the ethical and moral obligations of both computer scientists and librarians.

Price, Gary. "Just Announced: 'Designing Equitable Foundations for Open Knowledge' Will Be Theme of 2018 International Open Access Week." infoDOCKET, *Library Journal*, May 24, 2018. https://www.infodocket.com/2018/05/24/theme-of-2018-international-open-access-week-to-be-designing-equitable-foundations-for-open-knowledge/.

Price explains the 2018 International Open Access Week theme, "Designing Equitable Foundations for Open Knowledge": moving beyond the simple argument for why openness is important and on to the work of creating open publishing systems in intentional, critical ways to ensure equitable solutions for a diverse, global community.

Sherratt, Tim. "Seams and Edges: Dreams of Aggregation, Access and Discovery in a Broken World." *Discontents* (blog), February 3, 2015. http://discontents.com.au/seams-and-edges-dreams-of-aggregation-access-discovery-in-a-broken-world/.

Search algorithms from Google and others have installed a certain way of understanding information, but in fact often disaggregate information from itself, removing it from its context except in the most simplistic word-association sense. Sherratt gives an example of Trove, a database of cultural heritage collections that attempts to replicate the serendipity and geographic/visual discovery of a physical archive or collection.

Creating Systems That Permit More Access to More People

Alexander, Bryan, Kim Barrett, Sioux Cumming, Patrick Herron, Claudia Holland, Kathleen Keane, Joyce Ogburn, Jacob Orlowitz, Mary Augusta Thomas, and Jeffrey Tsao. "Report from the Information Overload and Underload Workgroup." *Open Scholarship Initiative Proceedings* 1 (2016): G8R30G. https://doi.org/10.13021/G8R30G.

The Open Scholarship Initiative working group identifies the dual problem of information "overload" and "underload"—a great wealth of information exists, but access to it is unequal and extremely limited—and concludes that open-access models address the second half of the problem but not the first. Any overhaul of the publishing system needs to be paired with solutions for the resulting increased overload of information: systematized solutions for curation, discoverability, and organization.

Baker, Matthew. "Be Creative, Determined, and Wise: Open Library Publishing and the Global South." *Computers in Libraries* 29, no. 10 (2009): 6–10.

Baker identifies the factors behind the so-called "digital divide," including access to the internet, increased censorship by governmental actors, and economic limitations at academic institutions in the Global South. Breaking each of these problems down, he suggests actions that libraries at these institutions can take to narrow the divide and argues that librarians are some of the most effective actors and allies to scholars in the fight for open access to knowledge.

Bonaccorso, Elisa, Reneta Bozhankova, Carlos Daniel Cadena, Veronika Čapská, Laura Czerniewicz, Ada Emmett, Folorunso Fasina Oludayo, Natalia Glukhova, Marc L. Greenberg, Miran Hladnik, María Eugenia Grillet, Mochamad Indrawan, Mate Kapović, Yuri Kleiner, Marek Łaziński, Rafael D. Loyola, Shaily Menon, Luis Gonzalo Morales, Clara Ocampo, Jorge Pérez-Emán, A. Townsend Peterson, Dimitar Poposki, Ajadi Adetola Rasheed, Kathryn M. Rodríguez-Clark, Jon Paul Rodríguez, and Brian Rosenblum. "Bottlenecks in the Open-Access System: Voices from Around the Globe." *Journal of Librarianship and Scholarly Communication* 2, no. 2 (2014): eP1126. https://doi.org/10.7710/2162-3309.1126.

A geographically diverse group of scholars highlight the drawbacks of "Gold" (author-funded) OA across a variety of economic, academic, and social contexts to show how prioritizing scholarly access over full scholarly participation ends up reinforcing colonialist power dynamics in academia.

Bourg, Chris. "Never Neutral: Libraries, Technology, and Inclusion." *Feral Librarian* (blog), January 28, 2015. https://chrisbourg.wordpress.com/2015/01/28/never-neutral-libraries-technology-and-inclusion/.

Bourg argues that libraries are not neutral repositories of information, but instead actively reinforce structures of societal bias through classification systems, both traditional and algorithmic. This bias can be addressed through changing the people participating in the creation of these systems in the tech and library worlds, but doing so is a matter of changing the culture of these spaces as much as it is about "diversity hires." The first step in culture change is awareness and acknowledgement of the exclusive, patriarchal culture that currently exists.

Cohen, Madeline, Maura A. Smale, Jill Cirasella, Cynthia Tobar, and Jessie Daniels. "Speaking as One: Supporting Open Access with Departmental Resolutions." *Journal of Librarianship and Scholarly Communication* 2, no. 1 (2013): eP1099. https://doi.org/10.7710/2162-3309.1099.

Individual scholars are often quick to personally commit to open-access pledges, but adoption at the university level has been incremental. This report describes the experiences, and, importantly, successes of librarians advocating university-level adoption of open access in the CUNY system, offering advice to other librarians hoping to leverage their position and broaden uptake of their open-access values.

Crissinger, Sarah. "Access to Research and Sci-Hub: Creating Opportunities for Campus Conversations on Open Access and Ethics." *College and Research Libraries News* 78, no. 2 (2017): 86–95.

Crissinger describes an event held on the Davidson College campus bringing together students, librarians, and faculty to use Sci-Hub as an entry point into discussions of access and ethics in publishing. Rather than just cautioning students not to make use of it, she argues, its existence can facilitate the discussions among scholarly communities that will eventually lead to systemic change that will broaden access and make Sci-Hub itself redundant.

Cruz, Laura, and Rachel Fleming. "Partnerships: The Engaged University and Library Publishing." *OCLC Systems and Services* 31, no. 4 (2015): 196–203.

Cruz and Fleming propose a model that positions the library as publishing partner rather than collector/customer, allowing individual open-access solutions from institutions embedded in and dedicated to serving their communities.

Czernowicz, Laura. "Inequitable Power Dynamics of Global Knowledge Production and Exchange Must Be Confronted Head On." *LSE Impact Blog*, April 29, 2013. http://blogs.lse.ac.uk/impactofsocialsciences/2013/04/29/redrawing-the-map-from-access-to-participation/.

Czernowicz argues that true international and equal academic participation will not be achieved through technological and financial interventions alone, but through teasing out and confronting the values that currently uphold the Global North's domination of the knowledge-sharing system and make Global South countries sites of Northern scholarship rather than producers of knowledge in their own right.

Ford, Emily. "Advancing an Open Ethos with Open Peer Review." *College and Research Libraries* 78, no. 4 (2017): 406–12.

Ford gives an overview of open peer-review efforts, advocating its use over closed review for reasons of time scale, accountability for reviewers, and broader contribution to scholarly knowledge.

Gearhart, Andrew, Mark Mattson, James O. Sullivan, and Sarah Pickle. "Infrastructure for Open Access: Mechanics, Economics, Politics." In *Open Access and the Future of Scholarly Communications*, edited by Kevin L. Smith and Katherine A. Dickson, 161–81. Lanham, MD: Rowman and Littlefield, 2016.

This paper uses the Penn State University Libraries as a case study for library-based OA publishing, outlining workflows, technical infrastructure, structures for sustainability, and the shifting relationship between library and institution in this new model.

Glushko, Bobby, and Rex Shoyama. "Unpacking Open Access: A Theoretical Framework for Understanding Open Access Initiatives." *Feliciter* 61, no. 1 (2015): 8–11.

This article defines open access and gives a series of rationales for librarians to use it for advocacy purposes.

Inefuku, Harrison W. "Globalization, Open Access, and the Democratization of Knowledge." *EDUCAUSE Review*, July/August 2017: 62–63.

Developments in information technology are already disrupting the unequal academic publishing system, but there are many challenges to making sure those disruptions actually democratize knowledge and improve access, participation, and production globally. Inefuku argues that overcoming these challenges is a matter of understanding context and doing anticolonial work as much as it is creating new business models and technological solutions.

Kansa, Eric. "It's the Neoliberalism, Stupid: Why Instrumentalist Arguments for Open Access, Open Data, and Open Science Are Not Enough." *LSE Impact Blog* (blog), January 14, 2014. http://blogs.lse.ac.uk/impactofsocialsciences/2014/01/27/its-the-neoliberalism-stupid-kansa/.

Kansa asks whether movements for openness really aim for real culture change in the academy or just openness and transparency for the further entrenchment of neoliberalism and corporate profit. He argues that any models for openness based on cost-cutting or accelerating speed of publication won't be enough to actually diversify and broaden knowledge participation and access.

Kember, Sarah. "Opening Out from Open Access: Writing and Publishing in Response to Neoliberalism." *Ada: A Journal of Gender, New Media, and Technology*, no. 4 (2014): article N31C1V51. https://doi.org/10.7264/N31C1V51.

Kember argues that open access is not the end goal, but the beginning of a repoliticization of scholarly writing and publishing and a decoupling of access from ethics, paving the way for true reform and ethical publishing practice.

Kutay, Stephen. "Advancing Digital Repository Services for Faculty Primary Research Assets: An Exploratory Study." *Journal of Academic Librarianship* 40, no. 6 (2014): 642–49.

This survey assessed primary research assets created and collected by librarians and archivists, collecting data on what kind of assets are created or collected, by whom, how they are preserved, and what attitudes exist toward them (e.g., should they be available online, etc.). The study is intended to be used for the development of policies around digitization and access to primary research documents.

Noble, Safiya Umoja. *Algorithms of Oppression: How Search Engines Reinforce Racism*. New York: NYU Press, 2018.

Noble examines algorithms, which increasingly control and contribute to human behavior and decision-making, although they are not neutral or objective mathematical formulas but build the biases of the data they're based on into their results. The lack of critical social theory among technologists means this bias becomes invisible, reinforcing white supremacy as the default and thus neutral information state.

Raju, Reggie. "Predatory Publishing from a Global South Perspective." *Library Publishing Coalition Blog*, February 7, 2018. https://librarypublishing.org/predatory-publishing-global-south-perspective/.

Beall's List of predatory publishers was based on criteria of excellence that overwhelmingly favored the Global North, and thus its definition of "predatory" had an oversized negative effect on publishers from the Global South. Raju argues for a redefinition of excellence, one drawn from whether or not papers published in a journal contribute to scholarship at large, and lays out a road map for moving forward and developing inclusive open-access practices.

Raju, Reggie, and Jeremiah Pietersen. "Library as Publisher: From an African Lens." *Journal of Electronic Publishing* 20, no. 2 (2017): e203. https://doi.org/10.3998/3336451.0020.203.

Raju and Pietersen argue that the library-as-publisher model should be adopted by African institutions in order to improve information flow in South-South and subsequently South-North directions.

Read, Kim Marsh. "Collective Voice for Collective Good: Library Consortia, Open Access, and the Future of Scholarly Communication." *Oregon Library Association Quarterly* 16, no. 3 (2010): 23–28.

By creating repositories, informational packets for faculty outreach, and training programs and participating in the formation of peer-review boards, Read argues, library consortia can play a more instrumental role in the widespread adoption and support of OA than either institutions or individuals on their own.

Rowntree, David. "Out of the Archive: Challenges and Opportunities for New Scholarly Access from Old Media Collections." *Black Camera* 1, no. 1 (2009): 171–85.

Conversations about access generally focus on what technology allows scholars to do with written works, but Rowntree uses the Film and Media Archive at Washington University as a case study for the challenges and opportunities of opening up other primary sources, such as photographs and filmed work. Access to the archive is especially important as much of it centers around African American history and the work of historical social movements.

Salaz, A. M., Nicole Johnston, and Clare Pickles. "Faculty Members Who Teach Online: A Phenomenographic Typology of Open Access Experiences." *Journal of Academic Librarianship* 44, no. 1 (2018): 125–32.

This study surveys teachers whose primary method of teaching is online and divides their open-access experiences into five different categories: resources for teaching, a method of publication, a social justice movement, "open-source" research, and "free for me"—that is, open to academic faculty, but not necessarily to a wider constituency.

Sondervan, Jeroen, and Kathleen Fitzpatrick. "Interview: Kathleen Fitzpatrick on Open Scholarship, Humanities Commons, and More." Open Access in Media Studies, April 19, 2018. https://oamediastudies.com/interview-kathleen-fitzpatrick/.

Open Access in Media Studies interviewed Kathleen Fitzpatrick about her work in open scholarship, the barriers and challenges to the widespread adoption of open access, monograph publishing, the role of libraries in an open publishing ecosystem, and what success looks like for nonprofit efforts in this space.

Sotudeh, Hajar, and Zahra Ghasempour. "The World's Approach toward Publishing in Springer and Elsevier's APC-Funded Open Access Journals." *College and Research Libraries* 79, no. 2 (2018). https://doi.org/10.5860/crl.79.2.257.

This study examined international tendencies to publish in Springer's and Elsevier's APC-driven OA journals and compared scholars' likelihood of publishing in said journals with the amount of financial support those scholars had to do so. They found that while Western, wealthier countries displayed the most willingness to publish, underdeveloped countries with less access to APC support still saw OA growth and acceleration.

Swauger, Shea. "Open Access, Power, and Privilege: A Response to [Jeffrey Beall's] 'What I Learned from Predatory Publishing.'" *College and Research Libraries News* 78, no. 11 (2017): 603–6.

Swauger critiques Beall's Predatory Publishing List based on four themes: his "dangerous nostalgia" for a time of authority and credibility that never really existed, his assertion of predatory publishing as a unique threat and not a part of a larger information literacy issue, his identification of "political correctness" as a problematic impetus behind advocacy for OA, and his claims that his own academic freedom was threatened for the publication of the list.

van der Graaf, Maurits, and Leo Waaijers. "How Could an Open Access Scholarly Journal System Look? A Scenario Analysis." White paper, January 13, 2017. http://digitalcommons.unl.edu/scholcom/38.

This article proposes a plan for flipping currently hybrid journals to APC-driven open access, examining the conditions necessary to do so and laying out next steps.

Veletsianos, George, and Royce Kimmons. "Assumptions and Challenges of Open Scholarship." *International Review of Research in Open and Distributed Learning* 13, no. 4 (2012): 166–89.

This article examines the assumptions made by open scholarship advocates and uses a critical technology studies lens to critique those assumptions, concluding that use of new access technologies alone won't necessarily advance the social justice goals of the movement.

Watters, Audrey. "From 'Open' to Justice." Presentation, OpenCon 2014, American University Washington College of Law, Washington, DC, November 16, 2014. http://hackeducation.com/2014/11/16/from-open-to-justice.

"Open" has become a buzzword co-opted by the same corporate interests the open access movement is attempting to disrupt and disempower. Watters argues that in order to actually work toward progressive social change in access movements, open access activists need to advocate not just for "openness" but for information justice.

Building Mission-Aligned Organizational and Financial Systems

Alonso, Carlos J., Cathy N. Davidson, John M. Unsworth, and Lynne Withey. *Crises and Opportunities: The Futures of Scholarly Publishing.* ACLS Occasional Paper. New York: American Council of Learned Societies, May 3, 2003.

This paper collects remarks by representatives of various stakeholders in scholarly communication on the problem of publishing, dissemination, and evaluation in a changing technological landscape.

Bourg, Chris, Ross Coleman, Ricky Erway, and RLG Partnership Research Information Management Roadmap Working Group. *Support for the Research Process: An Academic Library Manifesto.* Dublin, OH: OCLC Research, 2009. http://www.oclc.org/research/publications/library/2009/2009-07.pdf.

This manifesto shifts the focus of new scholarly communication strategy from attempting to understand the role of existing institutions—particularly libraries—to attempting to understand the betterment of scholarship and the research process itself and what a support structure for a better research process might look like. It includes a ten-step call to action for academic libraries.

Crissinger, Sarah. "A Critical Take on OER Practices: Interrogating Commercialization, Colonialism, and Content." *In the Library with the Lead Pipe*, October 21, 2015. http://www.inthelibrarywiththeleadpipe.org/2015/a-critical-take-on-oer-practices-interrogating-commercialization-colonialism-and-content/.

Much of the conversation on open educational resources centers around shared practices and shared values, not shared risk. In this article, Crissinger explores the possibility that data have become another in a long line of resources exploited by colonialist, capitalist forces, especially as the primary motivators of OER are embedded at increasingly corporatized institutions, and breaks down the risk of uncritical advocacy of OER absent an understanding of that context.

Crow, Raym. *Publishing Cooperatives: An Alternative for Society Publishers.* A SPARC Discussion Paper. Washington, DC: Scholarly Publishing and Academic Resources Coalition (SPARC), February 2006. https://sparcopen.org/wp-content/uploads/2016/03/cooperatives_v1-2.pdf.

This discussion paper puts forth a vision of how a new model of publisher cooperatives could potentially provide a new path to sustainability for society publishers.

Crow, Raym. *Sustainability of Open Access Services: Phase 3: The Collective Provision of Open Access Resources*. Washington, DC: Scholarly Publishing and Academic Resources Coalition (SPARC), 2013. http://www.chainbridgegroup.com/images/collective-provision-of-oa-services.pdf.

This report outlines key factors in sustainability planning specific to open-access resources, including discussion of collective models of support.

de jesus, nina. "Locating the Library within Institutional Oppression." *In the Library with the Lead Pipe*, September 24, 2014. http://www.inthelibrarywiththeleadpipe.org/2014/locating-the-library-in-institutional-oppression/.

de jesus examines the library as an Enlightenment institution through the "three logics" of white supremacy (slavery, Indigenous genocide, and Orientalism) in order to show that while libraries embody Enlightenment ideals, those ideals are shaped by the forces of oppression, and libraries should seek instead to embody a new set of values based in anticolonialist thought, breaking down concepts of intellectual property and publishing in particular.

Eatman, Timothy K., Gaelle Ivory, John Saltmarsh, Michael Middleton, Amanda Wittman, and Corey Dolgon. "Co-constructing Knowledge Spheres in the Academy: Developing Frameworks and Tools for Advancing Publicly Engaged Scholarship." *Urban Education* 53, no. 4 (2018): 532–61.

This article gives an overview of the benefits of, challenges to, and tensions inherent in publicly engaged scholarship, particularly the idea of scholarship beneficial to oppressed groups being produced by a hegemonic structure that has historically oppressed them.

Farrell, Maggie. "Leadership and Social Justice." *Journal of Library Administration* 56, no. 6 (2016): 722–30. https://doi.org/10.1080/01930826.2016.1199147.

This paper explores the pressures and opportunities of library leadership, acknowledging the ways in which library administrators have to balance serving a broad constituency with a variety of politics and viewpoints while emphasizing the library's unique positionality to advancing social justice aims.

Fister, Barbara. "Liberating Knowledge: A Librarian's Manifesto for Change." *Thought and Action,* Fall 2010: 83–90.

Fister lays out the artificial scarcity of academic knowledge and the fragility of the lease system of digital journal subscriptions for increasingly economically unstable academic libraries and offers a Marxist alternative, described in a manifesto for change. Her Liberation Bibliography arises out of outrage and solidarity rather than cost-saving and includes breaking down the distinction between scholarly and nonscholarly knowledge, recognizing librarian complicity in injustice systems, and advocating for living up to the ideals inscribed in mission and values statements of institutions of higher learning.

Franklin, Brinley. "Surviving to Thriving: Advancing the Institutional Mission." *Journal of Library Administration* 52, no. 1 (2012): 94–107.

This article repositions the priorities of libraries away from collections and toward research productivity for their students and faculty that aligns with the priorities of their home institution.

Gerolami, Natasha. "The Library Assemblage: Creative Institutions in an Information Society." *Journal of Documentation* 71, no. 1 (2015): 165–74.

Gerolami argues that in order to leverage libraries as social justice actors, we have to treat them as creative assemblages rather than institutions in a market-based system of information dissemination.

Gil, Alex. "The User, the Learner and the Machines We Make." Minimal Computing, May 21, 2015. http://go-dh.github.io/mincomp/thoughts/2015/05/21/user-vs-learner/.

Following his version of minimalist computing, Gil breaks down new technology creation in the academy to this question: What do we need in order to accomplish the broadest shared goal of humanities workers—in his words, "the renewal, dissemination, and preservation of the scholarly record"? He outlines some answers to this question from the perspective of the user (the academic) and the learner (the student, whether formal or informal).

Houghton, John W. "Economic Implications of Alternative Scholarly Publishing Models." In *A Handbook of Digital Library Economics*, edited by David Baker and Wendy Evans, 125–41. Oxford: Chandos, 2013. https://doi.org/10.1016/B978-1-84334-620-3.50011-8.

This report describes the economics of three models of alternative scholarly publishing in the UK (subscription publishing, open-access publishing, and self-archiving) and examines the implications of each for the ecosystem of scholarly communication, attempting to ascertain which would be most the cost-effective shift from traditional publishing models.

Maron, Nancy L., and Sarah Pickle. *Sustaining the Digital Humanities: Host Institution Support Beyond the Start-Up Phase*. New York: ITHAKA S+R, 2014. https://doi.org/10.18665/sr.22548.

This report uses four detailed library-based institutional case studies to examine the full publishing workflow for digital scholarship projects on campus, with the aim of helping library leaders and administrators develop better campus-level coordination of services. The report includes the Sustainability Implementation Toolkit for those wishing to conduct similar research and decision-making themselves.

Neylon, Cameron. "Openness in Scholarship: A Return to Core Values?" In *Expanding Perspectives on Open Science: Communities, Cultures and Diversity in Concepts and Practices*, edited by Leslie Chan and Fernando Loizides, 6–17. Amsterdam: IOS Press, 2017.

Neylon positions "openness" in all its many highly contextual facets as not something in opposition to the traditional work and values of academia but in fact core to their underpinnings and a natural extension of the work academics can and should strive to enact.

Nica, Elvira. "Has the Shift to Overworked and Underpaid Adjunct Faculty Helped Education Outcomes?" *Educational Philosophy and Theory* 50, no. 3 (2018): 213–16.

Nica argues that there are very few measures in place to actually evaluate the effect of the adjunctification of academic faculty on student learning outcomes. In addition, lack of time, dedicated office space, and structural influence and a high turnover rate mean very little opportunity for mentorship from adjunct faculty to students or from tenured faculty to adjuncts, meaning there is little upward mobility for most non-tenure-track faculty and an increasingly high turnover rate.

Norris, Timothy. "Morality in Information Ecosystems." *CLIR Connect* (blog), September 18, 2014. https://connect.clir.org/blogs/tim-norris/2014/09/18/morality-in-information-ecosystems.

Norris acknowledges that the "information ecosystem" metaphor is useful, but cautions that it's not precise—an ecosystem is an interaction between diverse actors and their environment with no moral or ethical intervention—and that library and information scientists by nature preserve and communicate information based on systems of value.

Peters, Michael A. "Managerialism and the Neoliberal University: Prospects for New Forms of 'Open Management' in Higher Education." *Contemporary Readings in Law and Social Justice* 5, no. 1 (2013): 11–26.

Decentralization and a neoliberal emphasis on management rather than administration means academic institutions are being run as businesses, with a focus on outputs rather than knowledge creation and research. Peters proposes new models of radical "open management" within new structures, utilizing new technologies to create new intellectual commons and knowledge sharing.

Rioux, Kevin. "Metatheory in Library and Information Science: A Nascent Social Justice Approach." *Journal of Education for Library and Information Science* 51, no. 1 (2010): 9–17.

A metatheory of library work is a relatively new idea, but one that is necessary in order to make sense of the field in an increasingly complicated landscape of actors. Rioux advocates that the metatheory to adopt would be one of social justice, returning to the ideals of freedom of information and of access in an active rather than a passive or lip-service one.

Scherlen, Allan, and Matthew Robinson. "Open Access to Criminal Justice Scholarship: A Matter of Social Justice." *Journal of Criminal Justice Education* 19, no. 1 (2008): 54–74.

Scherlen and Robinson argue that criminal justice scholarship critical of law enforcement faces unusually high barriers to publication and biased peer review and that in order for the full breadth of scholarship to see publication, criminal justice scholars must advocate for open-access models of academic publishing.

Tuhiwai Smith, Linda. "Decolonizing Knowledge: Toward a Critical Indigenous Research Justice Praxis." In *Research Justice: Methodologies for Social Change*, edited by Andrew J. Jolivétte, 205–11. Bristol, UK: Policy Press, 2015.

Writing from the perspective of a Māori critical information scholar, Tuhiwai Smith argues that creating change is about more than presenting the facts of research. It's about mobilization: of opinion, experience, language, discourse, and most importantly of community leaders. Researchers on their own cannot influence public policy. They're one aspect of a communicative structure that must involve the communities they serve in order to be effective agents for social justice.

Willinsky, John, and Matthew Rusk. "If Funders and Libraries Subscribed to Open Access: The Case of eLife, PLOS, and BioOne." PeerJ Preprints, November 4, 2017. https://doi.org/10.7287/peerj.preprints.3392v1.

This preprint article uses three nonprofit biomedical publishers as case studies in different publishing funding models, examining cost breakdowns for direct funding and library support and how that maps onto the cost breakdowns for OA efforts. Based on these data, it suggests a model using publishing data management structures to scale OA beyond APC-driven journals.

Advancing Innovation in Academic Libraries

Antonucci, Carl, and Sharon Clapp, eds. *The LITA Leadership Guide: The Librarian as Entrepreneur, Leader, and Technologist.* Lanham, MD: Rowman and Littlefield, 2017.

This book includes chapters on the many roles librarians play in the current scholarly communication landscape, highlighting the different skill sets involved in creating positive change in all the areas in which librarians work.

Camille, Damon, and R. Niccole Westbrook. "Building a Program That Cultivates Library Leaders from within the Organization." *Journal of Academic Librarianship* 39, no. 6 (2013): 447–50. https://doi.org/10.1016/j.acalib.2013.10.012.

Camille and Westbrook describe a project between the Libraries Training Committee and the Human Resources department at the University of Houston designed to give emotional intelligence training to new library leadership.

Carpenter, Maria, Jolie Graybill, Jerome Offord, and Mary Piorun. "Envisioning the Library's Role in Scholarly Communication in the Year 2025." *portal: Libraries and the Academy* 11, no. 2 (2011): 659–81.

This report identifies six possibilities for the future of scholarly communication based on projections of economic change and the shifting roles of libraries and other institutions. Twenty ARL directors provided feedback on the scenarios, including factors like desirability and likelihood of accuracy.

Casey, Anne Marie. "Strategic Priorities and Change in Academic Libraries." PhD diss., Simmons College, 2011. ProQuest Dissertations and Theses.

Casey analyzes library response to the 2007–2009 economic recession through three case studies of academic libraries at public universities in California and Michigan. She builds out an understanding of administrative priorities and argues the importance of the alignment of institutional and library planning.

Conerly, Rosalind D. "Campus Change Agents: Examining the Experiences of Cultural Center Scholar Practitioners at a Predominantly White Institution." EdD diss., University of Southern California, 2017. ProQuest Dissertations and Theses.

This dissertation presents a qualitative study of professional staff overseeing black, Asian, Latino, and Native American cultural centers at a predominately white institution, examining how leaders in these centers can work with stakeholders in the institution to help build social and cultural support systems for the minority students they serve.

Davis-Kahl, Stephanie, Teresa A. Fishel, and Merinda Kaye Hensley. "Weaving the Threads: Scholarly Communication and Information Literacy." *College and Research Libraries News* 75, no. 8 (2014): 441–44.

In 2013 the ACRL published a white paper entitled *Intersections of Scholarly Communication and Information Literacy: Creating Strategic Collaborations for a Changing Academic Environments*, arguing that while information literacy and scholarly communication have traditionally been treated as separate fields and outreach activities, they must work in collaboration in order to best serve their communities in a shifting academic landscape. This article describes the work of the Scholarly Communication and Information Literacy Task Force in bringing those collaborations to their own libraries.

Dewey, Barbara Irene. "Leading the Library by Leading the Campus: A Dean's Perspective." *Library Leadership and Management* 29, no. 1 (2014). https://journals.tdl.org/llm/index.php/llm/article/view/7099.

This article highlights the overlooked responsibilities of library deans and other senior leadership, including their leadership responsibilities to the rest of the institution, arguing that libraries are particularly well-suited to the kind of community engagement necessary for important values-based work such as diversity, online education, and mindful governance.

Eddy, Mark A., and Daniela Solomon. "Leveraging Librarian Liaison Expertise in a New Consultancy Role." *Journal of Academic Librarianship* 43, no. 2 (2017): 121–27.

This case study explores the potential role of librarian as consultant, functional specialist, and subject expert in new models for publication. It explains the contributions librarians make to editors to improve discoverability, search functionality within a journal, and metadata standards.

Eger, Thomas, and Marc Scheufen. *The Economics of Open Access: On the Future of Academic Publishing.* Northampton, MA: Edward Elgar Publishing, 2018.

This book presents findings from a survey of over 10,000 respondents from twenty-five countries and across scholarly disciplines on knowledge about and attitudes toward the academic publishing industry, illuminating the economic underpinnings of the fight to shift to open-access models of disseminating scholarly knowledge.

Erway, Ricky, and OCLC Research. *Lasting Impact: Sustainability of Disciplinary Repositories*. Dublin, OH: OCLC Research, 2012. https://www.oclc.org/content/dam/research/publications/library/2012/2012-03.pdf.

The changing landscape of scholarly communication means some libraries are looking to work with, or begin their own, disciplinary repositories. This report profiles seven repositories across various disciplines on the basis of business model and sustainability in order to inform librarians on their path forward.

Finlay, Craig, Andrew Tsou, and Cassidy Sugimoto. "Scholarly Communication as a Core Competency: Prevalence, Activities, and Concepts of Scholarly Communication Librarianship as Shown through Job

Advertisements." *Journal of Librarianship and Scholarly Communication* 3, no. 1 (2015): eP1236. https://doi.org/10.7710/2162-3309.1236.

Finlay and colleagues compare over 13,000 job advertisements for academic librarianship over eight years (2006–2014), examining the prevalence of various scholarly communication terms over time. They discovered that requirements for active experience in scholarly communication activities have gone up and requirements for passive knowledge about scholarly communication have gone down.

Fyfe, Aileen, Kelly Coate, Stephen Curry, Stuart Lawson, Noah Moxham, and Camilla Mørk Røstvik. "Untangling Academic Publishing: A History of the Relationship between Commercial Interests, Academic Prestige and the Circulation of Research." Zenodo, May 25, 2017. http://doi.org/10.5281/zenodo.546100.

This paper gives a historical overview of the business practices and cultural positionality of academic publishing over the twentieth century and argues that current technological changes have pushed the impetus for change in the publication system too far toward economic concerns.

Fyfe, Bruce, Catherine Steeves, and Nicole Nolan. "Charting Our Course through Reframing—Library Leadership in a Sea of Change." *Proceedings of the IATUL Conferences*, 2016, paper 3. http://docs.lib.purdue.edu/iatul/2016/wrkforce/3.

This paper applies the theoretical academic leadership frames identified by Bolman and Gallos in their 2011 book *Reframing Academic Leadership* to the Western Libraries change initiative, working through the challenges and complexities of leadership in order to remove barriers to positive change.

Giesecke, Joan, and Charlene Maxey-Harris. "Cultural Competencies in Authentic Leadership." In *Workplace Culture in Academic Libraries: The Early 21st Century*, edited by Kelly Blessinger and Paul Hrycaj, 111–24. Chandos Information Professional Series. Oxford: Chandos, 2013. https://doi.org/10.1016/B978-1-84334-702-6.50007-1.

This chapter argues the importance of developing cultural competencies among leadership and staff in order to improve diversity in academic libraries. It presents a case study in changing work culture through staff development and intentional diversity training.

Graybill, Jolie O. "Millennials among the Professional Workforce in Academic Libraries: Their Perspective on Leadership." *Journal of Academic Librarianship* 40, no. 1 (2014): 10–15. https://doi.org/10.1016/j.acalib.2013.09.006.

This survey examines whether millennials in the academic library workforce view themselves as leaders, what qualities they associate with leadership, and what opportunities for leadership they see in the structure of their jobs. It compares these results with attitudes toward leadership from other, older populations, concluding among other things that millennials value building working relationships with others significantly more than current library leadership.

Harris-Keith, Colleen S. "The Relationship between Academic Library Department Experience and Perceptions of Leadership Skill Development Relevant to Academic Library Directorship." *Journal of Academic Librarianship* 41, no. 3 (2015): 246–63. https://doi.org/10.1016/j.acalib.2015.03.017.

This report compares library departments based on the qualities and skills they give their workforces and how valued those skills are in leadership positions. It finds that training for many of the practical leadership skills necessary for library administration is available only once someone has already attained a directorship or equivalent position.

Harris-Keith, Colleen S. "What Academic Library Leadership Lacks: Leadership Skills Directors Are Least Likely to Develop, and Which Positions Offer Development Opportunity." *Journal of Academic Librarianship* 42, no. 4 (2016): 313–18. https://doi.org/10.1016/j.acalib.2016.06.005.

This paper examines the professional development opportunities of library leadership, finding a dearth of training in fund-raising and donor relations, school safety issues, legal issues, compliance issues, and facilities planning, especially for those in positions lower than director or assistant director.

Jantz, Ronald C. "Innovation in Academic Libraries: An Analysis of University Librarians' Perspectives." *Library and Information Science Research* 34, no. 1 (2012): 3–12. https://doi.org/10.1016/j.lisr.2011.07.008.

Jantz conducted structured interviews on innovation in academic libraries with university librarians in six institutions, exploring the importance of supportive leadership, risk-taking, and nontraditional innovation and the ways in which institutional and professional norms might limit genuine innovation.

Laitinen, Markku, and Jarmo Saarti. "Evidence Based Service Change: Remodelling the Academic Libraries for the Post-digital Era." *Qualitative and Quantitative Methods in Libraries* 3, no. 3 (2017): 611–18.

This case study of a Finnish academic library uses trend analysis to understand the shift of academic libraries as a whole from collection-based services to access and digital source management. Building from that study, it offers recommendations for gathering statistics from other libraries internationally.

Leadley, Sarah. "Reflections on Diversity and Organizational Development." *Reference and User Services Quarterly* 54, no. 4 (2015): 6–10.

This column speaks to the importance of diversity as an opportunity to build a strong community around libraries and improve the work of scholarly communication in general. It gives an overview of the work of the Equity, Diversity, and Social Justice Team at the University of Washington.

Lim, Adriene. "Against the Odds: Reflections on Asian American Identity and Multicultural, Shared Leadership in Academic Libraries." In *Asian American Librarians and Library Services: Activism, Collaborations, and Strategies*, edited by Janet Hyunju Clarke, Raymond Pun, and Monnee Tong, 233–45. Lanham, MD: Rowman and Littlefield, 2018.

Lim reflects on two decades of library management, considering the importance of increased Asian American and other minority inclusion in positions of leadership in academic libraries and the various barriers to entry that librarians of color face. She emphasizes the growing multiculturalism of the population libraries and academic institutions serve, the strength a breadth of cultural perspective brings to the creative problem-solving asked of library leadership, and the necessity of making empathy an institutional and professional norm.

Lombard, Emmett. "Gender and Leadership in Academic Libraries." *Journal of Academic Librarianship* 44, no. 2 (2018): 226–30. https://doi.org/10.1016/j.acalib.2018.02.003.

This survey measured staff perception of three obstacles to leadership—family, "double blinds," and social capital—and how they apply to male and female leaders within academic libraries. The article adapts suggestions by Alice Eagly and Linda Carli about leadership equity to the specific context of academic libraries.

Lynch, Clifford A. "Updating the Agenda for Academic Libraries and Scholarly Communications." *College and Research Libraries* 78, no. 2 (2017): 126–30. https://doi.org/10.5860/crl.78.2.16577.

In this guest editorial for *C&RL,* Lynch suggests restructuring the scholarly communications agenda around opening up access to current research articles, making historical scholarly material accessible, supporting preprint servers, and—in his view perhaps most importantly—conducting ongoing stewardship of the current scholarly and cultural record.

Lyon, Becky J., Kathel Dunn, and Sally Sinn. "Leveraging Partnerships to Develop a Strong and Diverse Workforce." *Journal of Library Administration* 51, no. 2 (2011): 231–41. https://doi.org/10.1080/01930826.2011.540554.

This article examines diversity efforts in academic health science libraries in order to better integrate libraries with campus organization, research institutions, and clinical settings and diversify the workforce across the health science field.

Maciel, Michael L., Wendi Arant Kaspar, and Wyoma vanDuinkerken. "(Desperately) Seeking Service Leadership in Academic Libraries: An Analysis of Dean and Director Position Advertisements." *Journal of Library Administration* 58, no. 1 (2018): 18–53. https://doi.org/10.1080/01930826.2017.1399711.

Maciel and colleagues discuss the leadership vacuum in academic librarianship, arguing that it speaks to a lack of emphasis on and understanding of a service leadership ethic in library department training.

Mihaljevic, Jasminka. "The New Competency Profile of Academic Libraries in the Function of Evaluation of Scientific Productivity." *Ekonomski Vjesnik* 28, no. 2 (2016): 535–49.

This article discusses the new competencies required of librarians if libraries are to play a role in setting the metrics and evaluation criteria of scientific inquiry. It describes the course of library education necessary so librarians can best acquire those competencies.

Neigel, Christina. "LIS Leadership and Leadership Education: A Matter of Gender." *Journal of Library Administration* 55, no. 7 (2015): 521–34. https://doi.org/10.1080/01930826.2015.1076307.

Neigel identifies a gap in LIS literature on the experience of women in leadership positions in academic libraries, especially in conversation with the gendered politics of librarianship as a field of study. She finds that the discourse of leadership represents a turn toward masculinized responses to the need for change and a continued devaluing of the "women's work" that has traditionally been the basis of the profession.

Ogburn, Joyce, Allegra Swift, and Emma Molls. "Scholarly Communication in the Context of Digital Literacy: Navigation and Decision Making in a Complex Landscape." Presentation, University of San Diego Digital Initiatives Symposium, San Diego, CA, April 24, 2018.

In this presentation at the USD Digital Initiatives Symposium, Ogburn and colleagues examined scholarly communication not in its own smaller sphere of libraries and publishing but as part of a greater interconnected landscape of the technology, research, economics, and student learning environments that comprise academia at large. They argue that in order to increase digital literacy and enact social justice values, it needs to be understood as such.

Paulus, Michael J., Jr. "Reconceptualizing Academic Libraries and Archives in the Digital Age." *portal: Libraries and the Academy* 11, no. 4 (2011): 939–52.

Paulus reevaluates the concept of preservation as a separate and discrete aspect of the life cycle of a scholarly work, arguing that librarians and archivists are taking on new roles in the creation and dissemination aspects as well. He states that taking this fact into account allows a model for twenty-first-century curation.

Puente, Mark A. "Developing a Vital Research Library Workforce." *Research Library Issues,* no. 272 (2010): 1–6.

Puente argues that the current economic and social situation of libraries calls for a new set of skills among library and information workers so that they can best serve the research community fast growing around them. This new workforce must be trained to speak to a constituency interested in collaborative learning, and one with a diversity of technological expertise and of cultural and national experiences and backgrounds.

Ryan, Patti, and Lisa Sloniowski. "The Public Academic Library: Friction in the Teflon Funnel." In *Information Literacy and Social Justice: Radical Professional Praxis,* edited by Shana Higgins and Lua Gregory, 275–96. Sacramento: Library Juice Press, 2013.

In the growing body of critical library work, libraries themselves are understood as hegemonic tools for colonization and Western domination of knowledge. Through case studies on library workshops on the Iraq War and the Occupy Movement, Ryan and Sloniowski offer suggestions for how to change that structure from within, resist the re-embedding of those values through neoliberalism, and shift the value system of libraries to one of social and communal responsibility.

Sutton, Shan C. "Time to Step on the Gas in Approaching the Intersections of Scholarly Communication and Information Literacy." *Journal of Librarianship and Scholarly Communication* 1, no. 3 (2013): eP1076. https://doi.org/10.7710/2162-3309.1076.

In the *JLSC's first* P^2 review, Sutton responds to the 2013 ACRL report from the Working Group on Intersections of Scholarly Communication and Information Literacy, identifying three themes (the coupling of scholarly communication instruction with experiential learning, the faculty impact of shifting scholarly communication programs toward students, and the integrated model's value to parent institutions and higher education) as worthy of further development and discussion.

Swygart-Hobaugh, Amanda J. "Information—Power to the People: Students and Librarians Dialoguing about Power, Social Justice, and Information." In *Information Literacy and Social Justice: Radical Professional Praxis*, edited by Shana Higgins and Lua Gregory, 219–46. Sacramento: Library Juice Press, 2013.

This chapter is a breakdown of the pedagogical theory and a content analysis of student work in an honors freshman seminar on critical theory and social justice frameworks in library and information sciences at Georgia State University.

Yu, Liangzhi. "The Divided Views of the Information and Digital Divides: A Call for Integrative Theories of Information Inequality." *Journal of Information Science* 37, no. 6 (2011): 660–79.

"Information poverty," "information divide," "knowledge gap," and "digital divide" are all terms understood and examined by a number of disciplines. Yu argues that they should be taken together and collected into a multidisciplinary framework, similar to Bourdieu's research on social inequality, in order to actually address the problems stemming from them.

Endnotes

Introduction

1. Association of College and Research Libraries, *Request for Proposals: Research Agenda on the Research Environment and Scholarly Communication System (Chicago: Association of College and Research Libraries, 2017),* https://acrl.ala.org/acrlinsider/wp-content/uploads/RFP-for-research-agenda-on-scholarly-environment.pdf.
2. ACRL Scholarly Communications Committee, *Establishing a Research Agenda for Scholarly Communication: A Call for Community Engagement (Chicago: Association of College and Research Libraries, 2007),* http://www.ala.org/acrl/sites/ala.org.acrl/files/content/issues/scholcomm/SCResearchAgenda.pdf.
3. Roger Schonfeld has been documenting this trend through his posts on *Scholarly Kitchen. See Roger C. Schonfeld, "Strategy and Integration among Workflow Providers," Scholarly Kitchen (blog), November 7, 2017,* https://scholarlykitchen.sspnet.org/2017/11/07/strategy-integration-workflow-providers/.
4. Association of College and Research Libraries, *ACRL Plan for Excellence (Chicago: Association of College and Research Libraries, 2011, rev. 2018),* http://www.ala.org/acrl/aboutacrl/strategicplan/stratplan.
5. Clifford Lynch, "Updating the Agenda for Academic Libraries and Scholarly Communication," *College and Research Libraries 78, no. 2 (2017): 126–30,* https://doi.org/10.5860/crl.78.2.16577; DLF Working Group on Labor in Digital Libraries, *Research Agenda: Valuing Labor in Digital Libraries (Washington, DC: Digital Library Federation, 2018),* https://wiki.diglib.org/images/d/d0/DLF_ValuingLabor_ResearchAgenda_2018.pdf; Micah Altman, Chris Bourg, Philip Cohen, G. Sayeed Choudhury, Charles Henry, Sue Kriegsman, Mary Minow, et al., *A Grand Challenges–Based Research Agenda for Scholarly Communication and Information Science,* MIT Grand Challenge PubPub Participation Platform, December 18, 2018, https://doi.org/10.21428/62b3421f.
6. SPARC, "Theme of 2018 International Open Access Week to Be 'Designing Equitable Foundations for Open Knowledge,'" news release, May 24, 2018, https://sparcopen.org/news/2018/theme-2018-international-open-access-week-designing-equitable-foundations-open-knowledge/.
7. For each of these terms, working definitions were based on a number of sources. A small selection of the thinkers who informed those definitions appears below, but these are merely representative of the larger discussions the report authors synthesized for working definitions. Additionally, the ALA Office for Diversity, Literacy, and Outreach Services maintains a glossary of terms, created by ALA members, which are used in conversations about equity, diversity, and inclusion, http://www.ala.org/aboutala/odlos-glossary-terms.

   Open: Rick Anderson, Seth Denbo, Diane Graves, Susan Haigh, Steven Hill, Martin Kalfatovic, Roy Kaufman, et al., "Report from the 'What Is Open?' Workgroup," *Open Scholarship Initiative Proceedings 1 (2016),* http://dx.doi.org/10.13021/G8XK5R; Ulrich Herb and Joachim Schöpfel, "Open Divide Emerges as Open Access Unfolds," in *Open Divide? Critical Studies on Open Access, ed. Ulrich Herb and Joachim Schöpfel (Sacramento: Litwin Books, 2018), 7–13,* https://doi.org/10.5281/zenodo.1206390; Mallory C. Kidwell, Ljiljana B. Lazarević, Erica Baranski, Tom E. Hardwicke, Sarah Piechowski, Lina-Sophia Falkenberg, Curtis Kennett, et al., "Badges to Acknowledge Open Practices: A Simple, Low-Cost, Effective Method for Increasing Transparency," *PLOS Biology 14, no. 5 (2016): e1002456,* https://doi.org/10.1371/journal.pbio.1002456; Public Library of Science, Scholarly Publishing and Academic Resources Coalition, and Open Access Scholarly Publishers Association, "HowOpenIsIt?" 2014, https://www.plos.org/how-open-is-it; Mark D. Wilkinson, Michel Dumontier, IJsbrand Jan Aalbersberg, Gabrielle Appleton, Myles Axton, Arie Baak, Niklas Blomberg, et al., "The FAIR Guiding Principles for Scientific Data Management and Stewardship," *Scientific Data 3 (2016): article 160018,* https://doi.org/10.1038/sdata.2016.18.

   Inclusive: Toni Anaya and Charlene Maxey-Harris, *Diversity and Inclusion: SPEC Kit 356 (Washington, DC: Association of Research Libraries, 2017),* https://doi.org/10.29242/spec.356; Michelle Baildon, Dana Hamlin, Czeslaw Jankowski, Rhonda Kauffman, Julia Lanigan, Michelle Miller, Jessica Venlet, and Ann Marie Willer, "Creating a Social Justice Mindset: Diversity, Inclusion, and Social Justice in the Collections Directorate of the MIT Libraries," Collections Directorate of the MIT Libraries, February 9, 2017, https://dspace.mit.edu/handle/1721.1/108771; Chris Bourg, "Never Neutral: Libraries, Technology, and Inclusion." *Feral Librarian (blog), January 28, 2015,* https://chrisbourg.wordpress.com/2015/01/28/never-neutral-libraries-technology-and-inclusion/; April Hathcock, "Making the Local Global: The Colonialism of Scholarly Communication," *At the Intersection (blog), September 27, 2016,* https://bit.ly/2dsgotJ; Katy Mathuews, "Moving beyond Diversity to Social Justice: A Call to Action for Academic Libraries," *Progressive Librarian 44 (2016): 6–27; Myrna Morales, Em Claire Knowles, and Chris Bourg, "Diversity, Social Justice, and the Future of Libraries," portal: Libraries and the Academy 14, no. 3 (July 2014): 439–51,* https://doi.org/10.1353/pla.2014.0017; Mega Subramaniam and Paul T. Jaeger, "Modeling Inclusive Practice? Attracting Diverse Faculty and Future Faculty to the Information Workforce," *Library Trends 59, no. 1–2 (2010): 109–27; William C. Welburn, "Creating Inclusive Communities: Diversity and the Responses of Academic Libraries," portal: Libraries and the Academy 10, no. 3 (2010): 355–63.*

   Equitable: Candise Branum and J. Turner Masland, "Critical Library Management: Administrating for Equity," *Oregon Library Association Quarterly 23, no. 2 (2017): 28–36; Laura Czernowicz, "Inequitable Power Dynamics of Global Knowledge Production and Exchange Must Be Confronted Head On," LSE Impact Blog, April 29, 2013,* http://blogs.lse.ac.uk/impactofsocialsciences/2013/04/29/redrawing-the-map-from-access-to-participation/; Paul T. Jaeger, Nicole A. Cooke, Cecilia Feltis, Michelle Hamiel, Fiona Jardine, and Katie Shilton, "The Virtuous Circle Revisited: Injecting Diversity, Inclusion, Rights, Justice, and Equity into LIS from Education to Advocacy," *Library Quarterly 85, no. 2 (2015): 150–71; Roger C. Schonfeld and Liam Sweeney,*

Inclusion, Diversity, and Equity: Members of the Association of Research Libraries: Employee Demographics and Director Perspectives (New York: Andrew W. Mellon Foundation, 2017), https://sr.ithaka.org/publications/inclusion-diversity-and-equity-arl/.

8. See, for example, the following pieces: Maria Carpenter, Jolie Graybill, Jerome Offord, and Mary Piorun, "Envisioning the Library's Role in Scholarly Communication in the Year 2025," *portal: Libraries and the Academy 11, no. 2 (April 2011): 659–81; Anne Marie Casey, "Strategic Priorities and Change in Academic Libraries" (PhD diss., Simmons College, 2011), ProQuest Dissertations and Theses; Barbara Irene Dewey, "Leading the Library by Leading the Campus: A Dean's Perspective," Library Leadership and Management 29, no. 1 (2014),* https://journals.tdl.org/llm/index.php/llm/article/view/7099; Barbara Fister, "Liberating Knowledge: A Librarian's Manifesto for Change," *Thought and Action, Fall 2010: 83–90; Bruce Fyfe, Catherine Steeves, and Nicole Nolan, "Charting Our Course through Reframing Library Leadership in a Sea of Change," Proceedings of the IATUL Conferences, 2016, paper 3,* http://docs.lib.purdue.edu/iatul/2016/wrkforce/3; Jennine A. Knight, "Academic Librarians as Change Champions: A Framework for Managing Change," *Library Management 38, no. 6/7 (2017): 294–301; Markku Laitinen and Jarmo Saarti, "Evidence Based Service Change: Remodelling the Academic Libraries for the Post-digital Era," Qualitative and Quantitative Methods in Libraries 3, no. 3 (2017): 611–18; Marlene Manoff, "Human and Machine Entanglement in the Digital Archive: Academic Libraries and Socio-technical Change," portal: Libraries and the Academy 15, no. 3 (2015): 513–30; Joyce Ogburn, "The Movement to Change Scholarly Communication Has Come a Long Way—How Far Might It Go?" Journal of Librarianship and Scholarly Communication 1, no. 1 (2012): eP1041,* http://doi.org/10.7710/2162-3309.1041; Charlotte Roh, "Scholarly Communication in a Time of Change: Considering the Impact of Bias, Diversity, and Traditional Publishing Structures as Scholarly Communication Moves to New Platforms and Systems" (presentation, California Academic and Research Libraries Conference: Academic Libraries in Times of Change, Redwood City, CA, April 14, 2018); Linda Tuhiwai Smith, "Decolonizing Knowledge: Toward a Critical Indigenous Research Justice Praxis," in *Research Justice: Methodologies for Social Change, ed. Andrew J. Jolivétte (University of Bristol, UK: Policy Press, 2015),* 205–11.

9. For the importance of practitioners as researchers, see, for example: Gaby Haddow and Jane E. Klobas, "Communication of Research to Practice in Library and Information Science: Closing the Gap," *Library and Information Science Research 26, no. 1 (Winter 2004): 29–43,* https://doi.org/10.1016/j.lisr.2003.11.010; Charles R. Hildreth and Selenay Aytac, "Recent Library Practitioner Research: A Methodological Analysis and Critique," *Journal for Library and Information Science Education 48, no. 3 (2008): 236–58; Peter Jarvis, The Practitioner-Researcher: Developing Theory from Practice.(New York: Jossey-Bass, 1998); Ronald R. Powell, Lynda M. Baker, and Joseph J. Mika, "Library and Information Science Practitioners and Research," Library and Information Science Research 24, no. 1 (2002): 49–72,* https://doi.org/10.1016/S0740-8188(01)00104-9; Donald A. Schön, "*Knowing-in-Action: The New Scholarship Requires a New Epistemology," Change 27, no. 6 (1995): 26–34; Rebecca Watson-Boone, "Academic Librarians as Practitioner-Researchers," Journal of Academic Librarianship 26, no. 2 (2000): 85–93.*

10. Peter Reason and Hilary Bradbury, "Introduction: Inquiry and Participation in Search of a World Worthy of Hyman Aspiration," in *Handbook of Action Research: Participative Inquiry and Practice, ed. Peter Reason and Hilary Bradbury (London: Sage, 2001), 1.*

11. Richard Couto, Sarah Hippensteel Hall, and Marti Goetz, "Community Change Context," in *Leading Change in Multiple Contexts: Concepts and Practices in Organizational, Community, Political, Social, and Global Change Settings, ed. Gill Robinson Hickman (Thousand Oaks, CA: Sage, 2009), 119–49.*

12. American Library Association, *Core Values of Librarianship (Chicago: American Library Association, 2004),* http://www.ala.org/advocacy/intfreedom/corevalues.

Research Agenda: People

13. The ACRL diversity standards, developed in 2012, can be found at Association of College and Research Libraries, *Diversity Standards: Cultural Competency for Academic Libraries (Chicago: Association of College and Research Libraries, 2012),* http://www.ala.org/acrl/standards/diversity. Also see the 2007 white paper, Teresa Y. Neely and Lorna Peterson, "Achieving Racial and Ethnic Diversity among Academic and Research Librarians: The Recruitment, Retention, and Advancement of Librarians of Color," *College and Research Library News 68, no. 9 (2007): 562–65,* https://crln.acrl.org/index.php/crlnews/article/view/7869.

14. The SPARC Author Addendum was first issued in 2006; version 3.0 is available here: "Author Rights: Using the SPARC Author Addendum," SPARC, accessed March 6, 2019, https://sparcopen.org/our-work/author-rights/brochure-html/. In 2008, eleven of the fourteen members of the Big Ten Academic Alliance endorsed a Statement on Publishing Agreements and Addendum; the current version is available here: Big Ten Academic Alliance, "Statement on Publishing Agreements and Addendum to Publication Agreements for BTAA Authors," December 7, 2016, http://www.btaa.org/docs/default-source/library/authorsrights.pdf?sfvrsn=b20a41e9_8.

15. See "Traditional Knowledge (TK) Labels," Local Contexts, accessed March 7, 2019, http://localcontexts.org/tk-labels/.

16. See also Ithaka S+R's 2017 Indigenous Studies Project (Danielle Cooper, "A New Project on Indigenous Studies Scholars," *Ithaka S+R [blog], November 27, 2017,* https://sr.ithaka.org/blog/a-new-project-on-indigenous-studies-scholars/), presented at the 2018 Joint Conference of Librarians of Color (Keahiahi Long, Anthony Sanchez, and Danielle Cooper, "Reflections on the Joint Conference of Librarians of Color, *Ithaka S+R [blog], October 23, 2018,* https://sr.ithaka.org/blog/reflections-on-the-joint-conference-of-librarians-of-color) and at the 2018 Library Assessment Conference (Danielle Cooper, "Session 11: Nontraditional Users: Perspectives on the Limits of Assessment: Ithaca S+R's Indigenous Studies Project," Library Assessment Conference, Program Abstracts, 2018, https://libraryassessment.org/program/schedule/program-abstracts/#Cooper).

17. In December 2018, the ACRL published Amy Nurnberger, Pamella Lach, Abigail Goben, Sandra De Groote, and Yasmeen Shorish, *ACRL Primer for Protecting Sensitive Data in Academic Research (Chicago: Association of College and Research Libraries, 2018),* https://www.acrl.ala.org/acrlinsider/archives/16710.

18. See, for example, ALA's 2006 report on diversity in the profession and its ongoing Diversity Counts initiative ("Diversity Counts," American Library Association, accessed March 6, 2019, http://www.ala.org/aboutala/offices/diversity/diversitycounts/divcounts) and ARL's 2017 SPEC Kit on diversity and inclusion (Anaya and Maxey-Harris, *Diversity and Inclusion). Some progress can be seen in demographic reports from ALA ("Librarianship and Library Staff Statistics," American Library Association, accessed March 6, 2019,* http://www.ala.org/tools/research/librarystaffstats) and ARL ("Demographic Trends in ARL Librarians," ARL Statistics, accessed March 6, 2019, http://www.arlstatistics.org/about/series/ss/use/demographic), and also in the recent report by Galbraith et al. that over the last thirty years the wage gap has closed when it comes to racial inequity, at least in ARL libraries (Quinn Galbraith, Heather Kelley, and Michel Groesbeck, "Is There a Racial Wage Gap in Research Libraries? An Analysis of ARL Libraries," *College and Research Libraries 79, no. 7 [2018]: 863–75,* https://doi.org/10.5860/crl.79.7.863). Ithaka S+R's recent study on diversity, inclusion, and equity (also focused on ARL libraries) provides a baseline for future research in this area and urges much more work to be done (Schonfeld and Sweeney, *Inclusion, Diversity, and Equity).*
19. See, for example, Juleah Swanson, Azusa Tanaka, and Isabel Gonzalez-Smith. "Lived Experience of Academic Librarians of Color," *College and Research Libraries* 79, no. 7 [2018] 876-894, https://doi.org/10.5860/crl.79.7.876. Antonia P. Olivas, *Choosing to Lead: The Motivational Factors of Underrepresented Minority Librarians in Higher Education* (Chicago: Association of College and Research Libraries, 2018).
20. Sarah Kalikman Lippincott, *Library as Publisher: New Models of Scholarly Communication for a New Era (ATG, 2017), "Starting or Growing a Publishing Program," "Organization, Staffing, and Partnerships," para. 2,* https://quod.lib.umich.edu/c/cb/mpub9944345. These results are also supported by the case studies found in Deanna Marcum, Roger Schonfeld, and Sarah Thomas, *Office of Scholarly Communication: Scope, Organizational Placement, and Planning in Ten Research Libraries (New York: Ithaka S+R, 2015),* https://doi.org/10.18665/sr.275206.
21. Steven Bell. *Course Materials Adoption: A Faculty Survey and Outlook for the OER Landscape* (Chicago: Choice/Association of College and Research Libraries, 2018). http://www.choice360.org/content/2-librarianship/5-whitepaper/bell-white-paper-october-2018/100318_bell_white_paper.pdf.
22. For those interested more specifically in a research agenda focused on digital library labor, please see the DLF Working Group on Labor in Digital Libraries, *Research Agenda, which outlines several areas for investigation.*
23. See, for example, Elizabeth Joffrion and Natalia Fernández, "Collaborations between Tribal and Nontribal Organizations: Suggested Best Practices for Sharing Expertise, Cultural Resources, and Knowledge," *American Archivist 78, no. 1 (2015): 192–237.*
24. See, for example, *Protocols for Native American Archival Materials* available online at http://www2.nau.edu/libnap-p/protocols.html, and Kimberly Christen, "Tribal Archives, Traditional Knowledge, and Local Contexts: Why the "s" Matters." *Journal of Western Archives* 6, no 1 (2015). http://digitalcommons.usu.edu/westernarchives/vol6/iss1/3.

Research Agenda: Content

25. The Review, Promotion, and Tenure Project is being conducted by Juan Pablo Alperin, Meredith T. Niles, Erin C. McKiernan, Lesley Schimanski, and Carol Muñoz Nieves. Learn more about this project to incentivize openness and accessibility at "Review, Promotion, and Tenure Project," ScholCommLab, accessed March 7, 2019, http://www.scholcommlab.ca/research/rpt-project/.
26. "Publons," Web of Science Group Clarivate Analytics, accessed April 29, 2019, https://publons.com/about/home/.
27. See, for example: Nicola Andrews, "Reflections on Resistance, Decolonization, and the Historical Trauma of Libraries and Academia," in *The Politics of Theory and the Practice of Critical Librarianship, ed. Karen P. Nicholson and Maura Seale (Sacramento: Library Juice Press, 2018), 181–92; Achille Mbembe, "Decolonizing Knowledge and the Question of the Archive," Wits Institute for Social and Economic Research, University of the Witwatersrand, Johannesburg, South Africa, May 2, 2015,* http://wiser.wits.ac.za/system/files/Achille%20Mbembe%20-%20Decolonizing%20Knowledge%20and%20the%20Question%20of%20the%20Archive.pdf.
28. Library Publishing Coalition, *An Ethical Framework for Library Publishing, ver. 1.0 (San Francisco: Educopia, 2018),* https://doi.org/10.5703/1288284316777.
29. "PubPub," MIT Press Massachusetts Institute of Technology, accessed April 29, 2019 https://www.pubpub.org/.
30. "Open Journal Systems," Public Knowledge Project Simon Fraser University, accessed April 29, 2019, https://pkp.sfu.ca/ojs/.
31. See, for example: Emily Ford, Wendi Arant Kaspar, and Peggy Seiden, "Diversity of ACRL Publications, Editorial Board Demographics: A Report from ACRL's Publications Coordinating Committee," *College and Research Libraries 78, no. 10 (2017): 548–51; Celia Sánchez Peñas and Peter Willett, "Brief Communication: Gender Differences in Publication and Citation Counts in Librarianship and Information Science Research," Journal of Information Science 32, no. 5 (2006): 480–85.*
32. For a sample of work looking at the issue of faculty productivity and the imbalance among research, teaching, and service, see, e.g., the following: Philip G. Altbach, "What Counts for Academic Productivity in Research Universities?" *International Higher Education 79 (2015): 6–7; Simon Cadez, Vlado Dimovski, and Maja Zaman Groff, "Research, Teaching and Performance Evaluation in Academia: The Salience of Quality," Studies in Higher Education 42, no. 8 (2017): 1455–73; John S. Levin and Aida Aliyeva, "Embedded Neoliberalism within Faculty Behaviors," Review of Higher Education 38, no. 4 (2015): 537–63; Ketevan Mamiseishvili, Michael T. Miller, and Donghun Lee, "Beyond Teaching and Research: Faculty Perceptions of Service Roles at Research Universities," Innovative Higher Education 41, no. 4 (2016): 273–85; Silvia Ines Monserrat and Claire A. Simmers, "Carolyn R. Dexter's Legacies: A Broader Perspective on Faculty Work Productivity and Impact." Journal of Management History 25, no. 1 (2019): 9–25.*
33. See, for example: Lynn P. Nygaard, "Publishing and Perishing: An Academic Literacies Framework for Investigating Research Productivity," *Studies in Higher Education 42, no. 3 (2015): 519–32; Robert H. Stupnisky, Reinhard Pekrun, and Stephanie Licht-*

enfeld, "New Faculty Members' Emotions: A Mixed-Method Study," Studies in Higher Education 41, no. 7 (2014): 1167–88; William H. Walters, *"The Faculty Subculture, the Librarian Subculture, and Librarians' Scholarly Productivity," portal: Libraries and the Academy 16, no. 4 (October 2016): 817–43,* https://doi.org/10.1353/pla.2016.0054.

34. Aaron E. Carroll, "Peer Review: The Worst Way to Judge Research, Except for All the Others," *New York Times, November 5, 2018,* https://www.nytimes.com/2018/11/05/upshot/peer-review-the-worst-way-to-judge-research-except-for-all-the-others.html.
35. "ACRL Impactful Scholarship and Metrics Task Force," Association of College and Research Libraries, accessed March 7, 2019, http://www.ala.org/acrl/aboutacrl/directoryofleadership/taskforces/acr-tfism.
36. "About HuMetricsHHS," HuMetricsHSS Humane Metrics Initiative, accessed March 7, 2019, http://humetricshss.org/about/.

Research Agenda: Systems

37. Daniel E. Atkins, Kelvin K. Droegemeier, Stuart I. Feldman, Hector Garcia-Molina, Michael L. Klein, David G. Messerschmitt, Paul Messina, Jeremiah P. Ostriker, and Margaret H. Wright, *Revolutionizing Science and Engineering through Cyberinfrastructure (Washington, DC: National Science Foundation, 2003), 5,* https://www.nsf.gov/cise/sci/reports/atkins.pdf, quoted in ACRL Scholarly Communications Committee, *Establishing a Research Agenda, 4–5.*
38. For more information about these projects, see Vega Academic Publishing System website, accessed March 9, 2019, https://vegapublish.com/; University of Minnesota Press's Library of Open-Access Titles: Powered by Manifold, accessed March 9, 2019, https://manifold.umn.edu/; Fulcrum website, accessed March 9, 2019, https://www.fulcrum.org/; and Humanities Commons website, accessed March 9, 2019, https://hcommons.org/.
39. "Humanities Commons Members," Modern Language Association, accessed April 20, 2019, https://hcommons.org/members/.
40. The methodology PKP uses to count journals is outlined in "OJS Usage," Public Knowledge Project, accessed March 6, 2019, https://pkp.sfu.ca/ojs/ojs-usage/.
41. Kenning Arlitsch and Carl Grant, "Why So Many Repositories? Examining the Limitations and Possibilities of the Institutional Repositories (IR) Landscape," *Journal of Library Administration 58, no. 3 (2018): 264–81,* https://doi.org/10.1080/01930826.2018.1436778.
42. Digital Preservation Network, "Community Announcement: DPN Sunset," December 4, 2018, accessed December 4, 2018, https://dpn.org (site discontinued); Roger C. Schonfeld, "Why Is the Digital Preservation Network Disbanding?," Scholarly Kitchen (blog), December 13, 2018, https://scholarlykitchen.sspnet.org/2018/12/13/digital-preservation-network-disband/.
43. Primary Trustworthy Digital Repository Authorisation Body Ltd. (PTAB), "ISO 16363," accessed March 9, 2019, http://www.iso16363.org/standards/iso-16363/.
44. "Section508.gov GSA Goverment-wide IT Accessibility Program," U.S. General Services Administration, accesssed April 28, 2019, https://section508.gov.
45. For more about ASGCLA's resources, see "About Us," ASGCLA website, accessed March 9, 2019, http://www.ala.org/asgcla/about.
46. For more about the Universal Accessibility Interest Group, see "Universal Accessibility Interest Group," Association of College and Research Libraries, accessed March 9, 2019, http://www.ala.org/acrl/aboutacrl/directoryofleadership/interestgroups/acr-igua.
47. For more on Editoria, designed to "build and customize streamlined, scalable book publishing workflows," ("Features," Editoria, accessed March 9, 2019, https://editoria.pub/features/), see Editoria website, accessed March 9, 2019, https://editoria.pub/.
48. "Scholarly Transformation Advice and Review (STAR) Team Charge," University of California Libraries, last updated January 9, 2019, https://libraries.universityofcalifornia.edu/sclg/star/charge. The STAR criteria and downloadable workbook are available here: "Scholarly Transformation Advice and Review (STAR) Team Criteria Summary," University of California Libraries, last updated January 31, 2017, https://libraries.universityofcalifornia.edu/sclg/star/criteria_summary.
49. Nancy L. Maron and Sarah Pickle, "Sustainability Implementation Toolkit: Developing an Institutional Strategy for Supporting Digital Humanities Resources," Ithaka S+R, last modified June 18, 2014, http://sr.ithaka.org/?p=22853. This includes a guided three-step process for evaluating where current resources reside on campus, an Excel-based framework for analyzing and visualizing overlaps and gaps in the digital project life cycle, and tools to facilitate key stakeholder discussions to develop campus strategy.
50. "Big Deal Cancellation Tracking," SPARC, accessed March 9, 2019, https://sparcopen.org/our-work/big-deal-cancellation-tracking/.
51. Nancy Maron, Kimberly Schmelzinger, Christine Mulhern, and Daniel Rossman, "The Costs of Publishing Monographs: Toward a Transparent Methodology," *Journal of Electronic Publishing 19, no. 1 (Summer 2016),* https://doi.org/10.3998/3336451.0019.103.
52. "Knowledge Unlatched," Knowledge Unlatched, accessed April 29, 2019, http://www.knowledgeunlatched.org.
53. "Open Library of Humanities," Open Library of Humanities, accessed April 29, 2019, https://www.openlibhums.org.
54. For more on the Mellon-funded project exploring the 2.5% concept, see "Mellon Grant Will Support Revamping Infrastructure for Digital Scholarship," Newsroom, Middlebury College, September 28, 2018, http://www.middlebury.edu/newsroom/archive/2018-news/node/594612.
55. Digital Public Library of America, "DPLA Update," November 14, 2018, https://dp.la/news/dpla-update.
56. Digital Preservation Network, "Community Announcement."
57. Chela Scott Weber, *Research and Learning Agenda for Archives, Special, and Distinctive Collections in Research Libraries (Dublin, OH: OCLC Research, 2017),* https://doi.org/10.25333/C3C34F. OCLC's Research Agenda highlights the importance of defining the skills library staff have that are relevant to open-source projects, including but not limited to coding.

58. See Center for Open Science and its work on reproducibility: ("Research Evaluates Scientific Ideas. We Evaluate Research," Center for Open Science, accessed March 8, 2019, https://cos.io/our-services/research/); on the challenges of reproducibility as well as some things that work, see "Checklists Work to Improve Science," *Nature 556 (2018): 273–74,* https://www.nature.com/articles/d41586-018-04590-7.
59. Carol Tenopir, Dane Hughes, Suzie Allard, Mike Frame, Ben Birch, Lynn Baird, Robert Sandusky, Madison Langseth, and Andrew Lundeen, "Research Data Services in Academic Libraries: Data Intensive Roles for the Future?" *Journal of eScience Librarianship 4, no. 2 (2015): e1085,* http://dx.doi.org/10.7191/jeslib.2015.1085.
60. "ACRL Digital Scholarship Section," Association of College and Research Libraries, accessed April 29, 2019, http://www.ala.org/acrl/aboutacrl/directoryofleadership/sections/dss/acr-dssec.
61. "ACRL Research Data Management RoadShow," Association of College and Research Libraries, accessed April 29, 2019, http://www.ala.org/acrl/conferences/roadshows/rdmroadshow.
62. Andrew Kirkpatrick, Joshue O Connor, Alastair Campbell, and Michael Cooper, eds., "Web Content Accessibility Guidelines (WCAG) 2.1," W3C Recommendation, June 5, 2018, https://www.w3.org/TR/2018/REC-WCAG21-20180605/.
63. See, e.g., Deque Systems, "Section 508 Refresh Update: ICT Final Rule Published," *Federal Government and Section 508 (blog), Deque, January 18, 2017,* https://www.deque.com/blog/section-508-refresh-news-ict-final-rule-update/.
64. Big Ten Academic Alliance, "Library e-Resource Accessibility: Introduction," accessed March 8, 2019, https://www.btaa.org/library/accessibility/reports.
65. Library Publishing Coalition, *Ethical Framework, ver. 1.0*
66. Notably, in spring 2019, the University of California system and Norwegian research institutions decided not to renew subscriptions with Elsevier. See "Open Statement: Why UC Cut Ties With Elsevier," March 20, 2019, https://osc.universityofcalifornia.edu/open-access-at-uc/publisher-negotiations/uc-and-elsevier. "Norwegian research institutions unable to reach agreement with Elsevier," March 12, 2019, https://www.uio.no/english/about/news-and-events/news/2019/unable-to-reach-agreement-with-elsevier.html.
67. Nicole Allen, "$1 Billion in Savings through Open Educational Resources," SPARC News, October 12, 2018, https://sparcopen.org/news/2018/1-billion-in-savings-through-open-educational-resources.
68. Everett M. Rogers, *Diffusion of Innovations, 5th ed. (New York: Free Press, 2003); Eunika Mercier-Laurent, Innovation Ecosystems (London: ISTE; Hoboken, NJ: John Wiley & Sons, 2011).*

Appendix 1

69. Mathuews, "Moving beyond Diversity."
70. For an annotated bibliography of work published between 2010 and 2015 on diversity in academic libraries, see Jenny Lynne Semenza, Regina Koury, and Sandra Shropshire, "Diversity at Work in Academic Libraries, 2010–2015: An Annotated Bibliography," *Collection Building 36, no. 3 (2017): 89–95.*
71. See, e.g., the following: American Library Association, "Diversity Counts: 2009–2010 Update," September 18, 2012, http://www.ala.org/aboutala/offices/diversity/diversitycounts/2009-2010update; Anaya and Maxey-Harris, *Diversity and Inclusion; Society of College, National and University Libraries (SCONUL), Research Project: BAME Staff Experiences of Academic Libraries (London: SCONUL, May 17, 2018),* https://www.sconul.ac.uk/sites/default/files/documents/Research%20Project%20-%20BAME%20staff%20experiences%20of%20academic%20libraries.pdf.
72. See the following: Juleah Swanson, Ione Damasco, Isabel Gonzalez-Smith, Dracine Hodges, Todd Honma, and Azusa Tanaka, 2015. "Why Diversity Matters: A Roundtable Discussion on Racial and Ethnic Diversity in Librarianship," *In the Library with the Lead Pipe, July 29, 2015,* http://www.inthelibrarywiththeleadpipe.org/2015/why-diversity-matters-a-roundtable-discussion-on-racial-and-ethnic-diversity-in-librarianship/; Jennifer Vinopal, "The Quest for Diversity in Library Staffing: From Awareness to Action," *In the Library with the Lead Pipe, January 13, 2016,* http://www.inthelibrarywiththeleadpipe.org/2016/quest-for-diversity/.
73. Anaya and Maxey-Harris, *Diversity and Inclusion, p. 8.*
74. See, e.g., the following: Anaya and Maxey-Harris, *Diversity and Inclusion; Kyung-Sun Kim and Sei-Ching Joanna Sin, "Increasing Ethnic Diversity in LIS: Strategies Suggested by Librarians of Color," Library Quarterly 78, no. 2 (2008): 153–77; Subramaniam and Jaeger, "Modeling Inclusive Practice?"*
75. See, e.g., the following: Anaya and Maxey-Harris, *Diversity and Inclusion; Mitch Fontenot, "Diversity: A Task Force: Survey of the Literature and Some Possible Trends for Academic Libraries," Louisiana Libraries 73, no. 1 (2010): 8–11; Rodney E. Freeman, "A Snapshot of Indiana's Librarians Leading in Diversity Fellowship Participants after the Program Has Concluded," Indiana Libraries 33, no. 1 (2014): 12–15; April Hathcock, "White Librarianship in Blackface: Diversity Initiatives in LIS," In the Library with the Lead Pipe, October 7, 2015,* https://bit.ly/1Pj087V; Eboni M. Henry, Eileen K. Bosch, Karen Quash, Leslie K. Griffin, Mario Ascencio, Monica Lopez, and Ray Pun, "Librarians of Color: The Challenges of 'Movin' On Up' (Part II)," (panel discussion, American Library Association Annual Conference, San Francisco, CA, June 27, 2015); Maha Kumaran, "Succession Planning Process That Includes Visible Minority Librarians," *Library Management 36, no. 6–7 (2015): 434–47; Becky J. Lyon, Kathel Dunn, and Sally Sinn, "Leveraging Partnerships to Develop a Strong and Diverse Workforce," Journal of Library Administration 51, no. 2 (2011): 231–41,* https://doi.org/10.1080/01930826.2011.540554; Chanelle Pickens and Ashleigh D. Coren, "Diversity Residency Programs: Strategies for a Collaborative Approach to Development," *Collaborative Librarianship 9, no. 2 (2017): 104–8; Schonfeld and Sweeney, Inclusion, Diversity, and Equity.*
76. See the following: Andrews, "Reflections on Resistance"; Karen E. Downing, "The Relationship between Social Identity and

Role Performance among Academic Librarians" (Ph.D. diss., University of Michigan, 2009); Mark A. Puente, "Developing a Vital Research Library Workforce," *Research Library Issues, no. 272 (October 2010): 1–6.*

77. See the following: Jaena Alabi, "To Be Seen and Heard: Realizing the Benefits of Diversity and Responding to the Needs of Minority Academic Librarians" (presentation, Mississippi Library Association Annual Conference, Natchez, MS, October 21, 2015); Rose L. Chou and Annie Pho, "Intersectionality at the Reference Desk: Lived Experiences of Women of Color Librarians," in *The Feminist Reference Desk: Concepts, Critiques, and Conversations, ed. Maria T. Accardi (Sacramento: Library Juice Press, 2017), 225–52; Ione T. Damasco and Dracine Hodges, "Tenure and Promotion Experiences of Academic Librarians of Color," College and Research Libraries 73, no. 3 (2012): 279–301; Trevar Riley-Reid, "Breaking Down Barriers: Making It Easier for Academic Librarians of Color to Stay," Journal of Academic Librarianship 43, no. 5 (September 2017): 392–96,* https://doi.org/10.1016/j.acalib.2017.06.017; Joyce K. Thornton, "African American Female Librarians: A Study of Job Satisfaction," *Journal of Library Administration 33, no. 1–2 (2001): 141–64.*

78. For a range of views, see the following: Bryan Alexander, Kim Barrett, Sioux Cumming, Patrick Herron, Claudia Holland, Kathleen Keane, Joyce Ogburn, Jacob Orlowitz, Mary Augusta Thomas, and Jeffrey Tsao, "Report from the Information Overload and Underload Workgroup." *Open Scholarship Initiative Proceedings 1 (2016): G8R30G,* https://doi.org/10.13021/G8R30G; Matthew Baker, "Be Creative, Determined, and Wise: Open Library Publishing and the Global South," *Computers in Libraries 29, no. 10 (December 2009): 6–10; Madeline Cohen, Maura A. Smale, Jill Cirasella, Cynthia Tobar, and Jessie Daniels, "Speaking as One: Supporting Open Access with Departmental Resolutions," Journal of Librarianship and Scholarly Communication 2, no. 1 (2013): eP1099,* https://doi.org/10.7710/2162-3309.1099; Sarah Crissinger, "Access to Research and Sci-Hub: Creating Opportunities for Campus Conversations on Open Access and Ethics," *College and Research Libraries News 78, no. 2 (2017): 86–95; Laura Cruz and Rachel Fleming, "Partnerships: The Engaged University and Library Publishing," OCLC Systems and Services 31, no. 4 (2015): 196–203; Emily Ford, "Advancing an Open Ethos with Open Peer Review," College and Research Libraries 78, no. 4 (2017): 406–12; Isaac Gilman, "Responsibilities and Rights: Balancing the Institutional Imperative for Open Access with Authors' Self-Determination," in Making Institutional Repositories Work, ed. Burton B. Callicott, David Scherer, and Andrew Wesolek (West Lafayette, IN: Purdue University Press, 2015), 69–85; Bobby Glushko and Rex Shoyama, "Unpacking Open Access: A Theoretical Framework for Understanding Open Access Initiatives," Feliciter 61, no. 1 (2015): 8–11; Margaret Heller and Franny Gaede, "Measuring Altruistic Impact: A Model for Understanding the Social Justice of Open Access," Journal of Librarianship and Scholarly Communication 4 (2016): eP2132,* https://doi.org/10.7710/2162-3309.2132; Harrison W. Inefuku, "Globalization, Open Access, and the Democratization of Knowledge," *EDUCAUSE Review, July/August 2017: 62–63; Paul Jones, "Digital Labour in the Academic Context: Challenges for Academic Staff Associations," Ephemera 10, no. 3/4 (2010): 537–39; Cameron Neylon, "Openness in Scholarship: A Return to Core Values?" in Expanding Perspectives on Open Science: Communities, Cultures and Diversity in Concepts and Practices, ed. Leslie Chan and Fernando Loizides (Amsterdam: IOS Press, 2017), 6–17; Thomas Padilla and Vicky Steeves, "Data Librarianship: A Path and an Ethic," Data Praxis (blog), dh+lib, April 4, 2018,* https://acrl.ala.org/dh/2018/04/04/repro/; Michael A. Peters, "Managerialism and the Neoliberal University: Prospects for New Forms of 'Open Management' in Higher Education." *Contemporary Readings in Law and Social Justice 5, no. 1 (2013): 11–26; A. M. Salaz, Nicole Johnston, and Clare Pickles, "Faculty Members Who Teach Online: A Phenomenographic Typology of Open Access Experiences," Journal of Academic Librarianship 44, no. 1 (2018): 125–32; Allan Scherlen and Matthew Robinson, "Open Access to Criminal Justice Scholarship: A Matter of Social Justice," Journal of Criminal Justice Education 19, no. 1 (2008): 54–74; George Veletsianos and Royce Kimmons, "Assumptions and Challenges of Open Scholarship." International Review of Research in Open and Distributed Learning 13, no. 4 (2012): 166–89.*

79. Audrey Watters, "From 'Open' to Justice" (presentation, OpenCon 2014, American University Washington College of Law, Washington, DC, November 16, 2014), http://hackeducation.com/2014/11/16/from-open-to-justice.

80. Nora Almeida, "Open Educational Resources and Rhetorical Paradox in the Neoliberal Univers(ity)," *Journal of Critical Library and Information Studies 1, no. 1 (2017): article 16, p. 2,* https://theidealis.org/open-educational-resources-and-rhetorical-paradox-in-the-neoliberal-university/.

81. Veletsianos and Kimmons, "Assumptions and Challenges," p. 180.

82. Almeida, "Open Educational Resources," 15.

83. Watters, "From 'Open' to Justice."

84. For more on this issue, see the following: Suzy Bear, "Building Libraries One Book at a Time," in *Aboriginal and Visible Minority Librarians: Oral Histories from Canada, ed. Deborah Lee and Mahalakshmi Kumaran (Lanham, MD: Rowman and Littlefield, 2014) 1–16; Matthew P. Ciszek and Courtney L. Young, "Diversity Collection Assessment in Large Academic Libraries," Collection Building 29, no. 4 (2010): 154–61; nina de jesus, "Locating the Library within Institutional Oppression," In the Library with the Lead Pipe, September 24, 2014,* http://www.inthelibrarywiththeleadpipe.org/2014/locating-the-library-in-institutional-oppression/; Harrison W. Inefuku and Charlotte Roh, "Agents of Diversity and Social Justice: Librarians and Scholarly Communication," in *Open Access and the Future of Scholarly Communication: Policy and Infrastructure, ed. Kevin L. Smith and Katherine A. Dickson (Lanham, MD: Rowman and Littlefield, 2016), 107–27; Mathuews, "Moving beyond Diversity"; Mbembe, "Decolonizing Knowledge"; Welburn "Creating Inclusive Communities."*

85. See Padilla and Steeves, "Data Librarianship."

86. See the following: Almeida, "Open Educational Resources"; Association of European Research Libraries (LIBER), *The Hague Declaration, December 10, 2014,* https://thehaguedeclaration.com/; de jesus, "Locating the Library"; Peter Johan Lor and Johannes Britz, "Knowledge Production from an African Perspective: International Information Flows and Intellectual Property," *International Information and Library Review 37, no. 2 (2005): 61–76.*

87. See the following: Association of College and Research Libraries (ACRL) Working Group on Intersections of Scholarly Com-

munication and Information Literacy, *Intersections of Scholarly Communication and Information Literacy: Creating Strategic Collaborations for a Changing Academic Environment (Chicago: Association of College and Research Libraries, 2013); Stephanie Davis-Kahl, Teresa A. Fishel, and Merinda Kaye Hensley, "Weaving the Threads: Scholarly Communication and Information Literacy," College and Research Libraries News 75, no. 8 (2014): 441–44; Tibor Koltay, Sonja Špiranec, and László Z. Karvalics, "The Shift of Information Literacy towards Research 2.0," Journal of Academic Librarianship 41, no. 1 (2015): 87–93; Joyce Ogburn, Allegra Swift, and Emma Molls, "Scholarly Communication in the Context of Digital Literacy: Navigation and Decision Making in a Complex Landscape" (presentation, University of San Diego Digital Initiatives Symposium, San Diego, CA, April 24, 2018); Charlotte Roh, "Scholarly Publishing, Information Literacy, and Social Justice" (presentation, University of San Diego Digital Initiatives Symposium, San Diego, CA, May 2, 2017); Patti Ryan and Lisa Sloniowski, "The Public Academic Library: Friction in the Teflon Funnel," in Information Literacy and Social Justice: Radical Professional Praxis, ed. Shana Higgins and Lua Gregory (Sacramento: Library Juice Press, 2013), 275–96; Shan C. Sutton, "Time to Step on the Gas in Approaching the Intersections of Scholarly Communication and Information Literacy," Journal of Librarianship and Scholarly Communication 1, no. 3 (2013): eP1076,* https://doi.org/10.7710/2162-3309.1076; Amanda J. Swygart-Hobaugh, "Information—Power to the People: Students and Librarians Dialoguing about Power, Social Justice, and Information," in *Information Literacy and Social Justice: Radical Professional Praxis, ed. Shana Higgins and Lua Gregory (Sacramento: Library Juice Press, 2013), 219–46; Eamon Tewell, "A Decade of Critical Information Literacy: A Review of the Literature," Communications in Information Literacy 9, no. 1 (2015): 24–43.*

88. See Patricia A. Matthew, "Tweeting Diversity: Race and Tenure in the Age of Social Media," in *Written/Unwritten: Diversity and the Hidden Truths of Tenure, ed. Patricia A. Matthew (Chapel Hill: University of North Carolina Press, 2016), 241–260.*
89. See the following: Almeida, "Open Educational Resources"; Brooke Erin Duffy and Jefferson D. Pooley, "'Facebook for Academics': The Convergence of Self-Branding and Social Media Logic on Academia.edu," *Social Media and Society 3, no. 1 (2017): 1–11; Eric Kansa, "It's the Neoliberalism, Stupid: Why Instrumentalist Arguments for Open Access, Open Data, and Open Science Are Not Enough," LSE Impact Blog, January 14, 2014,* http://blogs.lse.ac.uk/impactofsocialsciences/2014/01/27/its-the-neoliberalism-stupid-kansa/.
90. See the following: Baker, "Be Creative, Determined, and Wise"; William F. Birdsall, "Human Capabilities and Information and Communication Technology: The Communicative Connection," *Ethics and Information Technology 13, no. 2 (2011): 93–106; Inefuku, "Globalization, Open Access, and the Democritization of Knowledge"; Rebecca M. Marrall, "Teaching the Digital Divide: Connecting Students to Community, Knowledge, and Service Learning," Library Philosophy and Practice (June 2014): article 1126,* http://digitalcommons.unl.edu/libphilprac/1126/; Liangzhi Yu, "The Divided Views of the Information and Digital Divides: A Call for Integrative Theories of Information Inequality," *Journal of Information Science 37, no. 6 (2011): 660–79.*
91. See the following: Almeida, "Open Educational Resources; de jesus, "Locating the Library"; Charlotte Roh, Emily Drabinski, and Harrison W. Inefuku, "Scholarly Communication as a Tool for Social Justice and Diversity" (presentation, National Diversity in Libraries Conference, University of California Los Angeles, Los Angeles, CA, August 12, 2016).
92. See Roh, "Scholarly Communication in a Time of Change."
93. See the following: Czernowicz, "Inequitable Power Dynamics"; Albert N. Greco, Robert M. Wharton, and Amy Brand, "Demographics of Scholarly Publishing and Communication Professionals," *Learned Publishing 29, no. 2 (2016): 97–101; Library Publishing Coalition, "An Ethical Framework for Library Publishing," ver. 1.0, (San Francisco: Educopia, 2018),* http://dx.doi.org/10.5703/1288284316777; Reggie Raju, "Predatory Publishing from a Global South Perspective," *Library Publishing Coalition Blog, February 7, 2018,* https://librarypublishing.org/predatory-publishing-global-south-perspective/; Jeroen Sondervan and Kathleen Fitzpatrick, "Interview: Kathleen Fitzpatrick on Open Scholarship, Humanities Commons, and More," Open Access in Media Studies, April 19, 2018, https://oamediastudies.com/interview-kathleen-fitzpatrick/.
94. See Kansa, "It's the Neoliberalism."
95. See the following: Baildon et al., "Creating a Social Justice Mindset"; Bourg, "Never Neutral"; de jesus, "Locating the Library"; Anne Gilliland, "Neutrality, Social Justice and the Obligations of Archival Education and Educators in the Twenty-First Century," *Archival Science 11, no. 3–4 (2011): 193–209; Randall C. Jimerson, "Archives for All: Professional Responsibility and Social Justice," American Archivist 70, no. 2 (2007): 252–81.*
96. See the following: Baildon et al., "Creating a Social Justice Mindset"; de jesus, "Locating the Library"; Hathcock, "Making the Local Global"; Kansa, "It's the Neoliberalism"; Sarah Kember, "Opening Out from Open Access: Writing and Publishing in Response to Neoliberalism," *Ada: A Journal of Gender, New Media, and Technology, no. 4 (2014): article N31C1V51,* https://doi.org/10.7264/N31C1V51; Stuart Lawson, Kevin Sanders, and Lauren Smith, "Commodification of the Information Profession: A Critique of Higher Education under Neoliberalism," *Journal of Librarianship and Scholarly Communication 3, no. 1 (2015): eP1182,* https://doi.org/10.7710/2162-3309.1182; Neylon, "Openness in Scholarship."
97. See the following: Alexander et al., "Report from the Information Overload and Underload Workgroup"; Kenneth R. Fleischmann, "Digital Libraries with Embedded Values: Combining Insights from LIS and Science and Technology Studies," *Library Quarterly 77, no. 4 (2007): 409–27; Manoff, "Human and Machine Entanglement."*
98. See the following: Inefuku, "Globalization, Open Access, and the Democritization of Knowledge"; Library Publishing Coalition, *Ethical Framework, ver. 1.0; Roh, "Scholarly Communication in a Time of Change."*
99. See the following: Alex Gil, "The User, the Learner and the Machines We Make," Minimal Computing, May 21, 2015, http://go-dh.github.io/mincomp/thoughts/2015/05/21/user-vs-learner/; Padilla and Steeves, "Data Librarianship."
100. See the following: Sara Dreyfuss and Marianne Ryan, "Academic Freedom: The Continuing Challenge," *portal: Libraries and the Academy 16, no. 1 (2016): 1–9; George Pearson and Heidi Lowry, "Hating Hate Speech: Debating Freedom and Tolerance in the Chicago IFRT Program," Intellectual Freedom Round Table Report 46, no. 2 (2000): 1–3.*
101. See the following: Freeda Brook, Dave Ellenwood, and Althea Eannace Lazzaro, "In Pursuit of Antiracist Social Justice: De-

naturalizing Whiteness in the Academic Library," *Library Trends 64, no. 2 (2015): 246–84; Julianne Buschsbaum, "Academic Libraries and the Remaking of the Canon: Implications for Collection Development Librarians," Library Philosophy and Practice (2009): article 266,* http://digitalcommons.unl.edu/libphilprac/266/; de jesus, "Locating the Library"; Greco, Wharton, and Brand, "Demographics of Scholarly Publishing"; Hathcock "Making the Local Global"; Inefuku and Roh, "Agents of Diversity"; Mbembe, "Decolonizing Knowledge"; Society for Scholarly Publishing, "On Being Excluded: Testimonies by People of Color in Scholarly Publishing," *Scholarly Kitchen (blog), April 4, 2018,* https://scholarlykitchen.sspnet.org/2018/04/04/excluded-testimonies-people-color-scholarly-publishing/; Roh, "Scholarly Communication in a Time of Change"; Tuhiwai Smith, "Decolonizing Knowledge."